I Am Light

180 days to remember who you are

I Am Light

180 days to remember
who you are

Lisa Annese

WORLDCHANGERS
M E D I A

Paperback ISBN: 978-1-955811-19-4
E-book ISBN: 978-1-955811-20-0
LCCN: 2022908140

First paperback edition: June 2022

Cover photo by Cynthia Stepien
Design & Typesetting by Bryna Haynes

Published by WorldChangers Media
PO Box 83, Foster, RI 02825
www.WorldChangers.Media

For my higher self and, as an extension, my boys
Anthony and Michael—it was all for us.

You are my first loves, light, and world.

Always remember that the truth is your destiny—it will
set you free and bring you back home . . . to you.

Praise

"I have personally witnessed, in real time, the transformative and healing path of Lisa Annese. Her blossoming growth into love, stillness, and acceptance from her many challenges and struggles over the years was an awe-inspiring journey to watch as her teacher.

Lisa's guidance and sage wisdom through our most difficult moments of life are truly a blessing, and her generosity in sharing her adversity is an act of selfless service to be treasured.

Lisa takes you step-by-step through your most testing and demanding times, whether it be your marriage, divorce, health dis-eases, children, friendships, and beyond. Her 180-day guidance will bring you back to center, to long-lasting moments of sustained calm and peace.

She can lead you because Lisa has walked this path. From her Darkness comes your Light."

Katherine Hamer, Master Teacher and Practitioner at The Singing Bowl & Sound Institute of New York and The Singing Bowl Studio

"I love the way she writes. I feel as though I am sitting with her at her kitchen table, enjoying a coffee, and feeling a big "Yes!" This book is so inspiring at this time, when questions such as "What is true about anything anymore?" and "What to believe anymore?" are so pervasive in the world now. She does not feel that she is a "poor-me" victim, and she gives a plan from her own life experience. She is using the Five Sutras for the Aquarian Age, two of which she shares: "There's a way through every block" and "When the time is on you, start; and the pressure will be off." Thank you for your wonderful book!"

Gurmukh Khalsa

"Lisa Annese's book, *I Am Light: 180 Days to Remember Who You Are*, is such a gift! Through stories, practices, and prompts, readers are gently guided to initiate and experience their own healing journey. This book delivers an approachable method to discovering one's inner light and pathway forward. Lisa lovingly helps us all to see that one's high purpose is discovered through presence and devotion, rather than chasing job titles or falling into hustle culture. I trust that anyone who picks this book up will benefit greatly and discover a world that feels softer, more beautiful, and promising, than the world they knew before experiencing Lisa's wisdom and insight!"

Meg Sylvester, Spiritual Entrepreneur, Author, Mentor

"In *I Am Light*, Lisa shares her heartfelt journey of personal transformation, artfully navigating divorce and life as a single mom using the consciousness raising technology of Kundalini Yoga and meditation. She reminds us of the power of listening to the whispers of our soul and finding the courage to give ourselves permission to live a life that aligns with our true purpose. Based on deep insights from her own personal journey to break free from convention, Lisa's message is clear: living as authentically in the world as we can is for our highest good, and for that of all beings. The framework of the book is a practical guide for the spiritually curious, those open to energetic tools designed to help peel away the mental and emotional clutter so we can experience genuine well-being physically, mentally, and emotionally. I highly recommend Lisa's empowering book for anyone sensing that it might be time to take that leap into uncharted waters in their own lives."

Christine Montenegro-Okezie, Certified Holistic Health Coach and Kundalini Yoga Teacher

"Lisa is a master of words (and life). Her story intertwined with the quotes and chakras make a captivating read. The words exude a certain energy that draws upon all the emotions. The reader is drawn out of their head and to their heart. It's truly a work of art.

You'll want to read this to discover yourself. Your true authentic self. To ask the questions you've never asked yourself before. To slow down and reflect on the life you've created for yourself. The way Lisa shares her story makes the reader able to feel through the words. Her vulnerability and rawness allows one to dive into their own selves to dig and find the higher vibration Lisa asks her readers to seek."

Nicole Marchand, Intuitive Reiki Master Healer, Medium, Psychic

"This journal book is a great tool for anyone looking to find clarity and direction for living their best life. Lisa shares her story in a raw and relatable way by her willingness to share her vulnerabilities with confidence, grace, and ease. She is an exceptional sound therapy healer and Kundalini Yoga teacher who lovingly encourages others to find their true passion and follow their inner light. Not only is this book a great introduction to the technology and practice of the Kundalini style of yoga, it's also formatted in an approachable and easy to use design for anyone looking for a little more guidance with journaling. I highly recommend this book for anyone ready to begin this journey of a lifetime!"

Linda McLachlan, MA, RDN, FMN, CLT, Functional Medicine
Dietitian-Nutritionist, Nutrition Matters, LLC
www.AllNutritionMatters.com

"Lisa Annese is a beacon of light for anyone seeking to redirect their own life and discover who they really are. In her book, *I Am Light*, Lisa offers clear directions to follow, using a transformative path of vibrational light, based on her personal experience of change. In a world where women can be swallowed up by everything that is supposed to be good, Lisa forged a path using sound and yoga, which established her own authentic path of personal truth and purpose. This brought her pure joy so she could experience and share about finding a life that really is good.

As a sound healer myself, my favorite part is the accompanying videos which offer powerful meditations and sound healing sessions that vividly express her passion and gifts. I was very impressed by the level of clarity and detail that made the steps easy to implement. I give Lisa's impactful book my highest recommendation for anyone serious about changing their own life for the better."

Karen Olson, Ph.D., Multi Billboard-topping musician, recording
artist, composer, Reiki Master, award-winning author, energetic sound
healer, and member of the New York Pops

"This book has a great title, an intriguing subtitle, and then delivers its promise with great charm. This is essentially a record of how the author realized that her life was not serving her essence and how she overcame this impasse in her life with resolution, courage, and yoga. Lisa documents the changes and challenges she needed to make through the rubric of the six key qualities that needed reevaluating:truth, joy, power, love, intuition, and the divine.

One of the key methodologies of self-healing and life transformation that Lisa discovers is the practice of Kundalini Yoga, which becomes the touchstone of her awakening. The landmark of Lisa's 40th birthday and the Covid-19 pandemic also play their part in the backdrop of events, spurring transformation and change as she finds the courage to embrace the darkness of the unknown.

In an effective workbook style of presentation, each of the 180 days ends with a homily-like statement encouraging self-reflection and profound inner dialogue. Different yogic techniques are judiciously introduced, with careful and accurate instruction given to encourage the reader to develop their own practice.

Lisa is delightfully discursive in choosing inspiring and apposite quotations to elucidate her text from such disparate luminaries as Rumi to RuPaul, and Kurt Vonnegut to Albert Einstein.

This is an honest, heartfelt document from an inspirational professional woman, mother, and yogini who presents a primer of applied yogic technology which will help many people to make positive changes in their lives."

Guru Dharam Khalsa, BAcC, RCHM, Director International School of Kundalini Yoga, iSKY

Contents

I AM JOY

I AM POWER

I AM INTUITIVE

I AM DIVINE

Introduction

The other day I was shopping for tea service items to offer to a group of women participating in a sound bath meditation at my healing center. As I walked the aisles of the store, I recognized how grateful I was for the life I've created. I felt a rush of joy fill me and warm my heart center as I counted the blessings in my life. A year prior, my life had lacked shape or form, but now it has meaning, is full of vitality, and is guided by my purpose. This all happened because I believed in myself and trusted that I could create the life I always dreamed of and wanted—and that's what I did.

I am grateful that I've created a healing center full of light, peace, and love. In this center, I share my spiritual gifts of sound healing, meditation, and yoga for members of my community. It's a welcoming space that brings people together and fosters connections for those who want to heal. When I intuitively play my instruments for others, I am blessed and in a state of flow for the first time ever. And I am doubly blessed in that I can do this and support my family and our future. I love how I can recognize the beauty and simplicity in the present moment by reflecting on the gifts that my life is giving me.

You see, I didn't always live my life this way. In the past, I over-complicated my life. It was fast-paced and I was always living ten steps ahead in the future. I didn't stop to reflect on my blessings—I was too busy to even notice they were happening.

In college, I majored in accounting, received my MBA, and became a CPA. For ten years I worked for Ernst & Young in New Jersey and New York. My positions were in accounting and human resources, where feeling overworked and under-joyed were cele-brated. This way of life resulted in stressful days and nights in a career that didn't bring me joy and lacked my life's purpose.

Following the expectations of my life path, I married, had two boys, and was grateful to be a stay-at-home mother. However, I con-stantly struggled because my soul recognized that something was missing. On the outside and on paper, everything looked perfect, but inside, my soul was slowly dying a painful death and my existence was getting darker and more uncomfortable as the years progressed. I understand now that it was because my true light and purpose were not able to shine brightly for me, or for the world to see.

In early 2020, I realized that I was neither happy nor fully alive—it was time to make a drastic change. I was going through the motions of life, but I was completely detached and could no longer recognize myself. My body was in constant pain and this helped me to recognize that a major change had to happen. I needed courage to make a difficult decision—one that came from the heart, not the head—to separate from my husband and move out of our family home. After my son was diagnosed with permanent hearing loss in the summer of that same year, this experience led to a bigger and more lasting change: divorce.

Next, an abundance of healing occurred, as yoga, meditation, and writing led me to identify and find my purpose to help others using the power of sound vibrations. I shared with you the back-ground of how my life was in my earlier years and how my life transformed because I chose to believe that I deserved something different. I craved the light that I knew was there, and I am truly blessed to live my "second life" as it is completely different, like night-and-day different, from my "first life."

Here, I share things that have helped me turn my life around from a place of darkness to one of lightness. I've always collected quotes, and value their deep meaning and teachings, which is why I chose to start each day with a meaningful quote. However, I don't particularly resonate with the individual authors of the quotes. Through examples and real situations from my past, you will get a glimpse into my life and the powerful moments that helped to transform the narrative of my life, and, in turn, the future of my two boys. My hope is that by reading this book, you'll begin to uncover your own light and truth.

Key Concepts

In this book, you may come across key concepts and terms from my spiritual practices that appear foreign to you. I have defined and summarized those items below for your reference.

Kundalini Yoga

I am a KRI Level 1 Kundalini yoga teacher. Kundalini is the only yoga that I connected with deep within my core. It's a very spiritual yoga practice and is focused on connecting with the truth of your soul, finding your light, moving the dormant energy that lies at the base of your spine, and elevating it to increase your awareness and consciousness. I wear white when I practice and teach as it strengthens and builds my aura, which is an extension of my energy field nine feet in all directions around me. Doing this protects me from negativity. I also preserve my energy by covering my crown chakra with a turban or head wrap.

Tuning in

We begin each practice by tuning in to the Adi Mantra, "Ong Namo Guru Dev Namo." This is our opening mantra, which translates to "I bow to the Divine wisdom of all that is" and "I bow to the Divine teacher within." We chant these beautiful Sanskrit words three times to connect with our higher self, the spiritual teachers who have come before us, and to remind us to trust the power of our own intuition. The leader of your life is you. Always remember that.

Kriya

A set of asanas or postures taught during a Kundalini yoga class, usually with a specific focus in mind to heal the body.

Conscious Breathing

Paying attention to your breath. Consciously managing your inhale and exhale patterns can have dramatic effects on your mind and body.

Mantra

A repetitive verse that, when regularly chanted, resonates with your soul and becomes part of your consciousness. It is also a form of sound healing.

Mudra

A position of the hands that locks or seals and guides energy flow and reflexes the brain, creating specific results in the mind and body. Here are some examples that work with your fingers:

- *Gyan mudra* is the seal of knowledge. It is practiced by touching the thumb tip to the pointer finger.

- *Shuni mudra* is the seal of patience, which is practiced by touching the thumb tip to the middle finger.
- *Surya mudra* is the seal of the sun, which is practiced by touching the thumb to the ring finger.
- *Buddhi mudra* is the seal of mental clarity, which is practiced by touching the thumb to the pinky finger.

Meditation

The silencing of your mind so your soul can speak. It is an opportunity to be present, patient, and receive the answers you are looking for. Think of it as hanging out with your soul.

Sound Healing

A form of meditation that uses the power of sound vibrations to relax the mind, body, and subconscious. In my practice, I utilize the power of chanting mantra, ancient Tibetan singing bowls, gongs, drums, chimes, and more to move stagnant energy from the body to help individuals heal and live from their highest self.

Closing Mantra

We close every Kundalini yoga class by chanting three long "Sat Naams." This translates to "Truth is my identity."

How to Use This Book

This book is a six-month discovery of your own light and an awareness of your path to truth. By the end, you will understand the different energy chakras and their impact and benefits to your body and soul when that area is open and strong.

The book's format covers 180 days, organized into six unique sections. Each has its own mantra and belief for you to connect with as part of your own beautiful existence.

Each new day starts with a unique quote that has deep meaning for me. I explore the theme using my own reflection, understanding, and correlation to my personal life. At the end, I include a journal prompt question for you, which is designed to help you reflect and connect with the subject matter. Writing and reflecting on my feelings brought me immense healing, especially with deep subject matter. I recognized that my subconscious was holding onto things that were no longer supporting my highest good. So please take the time to reflect and process as well.

After the daily reading, I invite you to complete the recommended yoga postures and meditations for that month, which will help you to move energy, increase your awareness, and feel more alive. This should only take twenty to thirty minutes each morning. Consider devoting this time to healing yourself and benefiting your highest good. You can read descriptions of the postures in the Appendix, or watch my short videos on the *I Am Light* web page below.

I have also created ten-minute sound healing recordings for each month, which you can listen to after the daily activities, at a later time in your day, or on the weekend. The sound healing recording will allow your body to deeply relax and enjoy the vibrations of ancient Tibetan singing bowls, gongs, drums, chimes, and more.

Offering your body the gift of rest and your mind the gift of peace is an act of self-love that only you can give yourself. Your body, mind, soul, and heart will thank you.

Access each month's asana videos, meditation, sound healing audio, and more at www.LisaAnnese.com/i-am-light

I Am

Truth

I Am Truth
DAYS 1–30

It took me forty years to be able to scream with excitement and enthusiasm the mantra, "I am truth."

It was an extremely powerful thing to feel deep within myself that I was finally walking my very own path of truth. This has not only enabled me to heal myself, but also impacted the future of my young boys.

To fully present to the Universe my true, authentic, and real self is a magnificent freedom. It is a gift and opportunity to learn, grow, and evolve into who God meant for me to be as I fulfill my purpose on this planet.

Living from your truth is an association with the first chakra energy center, at the root area, located at the end of the spine between the anus and the sexual organs, in addition to the fifth chakra energy center, located at the throat area.

Key areas reflected in this chapter as it relates to living your own path of truth are as follows:

As it relates specifically to strengthening the first chakra, you will understand:

- To have trust and faith in God, Universe, Source, etc., at the foundation.

- The importance of feeling safe, secure, and grounded, and trusting that your basic needs are met.
- That the root area is associated with the Earth element. Therefore, connecting to nature, living life with simplicity, and focusing on the present are key qualities for this area.
- That it is important to connect with your roots and to pay attention to heal your inner child (who you were, your interests, having a playful side, etc., before societal influences may have changed you).
- That when you're vulnerable, you are allowing yourself to be opened up and exposed. Doing this in your life enables you to strengthen the first chakra and live for your truth.

As it relates specifically to strengthening the fifth chakra, you will understand:

- How to give your body prana or the life force energy needed to not only survive but also thrive through conscious breathing.
- The power and impact of speaking your truth through your voice, both to your peers and your children, and through using your own voice to chant a song.
- How to be a teacher for others and understand that the best teachers help you grow.
- That when you live your truth you are leaving your markings on those around you on your path. Presenting yourself to the world as authentically as you can serves your highest good.
- The importance and recognition that your soul has a unique gift and truth, and your purpose is to live as that person.

Tune In with the Adi Mantra
"Ong Namo Guru Dev Namo"

To center yourself in the higher self before practicing Kundalini yoga, chant the Adi Mantra three times.

Ong Namo Guru Dev Namo" translates to "I bow to the Divine wisdom of all that is" and "I bow to the Divine teacher within."

HOW TO PRACTICE

- *Posture:* Sit in Easy Pose, with the spine erect.
- *Eye Position:* Eyes slightly closed, focused at the Third Eye, which is the point between the brows.
- *Mudra: Prayer Pose.* Place the palms of the hands flat together to neutralize the positive (right, or male) and negative (left, or female) sides of the body. Your thumbs should press against the sternum and your forearms will be parallel to the floor.
- *Conscious Breathing:* Gently inhale through your nose, feel the breath fill up your belly, fill up your lungs, and expand your rib cage. On the exhale from your nose, recognize the breath leaving your body. When ready to "tune in" with the Adi Mantra, inhale and exhale deeply from the nose and begin chanting the mantra three times.

Asanas

The asanas listed below focus on strengthening both the energy centers at the root and throat areas. It is recommended that you hold each posture for one to two minutes with a slight rest in between. Remember to focus within while holding the postures and while resting, keep your eyes closed, focusing on the Third Eye, the point between the brows. This will allow you to focus on yourself and build your intuition, plus learn to trust your own power and ability.

- Neck Rolls
- Cat-Cow
- Crow
- Cobra
- Pelvic Lifts

Find a description of each posture in the Appendix on page 417.

Meditation
"Sat Naam"

This is a good meditation for someone who is new to meditation or who wants to develop the ability to concentrate. It is known as a *bij* or seed mantra because the seed contains the knowledge of the fully grown tree within itself. The essence or seed is the identity of truth embodied in condensed form. Chanting this mantra awakens the soul and leads you to your destiny.

- *Mantra:* "*Sat Naam*"
- *Translation:* "Truth is my identity." *Sat*: Truth, the reality of one's existence. *Naam*: identity.

HOW TO PRACTICE

- *Posture:* Sit in Easy Pose, with the spine erect.
- *Eye Position:* Eyes slightly closed, focused at the Third Eye, which is the point between the brows.
- *Mudra:* Place your left arm so that it's comfortably resting on your left leg. With the four fingers of the right hand, feel the pulse on the left wrist. Lightly place the

fingers in a straight line, so you can feel the pulse in each fingertip. On each beat of the heart, mentally hear the sound, *"Sat Naam."*

- *Time*: Continue for three minutes. Build to eleven minutes.

Deep Relaxation

- *Posture:* Lie on your back in Corpse Pose. With your eyes closed, place your arms at your sides, with palms facing up. Allow your body to rest, process, and absorb the movement of energy.
- *Time:* One to three minutes minimum.

Ending Prayer

To close your Kundalini practice, chant three long *Sat Naams.*

Sound Healing

Enjoy this month's ten minute Sound Healing ensemble to further relax your mind and body. Consider listening during deep relaxation or at another time during your day when your body could benefit from and enjoy the beautiful healing gift of sound and vibrations.

Access this month's asana videos, meditation, sound healing audio, and more at www.LisaAnnese.com/i-am-light

Day 1

"A spark of Divine light is within each of us."
Pope Francis

We are all beams of light. All of our experiences and connections as an energy exchange connect us and each other to the power of the Divine, whether we call it Source, Creator, God, or Universe. I believe that there is a higher power connecting all that we are doing, and it is perfectly aligned to teach our soul lessons. That power is our guiding light, which exists in all of us.

Knowing that light comes from darkness, through the power of faith, we all have the ability to turn our darkness or everyday challenges, troubles, ill-feelings, and concerns into light.

To me:

- Light is knowledge
- Light is wisdom
- Light is power
- Light is courage
- Light is energy
- Light is sunshine
- Light is positivity
- Light is strength
- Light is grace
- Light is gratitude

- Light is love
- Light is faith
- Light is hope
- Light is truth
- Light is intuitive
- Light is conscious
- Light is life

My own personal journey from dark to light was my path of awareness, spiritual awakening, elevated consciousness, love, and truth. This was only possible due to my intense feeling that I was not living as my true, authentic self.

Every day that passed, my soul was slowly dying a painful death as I was living a lie, which negatively impacted my physical, mental, spiritual, and emotional bodies. I lived in fear about what would happen if I eventually told the truth: my relationship and marriage was no longer serving my higher good. I had a fear of the unknown, others' reactions, and the probable outcome for myself and my young boys. Finally, deciding from my heart to follow the path of light and truth, I faced my fears, with no certainty about the outcome of my future.

Healing from the inside out wasn't an easy task, but the lessons learned have been greater than my wildest dreams. Now that I am finally living for myself, I am free, and I am home.

My mantra and belief is: "I am light;" and you are too.

How do you define light in your life?

Day 2

"There comes a time when you have to let everything fall apart. When you have to stop fighting for a life you've outgrown and trust that you will be okay, even if you can't see how right now. For a while everything may feel messy and hard, and you may feel scared and lost. Embrace the fear. Embrace the uncertainty. Embrace the loss. The dark tunnel of change leads to the light of possibility, but first you have to go through it."

Lori Deschene

My fortieth birthday was on March 4, 2020. This quote found its way to me two days later; it documented in print how I was feeling about the state of my marriage, relationships, and life at that moment in time. Believing in the power of synchronicity and that nothing is a coincidence, I began to reflect on the deeper meaning behind this message as it related to my own journey.

Before my spiritual awakening, I was living "in the dark." It was a very shallow existence, and I wasn't even truly alive. My feelings and outlook stayed at surface level, rather than delving into the deep. Life in the shallow end was painful, but I wasn't aware as I lacked the proper tools needed to handle my emotions and everything else. I played life safe. I was bored and living for everyone else, putting their needs before mine. I had no defined purpose and, in fact, I didn't really like myself very much. My life was in constant motion with an overall sense of stress. Life seemed complicated and I barely had time to breathe.

My pain led to my awakening and path to healing, and it was years in the making. It first manifested as health concerns, which led me to heal my body, then heal my mind, and finally my spirit.

Looking back at what I know now, the health of my body was very poor. When I took control in November 2016, I was holding onto unreleased emotions from not living my life with authenticity. These emotions were causing immense health concerns: gut issues, adrenal fatigue, anxiety, insomnia, obesity, and hormonal imbalances.

In February 2017, I began to focus on my mental health and was beyond grateful for my therapist, who has essentially put me back together. Today, neither of us recognize the "old Lisa" anymore.

Lastly, healing my spirit happened with the regular practice of Kundalini yoga, which has been part of my life since March 2018. This eventually led me to become a teacher so I could help heal others and share the work that had such a deep impact on my life.

Emerging from the tunnel, there is light. I love myself. I have a defined purpose. I am more still, present, and calm. I now know how to navigate my emotions. Conscious breathing and regularly moving energy has helped allow life to flow naturally as intended, connecting and trusting in the power of the Universe.

For me, I often describe this as my "Rising Phoenix" moment. The Rising Phoenix woke from the ashes of death and created a new existence full of life and vitality. I am proud of my awareness, experiences, and courage to go through the tunnel.

Identify and reflect on your own personal experiences with a dark versus light situation.

Day 3

"I truly believe that every single person has to go through something that absolutely destroys them so that they can figure out who they truly are."
Unknown

In May 2020, at the beginning of the COVID-19 pandemic, while the world was living in "quarantine," I shared my truth and separated from my husband. After ten years of marriage, I found an apartment and moved out of the home I'd built. My young boys, who are my everything, were with me only 50 percent of the time and I had to heal on my own.

I recognize that many people died unwillingly during the pandemic. At this time, I felt like my soul was dying, and I wanted to live. This was not a decision that I woke up with one morning, rather it was an inevitable choice that I kept pushing away. I pushed until finally I was ready to venture out of the safety net of my current existence into the wild waters of the unknown.

Before my awakening, I always lived from the comfort of my headspace. I didn't connect with my feelings when deciding anything. But this choice to separate? It was a decision of the heart solely made on my own. I trusted my inner power and intuition. My path was to separate as there were things that I wanted out of my life that would never be possible living in a marriage that was no longer serving my highest self.

I knew that my soul did not feel right anymore. So, with the power of faith, my own intuition, healing tools like Kundalini yoga, meditation, breathwork, my therapist, and a few close friends and family for support, I did the unthinkable . . . move from a comfortable existence with a known destination to one of discomfort and onto a path that had no map. I was the map. But I'm also a Pisces; I don't fear the depths of the water, even from a place I have never swam before.

In August 2020, my youngest son, Michael, who was seven at the time, was diagnosed with permanent hearing loss and required hearing aids; without them, he is considered deaf. I'm beyond grateful for the medical support we received. And it was a huge pill to swallow and absorb. Only a few months into my new journey, it was a big undertaking into another unfamiliar world, to now live with a child who's labeled as "legally disabled."

Michael's hearing loss became my greatest blessing in numerous ways. It connected me to my boys in a different way and forced me to really slow down and prioritize. From an emotional perspective, his diagnosis helped me recognize that I needed a partner to support the person who I had evolved into now, not who I was when we married ten years earlier.

In September 2020, I made the difficult decision to finalize our marriage and begin the divorce process.

Do you have a past issue or problem that has become your greatest blessing? How has this event changed your life?

Day 4

*"Our children can be our greatest teachers if we
are humble enough to receive their lessons."*
Bryant McGill

My oldest son, Anthony, turned ten on August 26, 2021; this milestone was a perfect opportunity for me to reflect on ten years as a mother.

Prior to Anthony's birth, I led a toxic existence, where everything always had to be perfect. At a family photoshoot in Central Park, in the heat of a June summer, I was concerned about my hair, our matching attire, and crafting the "perfect" photos of a ten-month-old baby. A baby whose only concern at that moment was living in the moment and having fun. Fun was never on my agenda, but stress and intensity were. Everything was planned out and complicated rather than being effortless and letting it all naturally flow as intended.

Flash-forward ten years to my son's birthday party where I was happier than I have ever been. I was only interested in one picture with my son to capture him doing his thing the way he wanted to do it, not me and what I had delivered or crafted. It was simple and fun. I was relaxed and able to remain present and witness the pure joy and happiness that exuded from my growing boy. My teacher.

My August, 26 (8.26) birthday boy represents double infinity with the repetition of the "8s." They offer a very powerful message and meaning for oneness—a reminder that we are all interconnected in this cycle of life. We're connected to ourselves and the Universe in the never-ending cycle of life and the power of unifying together as one. Allowing one to be and act as they want is a lifelong special gift. And it requires presence, not perfection.

My two boys are my greatest teachers. We are all growing daily and constantly learning from each other. I am beyond blessed that they chose me to be their mother, light, and guide on their journey. They also taught me the real meaning of love.

The gift of spirituality from them to me and me to them is priceless. This is a feeling of peace. And so be it.

Reflect on your own personal experiences receiving recent lessons from a child. How have these lessons changed the way you're currently living?

Day 5

"The world tells us to seek success, power, and money;
God tells us to seek humility, service, and love."

Pope Francis

In February 2019, I came across this quote on a digital billboard on the side of a major highway in New Jersey. Because it was digital, the message kept changing. By the time I reached the billboard, it was gone. Afterwards, I searched the internet for the quote because it was so very powerful, real, and true.

At this time in my life, I was regularly attending Kundalini yoga classes, beginning my journey of healing my spirit and monthly visiting my holistic doctor, Dr. Chris, who was healing my physical body of various ailments. While I was nowhere near spiritually enlightened, I was open to understanding my world from a greater depth and perspective.

This quote stood out because it directly described Dr. Chris, whom I was driving to see when I first spotted it. Looking back, this was no coincidence. It was the Universe connecting this quote with my doctor: a selfless healer whose service is literally in his blood as a second-generation chiropractor and nutritionist. I jokingly nicknamed him "Mr. Humble," as he often heals people (like myself) who are desperate and have entertained all other avenues before becoming his patient.

He works effortlessly and love permeates the ways in which he helps others. He's very humble and treats his gift as "just my job" or "it's just science." However, his uniqueness lies in his strong faith in the power of God guiding him. He believes that "God is working through my hands." His pleasant, respectful, and patient demeanor greets everyone who walks through his office door, and he places immense faith and trust in God's guidance of his talent.

At this time, nobody in my life had such an immense faith or strong sense of spirituality. It was refreshing and a great source of light in my darkened world. He became a teacher of mine and his connection undoubtedly strengthened my faith, internal light, and my own sense of self.

Dr. Chris is a true, real-life example and role model for us all. Living for power and money feeds one's ego, but living humbly with service and love feeds one's soul.

While there are different ways to go about our daily existence, serving and helping others has been my true nature since a young age. I'd forgotten this, but it came full circle for me during my spiritual awakening and awareness once my spiritual name was identified.

My soul's purpose and mission in this lifetime is to serve others with God's Divine love and light as my one-pointed devotion. This mission is a true blessing for me; and, when you follow your mission, you'll find fulfillment as well. I'll discuss the soul's purpose more in the "I am Power" chapter.

Are you living from a place of feeding your ego, also referred to as one's self-image, or are you feeding your soul and consciously connecting with your true self? If you feel like you're living more from an ego perspective, would you be open to shifting, and what's one way you could do so?

Day 6

Footprints in the Sand

"One night I had a dream. I dreamed I was walking along the beach with the Lord. Across the sky flashed scenes from my life. For each scene, I noticed two sets of footprints in the sand: one belonging to me, and the other to the Lord.

"When the last scene of my life flashed before me, I looked back at the footprints in the sand. I noticed that many times along the path of my life there was only one set of footprints. I also noticed that it happened at the very lowest and saddest times in my life.

"This really bothered me, and I questioned the Lord about it: 'Lord, you said that once I decided to follow you, you'd walk with me all the way. But I have noticed that during the most troublesome times in my life, there is only one set of footprints. I don't understand why when I need you most, you would leave me.'

"The Lord replied: 'My son, my precious child, I love you and would never leave you. During your times of trial and suffering, when you see only one set of footprints, it was then that I carried you.'"

Mary Stevenson

During the summer of 2019, I was lost and confused about my future, my direction, and my marriage. It was a very dark time for me. However, I felt a calling that was outside of my regular routine: to attend the daily morning mass at my church.

I attended mass alone while my boys were at camp. Alone in my thoughts, I relied on the power of being in the presence of God's home with other parishioners, the daily gospel reading, and reflection from my pastor for uplifting words. They were a light to guide and direct.

This exercise offered me comfort and peace. It allowed me to be present to the opportunity to slow down and enjoy the gifts received from being in attendance. I valued and enjoyed my solitude as it was gentle and soothing for my soul while I also felt uplifted and carried by the teachings.

At this low point in my journey, I was reminded about a favorite poem that Dr. Chris had shared with me that is framed and hanging on a wall in his office. "Footprints in the Sand" is a daily reminder to have faith in the power of God who will be there for you, even during those darkest moments.

Growing up, I was raised with beliefs in the Catholic faith, but we weren't active parishioners. As a result, the power of faith and trust in God wasn't a natural extension for me to look to for guidance. Possessing trust in God (or the Divine) as a foundation strengthens the first chakra. It gives one a great support system to build upon when you know your roots are grounded, safe, and secure.

Reflect on your personal experiences trusting in God, Universe, Source, or higher power. Where have you found comfort and peace?

Day 7

"To trust God in the light is nothing, but to trust him in the dark—that is faith."
C.H. Spurgeon

Oxford Languages defines faith as "complete trust or confidence in someone or something."

This is a reminder to have faith over fear even in the dark, for faith lights the dark.

You can't see, hear, smell, taste, or touch faith. Instead, you trust and believe that you're being led on the right path and journey.

Relying on your strong sense of inner intuition and belief in a higher power, Universe, God, Source, etc. motivates and uplifts you to continue on during those darkest moments.

So many of us carry fear on a regular basis. According to Oxford Languages, fear is "an unpleasant emotion caused by the belief that someone or something is dangerous, likely to cause pain, or a threat."

Fear of the unknown and unexpected happens when you're no longer living in the present, but rather spending time in the future. Painful emotions arise, which lower your vibration. That fear of the future, though? Nobody knows if those fears will ever come to fruition and become a reality.

Faith over fear is consciously choosing to believe and choose the power of God, regularly and every time a potential dark moment occurs.

As we learned on Day 2, there's always light at the end of the tunnel, but you must go through the tunnel to experience the darkness and turn toward the light. And so be it.

Reflect on a dark time in your past. How did your faith enable you to overcome the situation?

Day 8

"I like people who get excited about the change of seasons, the sound of water, watching a sunset, the smell of rain, and starry nights."
Brooke Hampton

Allowing ourselves to be present and still is life-changing and price-less. There is always so much to do and it's easy to miss the beauty and value in living in the present moment. The never-ending to-do lists, the external pressures, and the distractions from social media easily prevent us from being present.

Connecting with nature and cultivating an awareness of its simple pleasures are often overlooked. Nature is a reminder about our insignificance in the grand scheme of the Universe. If we stop to take the time to recognize and appreciate it, we'll see that the Universe has the capabilities to create such beauty all around us. There is beauty, calmness, and peacefulness to be found in just being, recognizing, and existing.

Before my spiritual awakening, I was nicknamed the "Energizer bunny" at work because I did everything so quickly. I was constantly in motion, completing tasks, always asking for more, never missing a beat. From a work perspective, the feedback was positive and so I believed that more equals better.

I continued that pattern while I was home raising my boys, unaware that for success as a mother, less can equal better. I was moving so fast that I missed the small important moments and was always looking for something to do next. I did not understand the value of being present and the peace it would bring to us. Instead, I'd brought my work ethic and drive for more to our home.

While I cannot go back and change my past, I can start with my present and recognize the beauty of less equals more, and ensure that mantra is part of my daily routine.

As my spiritual journey strengthened, I started to notice the beauty of sunrises and sunsets. They soothed and nurtured my soul, especially if they happened to occur near the water. As a Pisces who connects with the water, it was a simple pleasure. Watching sunsets is pure joy and a gift that changes daily. They offer reflection and the awareness that the day is ending. We all have another chance to start over the next day. Our past remains in the past, and we focus on what will be in the present and beyond.

Reflect on a time you allowed yourself to be present and recognize the beauty of nature. Do you recall what was so captivating? How did it make you feel?

Day 9

"I feel like I should want more, but I don't. I want less. Less stuff, less rushing, less stress, less noise. I want simplicity."
Brooke Hampton

Oxford Languages defines simple as "easily understood, or done; presenting no difficulty;" and "plain, basic, or uncomplicated in form, nature, or design." Considered in this way, living with simplicity is choosing peace and contentment over something that could cause you more stress and difficulty.

As I just shared, while raising my young boys I recognized that less equals more in most circumstances and situations. I began to see that when I focused on living with simplicity, my life was more manageable and enjoyable for me and, as an extension, my boys.

This awareness began to trickle down into all aspects of our daily routines and lives. I felt I was a more attentive and happier mother and person. I became less stressed and rushed when I chose to simplify. Because my energy vibe shifted from intense to calm, I was also more pleasant around others.

In my divorce, I chose to downsize from a large, 4,000+ square foot house to a small 1,000 square foot apartment. It was a huge change and adjustment for two very active boys and their mother, who were used to the luxury of extra space and storage for all their belongings.

I quickly saw that my boys and I had to learn how to live more simply with fewer possessions. Choices had to be made about holding onto extra stuff—which felt heavier and constricting—or learning to live with less, which felt lighter and freer in our new home.

Needless to say, we chose to feel lighter and do not miss holding onto the extra space and things that previously weighed us down. A change that was not easy based on past experiences, but well suited for the present moment.

Reflect on your own personal experiences with choosing to simplify an aspect of your life. How did it make you feel?

Day 10

"When your life doesn't add up, start subtracting."
Unknown

Before my spiritual awakening, I lived my life as a people pleaser, always saying yes to helping someone else. I loved how fulfilling and rewarding it felt to help others. But at the same time, I lacked boundaries. More often than not, by constantly saying yes to others, I was saying no to me. As a result, I began to feel overwhelmed. It felt like I lacked personal control and that my life was chaotic.

Continuing with the theme of less equals more, we may recognize over time that having too much on our daily list of responsibilities can be a recipe for disaster.

This becomes a personal decision and a reflection that we can't always do it all. Saying no respects your own boundaries. It creates more awareness and control over your day. It decreases pressure and simplifies things.

Creating healthy boundaries strengthens your fifth chakra at the throat as you need to communicate and speak up for yourself. However, speaking up to simplify one's life also allows you to feel more secure, safe, and grounded in your existence, which strengthens the first chakra at the root.

The question becomes: "What are you comfortable saying no to?"

When my children were younger, I volunteered at their school in different leadership capabilities. This gave me a sense of purpose and respect and fulfilled my desire to feel connected. But I always took on too much.

In my last year volunteering in this capacity, I struggled with feeling that I had outgrown my role and duties, but I still held on. Then, the Universe shared this quote with me. It was exactly what I needed to understand. I was still trying to accomplish too much as I managed a difficult divorce and all my other responsibilities.

I became aware that it was time to resign from my duties on the school board. In doing this, I removed a huge commitment from my daily workload, which took some time internally to process and understand. Ultimately, this decision was what was needed on my path as it allowed me to feel lighter and, as a result, simplified my life.

Reflect on something that you subtracted from your life that made you feel lighter. How has that decision impacted your path?

Day 11

*"When we make an effort to include things we love in our
everyday lives, the benefits are tenfold; we are happier, healthier,
more present, and more resilient to stress."*
Dr. Mark Hyman

Early on in my therapy journey, Pam recognized that I needed to connect more with myself and better balance the different aspects of my world. As such, she would often discuss and have me reflect on myself by using a "balance wheel" activity. This helped develop an awareness that improvements in my day-to-day activities would allow me to feel more fulfilled, balanced, and happier.

Before Pam, I lived my life 100 percent for my kids, often neglecting my own personal needs, wants, and desires in favor of theirs. It's not that anything was wrong with this approach; however, for me, it was no longer serving my highest good.

It was an important and necessary recognition for me that I previously hadn't received the proper mental health tools or training to build a better quality of life. Until Pam. This four-and-a-half-year journey has been life-changing in many aspects of my life.

I worked on the "balance wheel" activity for at least six to nine months. Pam would refer back to it at different appointments until she felt I understood and was living with more balance. The "balance wheel" allows you to look at your day—divided into eight sections—and reflect on how you allocate your time within each section.

It includes the following sections of your life:

- Physical Environment
- Fun / Recreation
- Personal Growth
- Relationships / Romance
- Family / Friends
- Health / Well-being
- Financial / Security / Money
- Career / Work

For me, this activity raised awareness. I saw that I was spending a disproportionate amount of time in some areas while completely neglecting other sections of the wheel. This caused me to feel unfulfilled and unhappy. I was not living my truth.

What was the truth? There were things from my past that sparked joy. I lacked purpose and goal setting. I didn't make time for relationships. These things, to name a few, were no longer a priority for me. I knew this because I didn't spend any time doing them. Instead, my days were overscheduled and allowed no extra time for anything fun, free, or spontaneous to brighten them.

Flash-forward to the present, where my life has more balance and enjoyment. This is a product of time talking in therapy, reflecting and applying the idea that there is value in connection with others and that I don't need to have everything scheduled. My life is constantly evolving.

Looking at the sections of the "balance wheel," which sections would you like to allocate more time to in your daily life?

Day 12

"The wound is the place where the light enters you."
Rumi

The wound is where we work. It is the root that needs to be healed from the inside out.

The wound represents an awareness of pain, suffering, and darkness that is carried around in your subconscious. It is a target and opportunity for immense internal healing, transforming darkness into light. Awakening the truth from within brings more peace to your life.

Allowing yourself to face the wound is the first step to recognizing its existence. An awareness and acceptance that your body is suffering brings the wound to the surface.

Relax into the pain as an opportunity to reflect and release what is no longer serving your higher self. As a result, you'll feel lighter and have an overall sense of calmness.

As shared in Day 2, my unresolved emotional issues or wounds went really deep. Fear, regret, loneliness, unfulfillment, insecurity, worthlessness, abandonment, and lacking self-love, among others, needed to be healed. I needed to forgive myself and my parents.

Carrying the unresolved trauma from those wounds caused physical and mental ailments that took time to heal. My answer was to go inwards and focus on my true self. Reflecting on my own personal needs, wants, and desires was the only way out, using the tools of communicating and spiritual healing methods.

Communicating issues or problems is life-changing. I was blessed to find my therapist, Pam, to help with my mental health, but therapy is simply talking to a trusted friend. You can feel so much better when you share with someone else who values you. A true professional is not always necessary.

My Kundalini yoga training evolved into a daily practice where the postures moved stagnant energy and stretched my muscles, bringing life back into my physical body.

I also learned how to implement conscious breathing techniques for difficult and stressful situations, and to meditate. I prefer chanting mantra meditations as an opportunity to increase my presence and allow the answers to my questions to intuitively come to life. Lastly, the power of sound vibrations further cleared energies that I may have been holding onto so I could feel at peace.

All these techniques helped me to feel more alive and heal my wounds; and it is what I am recommending for all of you to implement on a daily basis through the use of this book. I am, and you are, a daily work in progress. I recognize that I am no longer striving for perfection. Instead, I offer myself grace and patience as I heal, as it is a marathon not a sprint. And so be it.

Are you aware of any wounds or issues that are currently weighing you down? When you bring awareness to those wounds, reflect on appropriate healing methods that could help you release them.

Day 13

"Use your wings to show you what you can become.
Roots to remind you where you're from."
Unknown

"Bi@#%, please. I'm from New Jersey."

This was a saying I recently saw on a pillow in a boutique gift store near where I live. Totally hysterical and true. A reminder that, yes, I am from New Jersey. Those are my roots and foundation growing up as a "Jersey Girl," living in a small suburb outside of NYC where a majority of the families were also Italian-Americans. The town and surrounding area were the basis for the famous HBO television series, *The Sopranos*. From the beginning, I connected with the show because those were my childhood experiences and memories.

Growing up, I was surrounded by my Italian culture: both at home and with people in my community. The family holiday traditions, language, food, festivals, etc. were a big part of my frame of reference with the rest of the world. In fact, as a teenager I was the "Bella Signorina" who was invited to ride on a float in the annual Columbus Day parade, something I was honored to be recognized for as my culture was very deeply rooted within my identity.

Attending a local college was my first "wake-up call" that the rest of the world wasn't like living in "Little Italy." I was exposed to other cultures and types of people who broadened my horizons. I entered the workforce with a thick Jersey girl accent where a close friend and colleague called me "Guido" as a play on my last name. It was totally out of love. Working in NYC, I was surrounded by so much diversity that I lost my cute accent, but I grew and learned to respect and appreciate other cultures around me.

In the present day, I still live in Northern Jersey, but further away from New York City, with more property. My town is regularly depicted on the television series *The Real Housewives of New Jersey*, which I watched for a few seasons but grew bored of because I couldn't relate to the characters. I know a handful of people in town who are Italian-Americans, but it's not the same type of experience I had growing up. Culture isn't binding us at our foundation.

My spiritual awakening brought me back to my roots and the remembrance of who I was before I grew up and was molded by the social norms and standards of others around me. I'd become driven by ego rather than my spirit. Along the way, I forgot my roots, who I was, and what I learned. I thought bigger was always better.

I loved my small town and childhood, but as an adult, I was always striving for more. I'm grateful that my wings helped broaden my experience and open my eyes to an existence I hadn't dreamed of. And I'm grateful that my strong foundation brought me back home.

The first Halloween after the separation, I took my boys back to my old neighborhood for trick-or-treating and it was their best experience to date. The families had so much Halloween spirit for themselves and others—nothing that I ever experience in our current town. I saw that growing up in my small town hadn't really been bad at all. It was filled with real, rich, and soulful experiences; and to me, that is what matters the most. And so be it.

When you reflect on the roots that built your foundation, does it seem like you're living more from a place of ego or spirit?

Day 14

"Home is where my boys are."
Unknown

There's no doubt about it, my boys are my light and love in this world. They influence and motivate all my decisions; they are my home. When I made the difficult decision to separate and eventually divorce from their father, I kept all of our emotional, spiritual, and mental needs in mind. I changed our family structure from a four-sided square to a three-sided triangle, with truth as our foundation. In architecture, the triangle is the strongest shape, having a strong base and providing immense support, and spiritually representing a path towards enlightenment.

My beautiful friend, Ali, and I are both "boy moms." We cherish this common ground and she gifted me the above quote on a home decor piece that she crafted specifically for me. I treasure this memento—it was an act of pure love.

Growing up, I was as girly as can be. I dreamed that I would have two girls, like my mom, as that was what my frame of reference and all my experiences were based on. My life changed during my second pregnancy when I found out we were having another boy. All my dreams of girl names, activities, and matching outfits evaporated. My boys are active, full of love and energy. They keep me on my toes and have helped me to shape and change how I view my world and existence. God had greater plans for me, that's for sure, and I wouldn't want it any other way.

Home is when and where my boys are with me. Our apartment doesn't feel the same without their activity, energy, excitement, and laughter. Even our puppy, Roco, acts differently in their presence. Our apartment is so full of life and I deeply appreciate time with them, both together and individually. Although they possess similar characteristics, their personalities and interests are completely different.

My bed is much fuller at night with their physical presence, but my heart is full of love. I may have less personal space, but I would never have it any other way. Early on in Michael's hearing loss journey, I recall driving back from a routine appointment that was a few hours away from our home, thinking, "I would go to the edge of the Universe to help my son get the right care that he needs." Our little triangle family is full of strength, love, and truth. As it should be.

Reflect on where you feel at home. Is it a physical place, person, feeling, or so on?

Day 15

"We are not defined by the family into which we are born, but the one we choose and create. We are not born, we become."
Tori Spelling

Growing up, I often felt like I didn't fit in with those around me. I often kept my true feelings to myself for fear of disapproval or judgment. I felt loved, supported, and well cared for, but there was always something missing.

That was until I finally met my tribe of spiritual yogis in teacher training. They became my go-to people for light, connection, and discussions about topics that fascinated me in a way that other conversations did not. They are my "soul family."

When I met these people, there was a comfort level and soul-deep connection. Our energies were aligned. I'd found something that I didn't even know was missing from my life—connection with others who were just as interested in healing themselves and others as I was.

Even as an adult, prior to this I never felt like I fit in anyplace. I went through the motions of what I was "supposed to do." I lived everything in my life this way, from choosing my college major to developing a career perspective, to building my marriage, and everything in between. I was feeding my ego versus feeding my spirit.

I didn't trust that I knew what was best for my needs, so I always deferred to others for direction. But the truth is, only I knew what was best deep down inside. I needed to remember not to seek direction from those who hadn't traveled to where I wanted to go. I needed to strengthen my intuition, which we will deep dive into in the "I am Intuitive" section.

Reflect on important relationships that have developed into your "soul family." How have these relationships changed your life?

Day 16

"No one can heal you the way you heal yourself,
and that's one of your greatest superpowers."
Unknown

"Ong Namo Guru Dev Namo" is the Adi Mantra that is chanted at the beginning of every Kundalini yoga practice. It allows you to tune in to higher states of consciousness and connect with yourself and the spiritual teachers who have come before.

The translation from Sanskrit is as follows:

"Ong Namo" means "I bow to the Divine wisdom of all that is."
"Guru Dev Namo" means "I bow to the Divine teacher within."

My own personal meaning is: "I call upon my higher true self, I call upon the Divine teacher within to lead and guide me in my practice." Furthermore, I have the power within me to transfer dark to light and lead me on my journey of truth.

This is a reminder that no one is coming to save you or me. We all need to rely on our own strength and power to lead the way.

Growing up I always thought, "I'll get a boyfriend and I'll be happy." Then it was, "I'll get married and I'll be happy." Finally, it became, "I'll have a child and I'll be happy." But I wasn't really happy.

I always relied on the power of another or something outside myself for completeness and direction; I never trusted my own self and intuition. That was before my spiritual awakening and my first Kundalini yoga class. I'd taken yoga in the past but never really connected with the teachings, and so I wasn't motivated to attend with any consistency, until Kundalini.

Kundalini was unlike anything I'd ever experienced. Class participants wore white, covered their heads, and welcomed me, the newbie. It was a very inclusive class full of love, light, and chanting (in a language I didn't understand). I had no idea what was happening. The postures were different, nothing about it was "sexy" compared to other yoga classes and each class taught a new kriya, or sequence of postures, designed to have a specific effect on the body. Classes concluded with a glorious gong bath to further clear energies, and then a calming meditation. All I knew was that I was hooked and wanted to feel as amazing as I did post-class, every day.

Kundalini yoga opened spiritual doors that I never knew existed. It offered an awareness that transported me into higher realms and provided the opportunity to finally connect to something I was so deeply passionate about. It was truly life-changing.

Now I have a healthier and more balanced outlook when it comes to future relationships. I understand that in a true spiritual connection and relationship one walks side by side, with a balance of male and female energies. Not dependent on the other for survival or existence, but perfectly complementing each other for their own growth and life experiences.

Reflect on your own superpowers. Have you been more reliant on others or yourself? How does that make you feel?

Day 17

"Your inner child is the real part of you that is pure, sincere, innocent, and solely connected to your heart. It is the source of your true identity. Awaken this part of yourself again. Be loyal to the real you and protect what is in your heart."

Unknown

Am I good? Am I safe? Am I loved?

These are the most basic and important questions at the heart and center of your inner child. When the answer to any of these questions is unequivocally yes, your inner child is at peace and secure. However, when there's doubt you start to lack the security and safety you once felt. This results in a disconnection from the inner child and, as a result, weakness at your root and foundation.

Healing my inner child strengthened my first chakra at the root. Reflecting back on who "Lisa" was as a child was, and is, a big piece of inner healing. She's the girl who was guided by her own free spirit and connected to her heart before social conditioning and the opinions of the world changed her. I wasn't strong enough to understand that I was doing myself a disservice by following others' opinions—from a desire for acceptance and inclusion—instead of following my own personal truth.

I know it can be painful to refer back to difficult memories from the past. But the truth is, in order to heal you must spend time being uncomfortable and reflecting on these intense emotional feelings.

Unresolved pain and trauma from the past will cause you present-day pain and trauma if they're not properly healed. You can't fully live in the present moment. Until you learn how to process and release, you'll live the same pain cycle. Past hurtful feelings don't serve one's higher self.

I wasn't a feeler growing up. My family didn't regularly discuss or communicate deeply about emotional feelings. Feelings got brushed aside and never properly handled. It wasn't my family's fault—none of us knew any better.

Now I get to break the cycle with my own boys. I communicate openly with the boys so they know I'm interested in their feelings and desires. I want to ensure their spirit and true self is being heard. This allows them to decide based on their own heartfelt feelings, allowing their true self to shine brightly, not through "Mommy's shadow." I use everyday occurrences as teachable moments to help change the family pattern.

> ***Reflect on any unresolved emotions from your inner child that may be preventing you from living for your highest self.***

Day 18

"We don't stop playing because we grow old;
we grow old because we stop playing."

George Bernard Shaw

Making fun a priority connects you to the childlike joys and simplicity of acting like a kid again. Allowing ourselves to act silly, carefree, and experience the pure joys that life has to offer strengthens our inner child. And as a result your root chakra becomes stronger.

I summarized my forty-first birthday with this quote: "Be like a kid again, they have little expectations and feel the joy, amazement, and excitement in the simplest things adults often take for granted."

My boys and I celebrated this birthday with an overnight stay in Hoboken, from a hotel overlooking the NYC skyline. My motive was to wake up watching the sunrise in my next year of life. This birthday was unique as it was just my boys and me—the first celebration post-separation. Recognizing that the past year was traumatic in so many ways for all of us, from moving into a new home, the pandemic, and bans on everything, I wanted to share this occasion with them by doing something special and out of character. It was beyond perfect and exactly as it was supposed to be.

From a suite hotel room with a view of the skyline, to special macarons, to a steakhouse for dinner, and Mommy's favorite breakfast place, we had a blast enjoying our quality time together. But the most memorable and favorite takeaway for them was a really cool park on the pier with an amazing slide; it was a child's dream playground, and free.

This experience made me question why, as adults, we complicate life by taking everything so seriously now.

This really fabulous park slide allowed me to "swing into forty-one" with pure joy and happiness; the best things in life really are the pure and simplest of them all. My boys taught me that I need to see and feel life through the eyes of a child again. The smallest teachers—who are wise beyond their years—bring the most amazing lessons.

Reflect back to a time when you were a child. What brought you joy and happiness. How did you spend your free time? Consider making time to add some of your childlike joys to your day, week, or weekend.

Day 19

"You can't pour from an empty cup. Take care of yourself first."
Unknown

I recall reading this quote countless times as a young, sleep-deprived mother, but never applying it to myself. Until my spiritual awakening I didn't really see the value of making time for my own self-care. However, now self-care and self-love has become a top priority. I understand that it's an investment in my future, not an unnecessary expense. And it's a continuous work in progress.

Most of my memories from early motherhood days are of energy depletion—feeling under-slept, undernourished, dehydrated, and overscheduled. With minimal mental capacity to be present, I reacted rather than being proactive. My fuse was short and I snapped when things didn't go as planned; I had no understanding of "let it go" or "go with the flow." And my nervous system could no longer keep up with the external demands I was placing on my body. I was experiencing a serious case of adrenal fatigue and the temple for my soul was on a steep decline towards deterioration.

Originally, I began to "fix" myself because I couldn't lose weight. My ego was stuck, worried about the external issues and my image, but in the end, I got to where I needed to be: uncovering the root causes of my body's suffering through the help of functional medicine. As I shared earlier, I had numerous health concerns when I began my functional medicine journey in November 2016. I believe that my lack of self-care and non-existent concern for myself were the root cause. I'd put everyone's needs before attending to myself and my body had had enough.

In the present day, I am more aware of the power of sleeping, which results in better reactions for my family; eating in regular intervals so I don't snap; understanding how to breathe during difficult times; making time to move my body; having regular interactions with friends for fun; and paying attention to the signs my body is giving me. I deserve the same amount of love, maybe even more, than I give to others.

> *Reflect on your own personal self-care routine. How do you make time for yourself? If you don't have a self-care routine, or if you'd like to have one, how can you be more aware of where you spend your time and energy, and how can you shift that so that you become a priority? What one small step could you start with today?*

Day 20

"Vulnerability is not winning or losing. It's having the courage to show up when you can't control the outcome."
Brené Brown

In the summer of 2018, I watched *Mamma Mia! Here We Go Again* in the movie theaters with my dear friend, Kim, whom I've known since college. *Mamma Mia!* was such a free-spirited movie: full of life, fun, and adventure. I watched in awe and amazement at the lead character's courage as she ventured through Europe, feeling her way through different locations until she found herself at home on a small Greek island. This fictional experience began my own internal reflection, as I recognized that I wished I had the courage to live as freely and take risks as Donna had in the movie. This tiny seed that I planted would soon grow.

I shared about this experience at a therapy session and Pam responded by giving me homework to watch Brené Brown's TED talk on vulnerability. I believe Pam chose this because she recognized that, at that point, I hadn't lived my life with vulnerability and I was now beginning to question some past choices. To be honest, I didn't even know what the word "vulnerability" meant as I had no previous exposure to it.

Brené Brown taught me about living life with vulnerability. She defines it as "uncertainty, risk, and emotional exposure. But vulnerability is not weakness, it's our most accurate measure of courage."

I lived my life very safely; risk-taking was not a quality of mine. I only did something if I knew the outcome or if I was positive that I could excel at it—a product of being a true perfectionist. I wasn't comfortable having difficult conversations and avoided conflicts at all costs.

Living this way was boring and shallow. I spent my life in my head, disconnected from my heart and feelings. Which is why the concept of "allowing one to be vulnerable" was completely foreign to me.

Understanding what it truly meant to live with vulnerability began to intrigue me. What would life be like to try something new without a guaranteed result? What would life be like if I dared to go beyond my comfort zone? Once I started to get the courage to become vulnerable, that is when life became more interesting.

Fast forward to the present. I am living life in the deep: a place where I generally feel alive and connected to my feelings now more than ever. Having deep conversations and experiences with like-minded individuals has become my saving grace and connects profoundly with my soul. I enjoy the beauty of the unknown and have gone into uncharted waters, like when I announced to my husband that I wanted to separate and get my own apartment during a pandemic in May 2020. My decision was a vulnerable one—the outcome was unknown, but I did it anyway as it came from my heart.

Perhaps the experience of allowing myself to be vulnerable can best be described by Anaïs Nin, who wrote, "I must be a mermaid. I have no fear of depths and a great fear of shallow living."

Allowing yourself to be vulnerable strengthens the root chakra. Reflect on a time when you allowed yourself to be vulnerable. How did you feel?

Day 21

*"Feelings come and go like clouds in a windy sky.
Conscious breathing is my anchor."*
Thich Nhat Hanh

In 2018, I began to recognize that during stressful or difficult situations I wasn't breathing at all. Uneasiness caused me to hold onto my breath and just push through. But this awful habit was no longer working for me. It left me feeling depleted of my energy, dizzy, and lightheaded. Slowly, I saw it was time for a change.

During a therapy session, Pam shared with me that she uses a decorative picture in her office that says "Breathe." It helps remind her of the power of breathing in her daily life.

Since I was committed to change, and I believed in the "Power of Pam," I knew I wanted an external reminder in my world. Shortly after, I found a bracelet that said "Breathe." I connected with it and I knew it was my answer. The bracelet is a daily reminder that I can carry with me so I remember to feed my body with the necessary energy it needs. Energy that helps it thrive, not just survive.

During my Kundalini yoga teacher training in 2019, I learned that our body views the breath as "prana." Oxford Languages states, "Prana is seen as a universal energy which flows in currents in and around the body." Pranayama is how to regulate one's prana or breath through techniques and exercises. I learned how to teach pranayama to others and include simple exercises in my own classes so that others have the tools necessary to help manage their own lives.

A quote from Pattabhi Jois says, "When the breath control is correct, mind control is possible." In other words, learning how to consciously control your breath improves the vitality of your mind and strengthens the fifth chakra at the throat center, which is connected to your area of truth.

Learning how to consciously breathe has been my own personal saving grace during difficult situations, and I am so grateful for the power to help myself when I need it the most. I connect so deeply with the power of the breath that, while writing this book, I tattooed the Sanskrit symbol for 'breathe' on my left hand. It's a constant reminder of the most basic and important thing we do daily. Plus, breathing is a tool and technique anyone can implement anywhere, not just on a yoga mat. And nobody has to know, unless you want to spread the light and help someone else who could benefit.

Have you noticed a connection between your breathing patterns and your actions? Reflect on your awareness and any associated feelings.

Day 22

Why Complicate Life?

"Missing somebody? . . . Call
"Wanna meet up? . . . Invite
"Wanna be understood? . . . Explain
"Have questions? . . . Ask
"Don't like something? . . . Say it
"Like something? . . . State it
"Want something? . . . Ask for it
"Love someone? . . . Tell it
"We just have one Life. Keep it simple."
Unknown

My marriage was built on a constant state of miscommunication, and sometimes no communication at all. I lived in fear of saying the wrong thing and I was afraid to share my whole self. I had to build up courage to ask about taking my yoga class. My goal in every conversation? To shield myself.

Moving into the light from darkness gave me the opportunity to shape mine and my boys' future in terms of communicating. I am preparing them to have difficult conversations, something that I only learned in my late thirties. It's a very important skill that only happened because of the darkness I was in, and I want to prepare my boys in a way that wasn't done for me.

Respecting and paying attention, which are both connected to communicating with others, are so crucial for one's emotional well-being. Communication minimizes confusion, keeps others updated, and gives people an understanding about what is happening. Being a strong communicator also strengthens your throat chakra as you use your voice to express yourself.

Post-spiritual awakening, I often overcommunicate my feelings, beliefs, and truths to both friends and strangers. If you have something to say, you should say it. You never know how those words can brighten someone else's day, just by speaking your own personal truth from the heart.

Reflect on your own personal communication style. Do you tend to over- or under-communicate? How could improving your communication style simplify your life?

Day 23

"Love is the door. Chanting is the key."
Bhagavan Das

A component of healing in Kundalini yoga is chanting mantras—this is one of my most favorite parts of my Kundalini yoga practice. I practice them daily. Chanting resonates deeply with the truth of my soul in a way I'd never experienced. Pure love and joy resonate through every cell in my body as I chant. It's definitely the answer and a door I never knew was missing in my life. Chanting is so close to my heart.

Mantra is a repetitive verse that, when regularly chanted, resonates with one's soul and becomes a part of one's consciousness. Oxford Languages defines mantra as "a word or sound repeated to aid concentration in meditation." It's usually chanted in Sanskrit and is derived from two roots: manas meaning "mind" and tra meaning "tool." As such, mantras are considered tools for thought; you can use them to focus and calm the mind, decrease stress, change your mood, improve your attention, and increase concentration.

When planning for this book, I wanted it to reflect my true authentic spiritual journey, so each section and the title are all based on mantras. "I am . . ." is an extremely powerful mantra for a person to connect with. It's an affirmation to motivate and inspire you to be your best self and affirm the way you want to live.

Chanting from the soul using the power of your voice deeply connects and strengthens the throat chakra. It is singing your truth for the world to hear.

"No matter what people think of you, always keep singing your own song. Always." Unknown

Reflect on how your body feels when you chant or sing. If you're uncomfortable with this, what are some of your hesitations?

Day 24

"Speak to your children as if they are the wisest, kindest, most beautiful, and magical humans on Earth, for what they believe is what they will become."
Brooke Hampton

In June 2020, I broke the cycle the day I decided to move out and live my path of truth. At the time, my boys were seven and eight. My separation and the eventual reality that we would be a divorced family aged my boys. They became more aware of their surroundings. And everything was a teaching and learning experience—it all became an energy exchange to me. Using love, kindness, and compassion as my foundation, it was best to explain why things were happening so they would understand.

Through it all, the underlying theme was, "No matter if it is difficult, always tell the truth." That is what I did and that is what I want them to feel comfortable doing. I was modeling a behavior for them to use in their future on their own paths.

No "Mommy Handbook" exists, especially when you're used to living as a traditional family and then become a non-traditional family. The best recipe for me was to take things slow, with lots of communication. I made sure to understand and respect my boys' feelings and desires as we were in unfamiliar waters.

I adamantly believe my boys should lead their own paths of truth and that starts with them having the courage to be their own real and authentic self.

This book of light is all for my boys. The opportunity to share my path with lessons for others and the turning of darkness into light is important, but my motivating factor is and always will be my boys. Society shows traditional-looking families with both parents living under the same roof. It's against the norm for parents to not live that way and the last thing I want them to feel is that there was something wrong with our own family structure. Just be yourself and everything will fall into place as it is intended to be.

Reflect on your own path of truth. Do you meet yourself with kindness, love, and compassion? If not, reflect on the changes you could make.

Day 25

"The voice can only reproduce what the ear can hear."
Dr. Alfred Tomatis

The ability to hear is directly connected to your own voice, and so is the ability to speak your truth. However, if you're not aware of or able to understand the sounds around you, then verbal communication becomes a challenge.

In August 2020, my angel, Michael, was officially diagnosed with bilateral permanent hearing loss at the age of seven. Without hearing aids, he's considered deaf.

Michael's hearing has always been slightly off and at times he lacked focus. He'd had some inconsistent hearing tests in the past and I'd also started to notice behavior concerns that were out of character for him. When I received an Akashic reading in July 2020, I learned that sound healing could help him. And we'd eventually understand what was wrong with his hearing, but I needed to be careful with his voice—this was the bigger concern.

Michael's diagnosis, although shocking, made sense. I wanted to do everything possible to help him, and so I became deeply fascinated with the power of sound healing. The more I learned about different sound instruments and their healing powers, the more I believed that I'd finally found my path and purpose. Sound healing facilitates the movement of energy in your body, especially with things that no longer serve you and may be causing disease and sickness. Bringing the cells in the body back to their original cellular level allows the body to release, restore, and heal. As I learned more, sound healing became an opportunity to help my son, myself, and others.

In doing research for my new sound healing path, I came across this quote and it all made sense. Michael has the ability to speak; that was never a concern. But his brain had to work really hard to understand the world around him. Prior to his diagnosis, he became very withdrawn. He struggled to trust or connect with others and constantly relied on me to respond or speak for him. If he didn't know where I was, he would panic.

Because the lack of hearing made it hard for him to understand what was happening around him, Michael suffered to be heard and understood. It was a very dark moment in the waves of his life, but darkness often brings light. Now Michael's life is radiant and shines brighter as he learns how to manage his disability. As I'm writing this, he's had his "new ears", as I often refer to them, for slightly over a year. He's done a 180-degree transformation. He is confident and vocal and other boys are attracted to his own bright light. On the baseball field, he's excelling as a pitcher and is an excellent team player. His peers see him as a role model and it's a beautiful sight for me to witness. Everything has changed now that he can hear and understand the world around him.

Reflect on your own ability to hear, to connect to your voice, and to understand the world around you. Were there situations in the past where your lack of understanding prevented you from putting your best self first?

Day 26

*"The best teachers are those who show you
where to look but don't tell you what to see."*
Alexandra K. Trenfor

My spiritual teacher, Kathy, taught me how to heal others with ancient Tibetan singing bowls, gongs, chimes, mind bowls, and other instruments. The Universe needed me to connect with this powerful woman as she held the key to open my heart and soul—both into all the beautiful ways sound could heal others, but also to heal myself in the process.

I was initially drawn to learn about the singing bowls and become a practitioner to help mitigate my son's hearing loss. I recognized that his hearing would never fully return, but I had high hopes that it wouldn't worsen. Furthermore, if I was going to spend time and energy to learn something new, there had to be a connection to help my family at the same time.

Since I began, Kathy continually shared with me, "When you give a healing, you get a healing." And this is so very, very true. The beautiful instruments had great power over my journey and amplified my connection to life, love, and spirit. Every healing I gave changed me and vibrated my soul higher.

Kathy is my teacher, my second therapist, my biggest cheerleader, and my friend. She has also gone through her own divorce process, referring to her first husband as her lessons. She's been a great resource—sent from the Divine for guidance and love—as I navigated my own difficult divorce. A divorce which was the opposite of the spiritual life I'd created. Kathy helped me recognize that my divorce process was my teacher and to view, understand, and manage it with grace, gratitude, and dignity.

Today, Kathy patiently listens to me as I share feedback learned from my healings on clients, spiritual updates from my own journey, or issues related to my divorce with compassion and understanding. Our training began with "All in Divine timing," which is a beautiful phrase indicating that everything happens exactly when it's supposed to happen and I'm no longer in control.

Kathy saw that this was where I needed to be and allowed me to figure it out for myself. Working regularly with sound and vibrations slowed me down tremendously. I learned about the power of energy, both my own and others'. I started to keep my energy, rather than giving it away so easily and wasting it on something not meant for me.

Teachers project the truth to help others; this projection connects with and strengthens your throat chakra. Kathy recognized my strong light and her role in guiding me to my purpose before I recognized my purpose myself—a purpose so pure and natural that it fell into place effortlessly. Living my purpose is an unexplainable feeling that can only be described as a perfect match. And so be it.

Reflect on a similar experience you've had with a teacher who, by sharing their truth, helped you. How has it inspired you on your own path?

Day 27

"Our fingerprints don't fade from the lives we touch."
Judy Blume

I am my boys' first everything. Their first home, first love, and first teacher. My fingerprints permanently remain on their souls even when we are apart. They're a direct extension and reflection of me through their actions, behaviors, and mannerisms. It's a huge responsibility and undertaking, which I didn't realize until post-spiritual awakening.

In February 2018, my boys were asked to be the ring bearers in a cousin's wedding, when they were four and six years old. Due to a rainstorm, the bride was late with a church full of guests. Beyond handsome and adorable in their matching tuxedos with tails and shiny shoes, my boys walked the aisle handing out bubbles to guests. Nobody asked them to do this; they'd decided between themselves that they should help pass the time. They are definitely helpers in this world; they are social and hospitable and brighten others' days with a joyful smile. These beautiful traits warm my heart, because of the sweetness and truth that they were learned from their mother.

As I shared on Day 26, teachers project the truth to help others; this connects with and strengthens your throat chakra. We all are capable of teachable moments with those around us. As the beloved

Mr. Rogers said, "The most important people in a child's life are that child's parents and teachers. That means parents and teachers are the most important people in the world."

Reflect on a time you received a teachable moment from someone you respected or provided a teachable moment for someone in need. Why was it so memorable?

Day 28

*"Sometimes what is meant for you can't find you
simply because you aren't being yourself."*
Maryam Hasnaa

In order to truly be yourself and live the path of truth, you must be comfortable with those around you in your environment and surroundings. You should feel safe and comfortable to fully express yourself, guided by your own internal spirit. This is evidence of a strong and balanced throat and root chakra.

Healing work takes time. We need to give ourselves patience, love, and kindness as we do the internal steps necessary to heal. Healing elevates one's vibration, so understanding what is meant for me today is not my final destination. We are constantly evolving and changing; in that process, what is meant for you also energetically changes as you elevate.

Being real is rare. Do it anyway. Be that way with yourself and others. The beautiful quote reminds you to be radiant and always be yourself. What is meant for you will always find its way, especially if you are living in the truth. It will feel good, natural, and effortless. Relax into life and be at peace knowing all that is meant to be will be.

Reflect on a person in your life who is real in how they present themselves. What do you notice? How does being around them help you be more real? Are there any characteristics of their life that can help you be truly yourself?

Day 29

*"Authenticity is the daily practice of letting go of who we
think we're supposed to be and embracing who we are."*
Brené Brown

Oxford Languages defines authentic as "of undisputed origins; genuine" and authenticity as "the quality of being authentic." To me
this means to live your life by being as real as real can be. And to
trusting your intuition at the soul level, even if it differs from the
social conditioning and norms around you.

On Day 3, I shared my truth that I decided to separate from my
husband. This difficult decision was based on my feelings, connecting my soul, heart, and intuition. I chose to live with authenticity
when I decided to leave my comfortable home and existence with
my husband for the unknown in a small apartment by myself. It
took a lot of courage to go against the societal norms of . . .

What will people think of me?

But I reminded myself about the powerful quote from
Marianne Williamson: "Ego says, once everything falls into place,
I will feel peace. Spirit says, find your peace and everything will fall
into place."

Putting my ego aside, I followed the path of my spirit to the
most authentic and genuine person that I could be. Nothing about
it was fake; it was real and I figured it out. I had to rely on myself
for what I believed was the right thing to do for my spirit. I became

more resourceful. And I had to trust myself, which I hadn't been capable of before this. It was my time to shine.

This was my journey. My life. I had the tools to thrive. I believed in the power of my faith and that everything would be OK at the other end of the rainbow. And it is.

Reflect on your life. Do you live most aspects of your life with authenticity? If not, how can you?

Day 30

"Find out who you are and be that person. That's what your soul was put on Earth to be. Find that truth, and everything else will come."
Ellen DeGeneres

We are all spiritual beings having a human existence. Our energetic souls were given a special purpose and truth for our time living on this planet; living this way truly connects us with our fullest potential and the power of our own unique spirit. As Pablo Picasso said, "The meaning of life is to find your gift. The purpose of life is to give it away."

How do I know if I am living my purpose?

When your spirit lives from a place of purpose, you're able to trust in a higher power and in your own intuition for direction and guidance. Life is lighter and it flows more naturally and with ease. You feel calm and full of joy and happiness with an overall sense that you are living as you should be.

According to my teachers, our soul's purpose and destiny can be found in our own spiritual name, which is tattooed on our forehead. Purpose is also referred to as living one's "dharma." My spiritual name is Prem Livjot, which was identified in December 2019.

Prem = Divine love
Liv = one-pointed devotion
Jot = reference to light

Taken together, this is translated from Gurmukhi (the alphabet of the sacred language of the Sikhs) as "the sacred Princess who embodies God's Divine love and light through the power of her one-pointed devotion." This very special name is my truth. As time has passed since that day, I've recognized that I have been naturally fulfilling my purpose or dharma in my daily interactions with others as an extension of who I am. It's a beautiful thing to shine your love and light for others in order to recognize that they themselves possess their own beautiful light as well.

Do you know who you are? Are you living as that person? If the answer is no, what is stopping you?

I Am

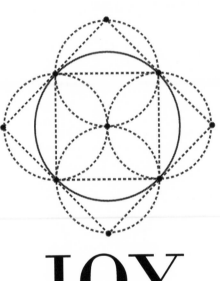

JOY

I Am Joy

DAYS 31–60

Living your life as if a river of joy flows within you is a beautiful expression of living from your highest good.

Choosing to allow the feeling of joy to embody you is an association with the second chakra energy center, at the sacral area, located at the sexual organs. Joy reverberating through you can be your leading feeling. In this chapter, you'll learn that living with joy strengthens and heals the second chakra.

As it relates to the second chakra, you will understand that:

- When you choose to live with joy, you can bring happiness into your life.
- Recognizing and connecting with your emotions and feelings strengthens the energy at the sacral area.
- It is important to have vitality within and true happiness with your own life.
- Water is the element associated with the sacral area, and learning to live life in the deep end and going with the flow are key components to strengthening this area.
- Having a creative flow of energy and allowing things to inspire you is key to bringing joy into your life.
- Human connections and relationships are powerful and

need to be maintained.

- It is important to live with passion.
- Having intimacy with another is not purely physical, but also the ability to see another's soul.
- Sexual energy is the creative force of the Universe.
- A balance between male and female polarities within yourself is necessary to maintain a healthy and balanced sacral area.
- The sacral area sources the creative energy for new life.

Tune In with the Adi Mantra
"Ong Namo Guru Dev Namo"

To center yourself in the higher self before practicing Kundalini yoga, chant the Adi Mantra three times.

Ong Namo Guru Dev Namo" translates to "I bow to the Divine wisdom of all that is" and "I bow to the Divine teacher within."

HOW TO PRACTICE

- *Posture:* Sit in Easy Pose, with the spine erect.
- *Eye Position:* Eyes slightly closed, focused at the Third Eye, which is the point between the brows.
- *Mudra: Prayer Pose.* Place the palms of the hands flat together to neutralize the positive (right, or male) and negative (left, or female) sides of the body. Your thumbs should press against the sternum and your forearms will be parallel to the floor.
- Consciously begin to breathe. Gently inhale through your nose, feel the breath fill up your belly, fill up your lungs, and expand your rib cage. On the exhale from your nose,

recognize the breath leaving your body. When ready to "tune in" with the Adi Mantra, inhale and exhale deeply from the nose and begin chanting the mantra three times.

Asanas

The asanas listed below focus on strengthening the energy center at the sacral area. It is recommended that you hold each posture for one to two minutes with a slight rest in between. Remember to stay within while holding the postures and while resting, keep your eyes closed, focusing on the Third Eye. This will allow you to focus on yourself and build your intuition, plus learn to trust your own power and ability.

- Butterfly
- Cobra
- Nose to Knee
- Back Rolls
- Baby Pose

Find a description of each posture in the Appendix on page 418.

Meditation
"Har Hare Hari Wahe Guru"

This mantra for creativity invokes the flow and cycle of creative activity. Using the primal force of creativity to rid one of the difficult situations in life can bring you through any block and opens up your own creative energy. Chanting this will open the primal force of creativity in your own life.

- *Mantra: "Har Haray Hari Wahe Guru"* (for pronunciation)

- *Translation:* "All aspects of the creator are bliss." This includes three qualities of "*Har*"

The transaltion is broken down as follows:
- *Har:* the seed potential of infinite creativity
- *Haray:* the flow of the creative force
- *Hari:* the completion of the creative force
- *Wahe Guru:* an expression of joy and wonder at the beauty of the process

HOW TO PRACTICE

- *Posture:* Sit in Easy Pose, with the spine erect.
- *Eye Position:* Eyes closed, focused at the Third Eye, which is the point between the brows.
- *Mudra:* Gyan mudra is the seal of knowledge. To form, put the tip of the thumb together with the tip of the index finger. Allow your palms to face up, resting them on your knees with your fingers resting on your legs.
- *Time:* Continue for three minutes. Build to seven minutes.
- *Helpful Tip:* Soundtracks are available to chant as you complete the meditation that can be found on any app that streams music. I like to chant this meditation along with the artist, Aurora.

Deep Relaxation

- *Posture:* Lie on your back in Corpse Pose. With your eyes closed, place your arms at your sides, with palms facing up. Allow your body to rest, process, and absorb the movement of energy.
- *Time:* One to three minutes minimum.

Ending Prayer

To close your Kundalini practice, chant three long *Sat Naams*.

Sound Healing

Enjoy this ten-minute sound healing ensemble to further relax your mind and body. Consider listening during deep relaxation or at another time during your day when your body could benefit from and enjoy the beautiful healing gift of sound and vibrations.

> **Access this month's asana videos, meditation, sound healing audio, and more at www.LisaAnnese.com/i-am-light**

Day 31

Choose Joy!

"Don't wait for things to get easier, simpler, better. Life will always be complicated. Learn to be happy right now. Otherwise, you'll run out of time."
Unknown

Oxford Languages defines joy as "a feeling of great pleasure and happiness." To me, it is the "golden ticket" of feelings—the ultimate positive feeling, where others are derived from, but it all starts with the power of joy.

Joy is a favorite feeling for both Pam and me, but it took me several years of therapy to recognize that it was missing from my life. In fact, prior to Pam, I wouldn't have ever described myself as "full of joy" or viewed anything as joyful. It wasn't a part of my vocabulary.

Before my spiritual awakening, I operated as a machine, living from my head rather than my heart. I was too busy to make time to recognize my feelings or the impact they would have on my life.

Choose to see joy—even during your darkest moments. You must recognize that there is always a silver lining to be found, a learning opportunity to uncover, or a pivotal moment that can propel you to a better place. When you view life from a place of joy, it elevates your vibration. The uplifted attitude that results can carry your soul on the right path for your journey.

"Do things that spark joy" is a favorite saying of Pam's and it's something I regularly implement throughout my day.

Now joy is a shared feeling of importance for Pam and me. Often, I "gift" her joy in the form of handmade crafted items, Christmas ornaments, or home decorations. My love language is to give gifts, so Pam is always a top recipient because she has helped me tremendously on my journey, plus she is appreciative and values my efforts.

Your life will change when you always choose joy. Every day.

How does your life improve when you view it through the eyes of joy versus a more negative feeling or emotion?

Day 32

"When you do things from your soul, you feel a river moving in you, a joy."
Rumi

If you have either lost your joy or want to experience joy, start living your soul's truth. Then you will find it.

In the summer of 2021, Pam told me to read *Broken Open* by Elizabeth Lesser. This Rumi quote is woven into the theme of the book. At the time, I was about nine months into a difficult and stressful divorce process with no end in sight.

This is my favorite book to date about spirituality; it is written about the author's own path of truth, leading to her own divorce after being "broken open" herself. It includes her journey, but also stories of others who have their own "broken open" truths. These truths have completely changed their lives. They've essentially become a "Twice-Born" person when their soul became more aware that they were living a half-lived life. According to Lesser, "Twice-Born people trade the safety of the known for the power of the unknown." Reading this confirmed for me that I am living as a "Twice-Born" person, and thereby experiencing my own phoenix process, as I mentioned on Day 2.

Lastly, according to Lesser, "Our lives ask us to die and to be reborn every time we confront change . . . When we descend all the way down to the bottom of a loss, and dwell patiently, with an open heart, in the darkness and pain, we can bring back up with us the sweetness of life and exhilaration of inner growth. When there is nothing left to lose, we find the true self—the self that is whole, the self that is enough, the self that no longer looks to others for definition, or completion or anything but companionship on the journey. This is the way to live a meaningful life—a life of real happiness and inner peace."

It was such a powerful feeling to read about someone else's journey through similar darkness and see that they'd chosen to follow the light of truth. It helped me recognize that I am not alone and that it is important to feel the river of joy in my body. This quote perfectly connects with the energies of the second chakra, located at the sacral area, as water is the element associated with this area.

Water is fluid and constantly free-flowing. We should cultivate an ability to "go with the flow" in life. Understanding that joy, like water, has the power and ability to be free-flowing in your life is priceless. This is the epitome of how we all should live—with our feelings flowing free, like water. I can't think of anything more powerful. And so be it.

Reflect on a time you felt joy flowing through you like a river.

Day 33

"Don't move the way fear makes you move. Move the way love makes you move. Move the way joy makes you move."

Osho

Fear, as a noun, is defined by Oxford Languages as "an unpleasant emotion caused by the belief that someone or something is dangerous, likely to cause pain, or a threat." The definition of the verb form of fear is "to be afraid of someone or something as likely to be dangerous, painful, or threatening."

Prior to my spiritual awakening, I constantly carried fear around with me. My mind would immediately go to the negative or the worst-case scenario in every situation. This caused a chain reaction of anxiety, uneasiness, and discomfort. I never allowed myself to focus on the possibility of a better outcome. The question, "What if this goes better than I expect and leads to an ultimate feeling of joy as an end result?" was unfathomable.

Why do we always do this? Are we programmed to fear the worst? I think so.

One of the important things I learned during my yoga training was to not let feelings go by the wayside. We need to fully embrace them internally and accept that they exist. If not, our subconscious bodies store them as an unhealed emotion. This causes pain until we recognize and ultimately release them. Connecting with our feelings and emotions strengthens our second chakra at the sacral area.

Let's change the narrative from the start by choosing to act from a place of joy or ultimately love rather than from a place of fear. Give yourself the love you need to heal, learn, and let go.

We tend to fear the worst, so we don't allow ourselves to feel the pain of disappointment or other probable negative emotions. That's why I focused on the negative or worst possible outcome and, in turn, lived in fear.

The true path to self-healing occurs when you allow yourself to recognize your own body's response to unpleasant feelings—even if it makes you feel uncomfortable.

As such, remember to choose the path of love over that of fear. Every day.

Lastly, as Yoda states, "Train yourself to let go of everything you fear to lose."

Reflect for yourself. How do you feel when you choose to live from a place of love or joy versus fear?

Day 34

"Be who you are and say what you feel, because those who mind don't matter and those who matter don't mind."

Dr. Seuss

This quote was printed on the top of a menu at a local restaurant where I dined with two close mom friends. We resonated with the words and how they reflected our relationships with each other and life.

I initially connected with these moms while planning and organizing school fundraisers. We were heavily involved with the same underlying reason: our kids.

Over the years, our relationship has grown and developed into a closer and deeper heartfelt connection. Now our conversations feel like home, and our time spent together is natural, real, and true. There is no judgment. It is free and glorious.

It makes me reflect on being in the presence of others who lack that strong connection. Those situations feel unnatural, conversations are forced, and true feelings about topics are often censored as they aren't on par with the others' feelings. My soul feels transported to a place that is far from home. A place where I no longer belong.

Understand that where you feel at home is where your attention and energy is best suited. Remember to speak your true feelings regardless of who is in your presence. Connecting and expressing those authentic feelings and emotions strengthens the second and fifth chakras.

Your truth matters and those who matter to you will thank you for sharing it with them.

> ***Reflect on how you speak your true feelings when you're with different people. Why or why not? How do you know when you feel at home?***

Day 35

"To the heart in you, don't be afraid to feel. To the sun in you, don't be afraid to shine. To the love in you, don't be afraid to heal. To the ocean in you, don't be afraid to rage. To the silence in you, don't be afraid to break."

Najwa Zebian

Our emotions and feelings play a huge role in our interactions with ourselves and the world around us. Unfortunately, many of those emotions are not appropriately felt or expressed and this causes havoc on our soul and body.

Karla McLaren says, "Emotions are the language of the soul." Before my spiritual awakening, I lived from my head not my heart. I was constantly thinking and processing using logic. I seriously ignored my emotions and so I didn't express my soul very well either.

Emotions and feelings weren't expressed in my marriage; we connected intellectually. It seemed to me that my husband would rather remain silent about an issue or concern instead of communicating something that he might later regret. Out of fear, I went along with this approach, to the detriment of my soul and truth. This caused a tremendous amount of unreleased and unhealed emotions to exist in my body.

Flash-forward to the present, I recognize that if I had the courage to face those emotions and feelings, it would have been to both our benefit and would have helped us both heal from the inside out.

Now I approach life through the power of my heart. I am more aware than ever how a situation, issue, or person makes my soul feel on the inside, and I am fully present and accepting of it. I can offer that awareness to my boys and truly understand how they feel. This motivates the direction of my decisions and ultimately their own paths.

Do you approach life with a focus on the logic of your head or the feelings in your heart? How is your approach working for you?

Day 36

*"Don't ask what the world needs. Ask what makes you come alive, and go do it.
Because what the world needs is people who have come alive."*
Howard Thurman

This quote was on the website of the Kundalini yoga studio I regularly attended—the same studio where I later became certified to teach. I immediately connected with the quote and the studio as the projection into the Universe was about vitality and feeling alive as a person. At the end of 2017, when I was looking for a yoga studio, I didn't feel alive. I was technically alive as I was walking and breathing, but my soul wasn't flourishing the way it is now.

I have collected quotes since I was a child and I keep a list of all the ones I've connected with or ones that have touched me in a special way. The owner of the yoga studio, Michele, was also a collector of quotes. They were all around her studio. I believe it wasn't a coincidence that I had a connection to her studio. And in my first book, I have the opportunity to create and put out into the Universe a compilation of quotes that have helped me on my own healing journey. This isn't a coincidence either.

You must live your life with vitality. It is crucial to your existence and ability to thrive in this world. Having a strong sense of vitality also connects with the second chakra. Oxford Languages describes vitality as "the state of being strong and active; energy." Also, "the power giving continuance of life, present in all living things."

We are all made of energy. To be alive with energy—alive with passion, vigor, and life—that is what it is all about.

The yoga studio I attended was like my second home. A beautiful, peaceful sanctuary full of love and light, it was on the second floor of a building. I recall feeling transported to a state of peace as I walked up those stairs to enter the studio. My soul knew I was approaching home with my people. I finally felt safe to be me.

This is where I knew I needed to be. I had found my sanctuary. My safe space.

Do you live with vitality? Have you found what makes you come alive?

Day 37

"When I was five years old, my mother always told me that happiness was the key to life. When I went to school, they asked me what I wanted to be when I grew up. I wrote down, 'happy.' They told me I didn't understand the assignment, and I told them they didn't understand life."

John Lennon

I absolutely love this quote. It connects to the heart and soul about life and what really matters at the end of the day. Every time I read it, I feel my heart smiling.

Ask yourself, "What will make me happy?"

When I was younger, I never asked myself this important question. It didn't motivate my decisions about the direction of my path. As I shared earlier, I made decisions from my headspace not my heart. Connecting with and trusting my feelings to guide me was outside of my frame of reference and comfort zone.

I majored in accounting in college because I was good at it; I knew I could get a job and it made my parents proud of me. In 2002, I passed all four parts of the CPA exam at one time, a huge deal, and was hired by one of the Big Four accounting firms. A few years later, I completed my MBA. In my mind I was set, but not my heart. My heart was unhappy.

Was this the definition of happiness? Absolutely not.

I was "checking the boxes" and looking outside myself for items on a checklist that would make me happy. However, the path of happiness was to connect with my soul's true desire and wants, which I would learn during my spiritual awakening.

I had a nice paycheck and credentials behind my name. I felt secure, but I was bored. There were passions and skills that I wasn't utilizing, and connecting with others was missing from my day-to-day responsibilities. I often dreamed about owning my own business and I recognized that aspects of my soul weren't fully living in my job as an accountant.

In 2005, I remember reading a magazine article called "How to be the It Girl" where the author wrote about her own path of considering becoming a lawyer because her parents would be proud of her, but she had visions of poking her eyes out with pencils. She later joined the school newspaper and recognized her passion for journalism. She changed her major and life path because she followed her truth and happiness.

After reading this article, I recognized that I wanted to poke my eyes out with pencils, and it showed. Living for my truth and passions was missing from my life. I knew at that moment I had to make a change, to connect with my soul and find my own happiness with myself.

Now, in the present I can say with 100 percent confidence that I am happy. I have no regrets for my past decisions and life choices as it was all part of my own plan for lessons and growth. I recognize that all those steps along the way have provided the foundation for my future. One that is brighter than I could have ever imagined.

Happiness with your true self is definitely the key to life. It becomes a domino effect around you when fully living from the heart space as intended.

Reflect on your own path. When you make decisions based on your happiness, how does that impact your life?

Day 38

"Don't wait for everything to be perfect to be happy."
Unknown

At bedtime, one summer evening in 2021, I felt myself smiling. I was present enough to capture happiness and gratitude in my body. This was the opposite emotion from what I'd felt when I woke up earlier that day. I'd woken up in the middle of the night, stressed about the current state of things. There was so much division and hate and I felt that, despite my efforts, my voice was unheard.

Emotions and feelings are powerful. Feelings of fear, anger, and hate put the body in a lower vibrational state, causing sickness. And those of love, joy, and gratitude have the opposite effect, which can raise your vibration. The ultimate goal is to maintain and live at a higher vibration, but that reality may not always be possible.

For me, during this particular instance, my morning meditation helped elevate my body to feel lighter and my mind to feel clearer. I raised my vibration and understood that I was approaching this difficult time in the wrong way. The answer was to approach with the power of love, not hate.

Happiness is a state of the mind; that is where our power lives. Our lives are full of daily challenges outside of our control, but we can control how we react and respond. It also helps to accept the reality that nothing is perfect. From a young age, I lived for perfectionism and thought that it was normal to spend excess energy for an unrealistic expectation. This constantly depleted me and now I recognize that it is far from the truth.

My best advice to all is to stay present, slow down, really feel what is happening around you, and appreciate the smallest things, with gratitude. Choose to be present over perfect, every time.

On that summer evening, I went to bed full of gratitude hearing my boys so lovingly wish each other, the dog, and me goodnight with kisses. Pure bliss to end our day, which created a ripple effect that carried over to the next day for us all to enjoy. And so be it, further understanding that, "The real secret to a fabulous life is to live imperfectly with great delight." Unknown

What are some ways in which your life might change if you choose present over perfect?

Day 39

"Life is about using the whole box of crayons."
RuPaul

I believe in using the whole set of crayons. Live your life using all the colors of the rainbow, as rainbows speak directly to your heart and soul. Feel all the feels. Experience all the experiences that are offered to you. Make the most of your time living and have no regrets. We are blessed to have the opportunity every day to start fresh and new and to allow the lessons of our past to remain behind us.

Be adventurous and creative. Fill your life with an array of colorful and vibrant experiences.

"Jobs fill your pocket; adventures fill your soul." Unknown

Those are the memories that we will take with us and leave us feeling fulfilled with joy. Living your life this way will strengthen your second chakra at the sacral area.

Lead a diverse life with no regrets, taking with you the knowledge and memories forever. The memories are like a treasure chest of precious jewels. Most people go through life safely and only utilize the "eight-color box." They stay on the shore and don't risk the waves of life to try something new or take chances.

However, I challenge you to take the risk, ride the waves, dive into the deep end, and be the "sixty-four-color box" with the sharpener in the back. It's an opportunity to try, try, and try again until you find your perfect color and fit.

Do you live your life as the colors of the rainbow? If not, how could you?

Day 40

"If there is magic on this planet, it is contained in water."
Loren Eiseley

Water is life. The human body is 70 percent water. We all rely on it for our survival and our bodies to function at optimal levels. As such, it is essential to our existence; it is also free-flowing and pure. Water is the element of the sacral chakra and accompanies the astrological sign of Pisces, which is represented by the fish. I am a Pisces and it is magical.

Key qualities of a Pisces include:

- Fluidity
- A giver
- Passionate
- Intuitive
- Emotional
- Healer
- Water lover
- Trusting of the process
- Connected to the Universe

As a Pisces, I thrive in the water. It's where I heal and feel the most alive. It's probably no coincidence that I learned to heal others with ancient Tibetan singing bowls that utilize water to deepen the healing process. Water also reminds us that life is best lived when we go with the flow. According to Spirit Daughter, "The magic is not in the fixed road, it's in the flow." As the most spiritual sign of the zodiac, Pisces' energy reminds us that we are in fact spiritual beings having a human experience.

As I reflect about the constant change that life brings (something I hated in my younger self, but happily embrace today), I recognize that some qualities of being a Pisces have always been there. I am also happy to recognize that, as I have grown, progressed, and healed, I have evolved "back home" to my true, authentic self as reflected in the qualities of a Pisces.

How do you feel about the magical healing powers of water? What is your favorite way to connect with water?

Day 41

"Go with the flow. Force nothing . . . let it happen . . .
trusting that whichever way it goes, it's for the best."
Mandy Hale

Even though I am a Pisces, it has taken many years to fully live and understand how to be in a flow state of life. In the past, if something I was looking forward to was canceled, I would feel disappointment, fear of the unknown, or uneasiness.

In the fall of 2021, I believe I mastered living with flow. At the time, I was teaching classes outdoors at supportive friends' homes (I'm grateful to have those relationships on my journey). One day, I had to cancel class because it was raining outside. The decision to cancel came with ease and I understood that something else would cross my path to occupy my morning. The unknown became more of an excitement and opportunity rather than the unsettled feelings I'd experienced in the past.

The rain helped me see that it was time to find a dedicated indoor space to host future healing events and classes. Well, that very day the Universe connected me with a lovely woman who was planning to attend my class that day. She was opening a local business and inquired about my interest in renting the space when it wasn't in use!

The power of awareness and of being present to the synchronicity of this energy exchange was in full force. The connection was effortless and not forced, which meant it belonged on my path. Allowing yourself to let go and trust the process is the key to living this amazing life, which is the greatest gift of all. Remember, "Flowing will get you places forcing never could." Spirit Daughter

Reflect on a time you mastered living your life in flow. How did you feel?

Day 42

"Promise me you will not spend so much time treading water and trying to keep your head above the waves that you forget, truly forget, how much you have always loved to swim."

Unknown

Life is not meant to be easy. It's meant to be lived in the deep. The reality is that it'll be hard at times and the harder it is, the deeper you have to go to heal and that is when life becomes more real. The Universe offers lots of lessons, learning experiences, and growth opportunities.

For me, deciding to file for a divorce from my husband and all the delicate intricacies included in that decision has been the heaviest experience of my life so far. However, it has catapulted me into a completely different person full of light, truth, and authenticity. I am alive for the first time and realer than real.

I've found that the key is to stay present and mindful as your day progresses to fully appreciate and be aware of the opportunities presented. Approach something difficult from a place of love rather than fear. Look for the silver lining and ask yourself, "What did I learn?" That is how you can transform the dark into light.

"The deepest oceans have the mightiest waves. Rising tide. Nowhere to hide. Go ahead, just dive. The deep is where we feel most alive."
Unknown

Some days are easy and some are hard, but you can learn to ride the waves with grace and gratitude.

What feelings come through when you live your life in the deep?

Day 43

*"Enjoy the little things in life because one day
you'll look back and realize they were the big things."*
Kurt Vonnegut Jr.

I adore this quote. To me it's a reminder of my boys and the reality that they won't be little forever. Allowing yourself to feel enjoyment on a regular basis strengthens the second chakra. It's important to enjoy the simple pleasures that we often take for granted every day. Before my spiritual awakening, I was scattered and unfocused. I over-complicated everything and wasn't present enough to really enjoy the little things the way I wanted to. And I knew that was the truth.

This quote was on a wood block in Marshalls, one of my favorite stores. It was probably 2018 when I saw and purchased it. I was following my spiritual awakening and I recognized that I wanted to slow down, be present, and enjoy the little, beautiful things in my life. My boys.

A beautiful sunset, a perfectly blue sky, a rainbow, laughter or a smile from your child, a sentimental note from a friend, a good book, a song, quality time with a grandparent, a hug from a friend, a meal, or celebration. The list is endless and different for each person. The key underlying factor is to be present enough to notice the good things that happen on a regular basis that connect with your heart and soul. These are the special things that will carry us and bring joy on our paths.

**What little things in your life bring
you joy? How can you include them
more in your day-to-day?**

Day 44

"Creativity is inventing, experimenting, growing, taking risks,
breaking rules, making mistakes, and having fun."
Mary Lou Cook

Oxford Languages defines creativity as "the use of the imagination or original ideas, especially in the production of an artistic work." The primary purpose of the second chakra energy center is creation. Specifically, creation of something new that never existed before. New life, projects, artwork, or a dance. Baking cookies, growing a garden, singing a song, writing a book, or taking a photograph. The list is endless and specific to your wants, desires, and Divine spirit. All driven by the energy from the sacral area.

Early on in my yoga journey, I attended a weekly series of Kundalini classes that focused on each chakra. Upon first hearing about the description of the second chakra and its main purpose of creativity, I was immediately intrigued, connected, and drawn to the mystical powers of this area.

As a child, I loved creating art projects, crafts, and baked goods. I loved using my creative powers to share handmade gifts with others. However, somewhere along the way, my love and passion for using my creativity was no longer part of my day-to-day life. I intentionally abolished the creative aspects of my life which had brought me so much joy. It was no longer a priority to create; I was too consumed with my job and other responsibilities. This lack of balance in my life was slowly killing me deep at the soul level.

Use the energy of this center to create something new for yourself, others, or the Universe. Allowing yourself to do this creates an opportunity for this area to be open and strong. In return, your spirit will feel fulfilled with joy and your life will remain fascinating.

What are some things in your life that you've created that bring you joy? How has creativity impacted your life?

Day 45

"Craft is passionately creating something with your hands."
Unknown

My creativity is often executed in the form of homemade crafts or baked goods for friends and family. I realized it is my love language to give gifts; I take it one step further by gifting with my own personal touch and love.

As a young girl, I had a minor obsession with Martha Stewart, the "Queen of Perfection," who grew up in the same hometown as me. Every Sunday morning, I would wake up to watch the *Martha Stewart Living* television show. I collected her magazines, cookbooks, and craft sets and replicated her doings in every way.

The truth was I always had a passion for, interest in, and love of creating things with my own two hands. I had the patience and understood the time value of gifting something from my soul.

Unfortunately, as I grew into an adult, I stopped crafting as much as I used to. Like other areas in my life, I chose to focus my time on my job responsibilities, marriage, and raising my boys.

That was until I separated from my husband and moved out into my own apartment. I had all these plans to conquer the world and make something of myself, to prove I could live independently. But I didn't account for the huge emotional release that happened at the same time.

My body was telling me to rest and I wanted to go. To prevent total burnout, I finally released control to the Universe and slowed down in a way that I'd never experienced before. It was healthy and 100 percent what my body was begging me to do. I needed to simplify so I could understand, process, and accept the major life changes that were happening.

Remembering my love for crafts became the saving grace to my soul and helped me to recall what I loved to do as a child. Focusing on creating soothed me and filled me with joy again. A feeling that I hadn't allowed myself to experience had returned and I was forever changed.

I turned to painting rocks, flowerpots, and seashells. I created needlework beaded ornaments and Christmas stockings as my daily work responsibilities. I often gifted these to people who've helped me on my journey as a token of my appreciation.

By stepping back to give myself the true love I needed and connecting with my soul through creating, I helped open, balance, and heal my lower chakras.

My divorce process, while far from pleasant, was a great gift in finding myself again. The self who was always there but needed to come into the light and be seen again.

How do you express your creativity?

Day 46

"Just don't give up trying to do what you really want to do. Where there is love and inspiration, I don't think you can go wrong."
Ella Fitzgerald

Inspiration is the motivational response to creative ideas. Oxford Languages defines inspiration as "the process of being mentally stimulated to do or feel something, especially to do something creative." It explains the transmission, not the origin, of creativity.

Owning my own business had been something I was inspired to do since I was in college. As an accounting major, I learned the necessary business fundamentals, plus an understanding of how to account for my own business transactions. During graduate school, I took a course in entrepreneurship and created a business plan for my dream business at the time: wedding planning. It was the perfect mix of organization, events, and perfectionism. As you can tell, I thrived on a life where numerous aspects had to be perfect.

As I shared earlier, when working as a CPA I had visions of poking my eyes out with pencils. It was not something I loved to do. I didn't wake up every morning with a passion for it. Love and passion are critical for your daily existence and my life was far from that. But I never gave up on my inspiration to be a business owner. Understanding this desire, I was grateful to have the opportunity to switch gears and work in human resources as a campus recruiter and project manager. In these roles, I gained experience in event planning; however, I recognized that owning my own event planning business no longer interested me.

Flash-forward to being a stay-at-home mother. I dreamed of other random ideas for my own business, but nothing ever progressed past this stage. Until my spiritual awakening.

I completed two yoga certifications in 2020 and became intrigued with the power of sound healing. I found my passion and purpose to help and heal others. As a result, I was ready, and I finally had the courage to implement and create my own business LLC for my spiritual healing practice. Healing others has become a natural extension of who I am and thus my way of life.

I never gave up on my deep love for and inspiration to own my own business. It was 20-plus years in the making and I am so beyond proud of myself for riding the waves, going with the flow, letting go of being a perfectionist, and truly feeling where my energy was best suited to live my soul's higher purpose.

What do you really want to do? Where do you find your inspiration?

Day 47

"The strongest drug that exists for a human is another human being."
Unknown

A real connection and relationship with someone who you love, value, and respect can change your mood about, perception of, or outlook on your day. Maintaining relationships with others strengthens the second chakra.

In March 2020, the COVID-19 pandemic caused us all to go into lockdown mode. It was a very scary and unprecedented time for everyone in the world. The focus of our day-to-day life went from a place of love to a place of fear. Fear of the unknown, fear for our health, and fear of what would happen next. I was scared, but I recognized that projecting fear into my home was not the best way to approach the situation for myself or my boys, who watch my every move.

It is no coincidence that I was finishing two different yoga certifications at this time. The Universe knew that I was a lighthouse to help others process and heal from the pandemic.

How did I manage the early onset of the pandemic? With the spiritual tools of yoga and meditation. It was my only way out. I also read spiritual literature, refrained from watching television, and avoided social media. This was my recipe to keep me sane—and it worked.

I am grateful for the close-knit family time that the lockdown provided; however, it also created fear of those outside of my immediate family. I was worried about getting my parents and other elders sick, so I limited my exposure to them. I also limited my interactions with close friends. I relied on these friendships and connections to help me keep going. According to Lois Wyse, "A good friend is a connection to life—a tie to the past, a road to the future, the key to sanity in a totally insane world."

At this time, I strengthened a relationship with a yogi from my training, Nicole, who I now refer to as my "soul sister," as we were divinely guided to meet, connect, and grow on our own separate journeys with the foundation of our desire to help and heal others on our path. Our lives are mirrors: we both have a background in accounting, we both turned to spiritual work, and we are helping each other to heal. Our relationship progressed from friends, to confidantes, to colleagues, and now soul sisters. From a business perspective, we have combined our healing powers to help move energy that others are holding in their bodies. Energy that prevents them from living from their highest self. I accomplish this through sound and vibrations, and Nicole from a reiki, psychic, and medium capacity.

I'm forever grateful for the connections we share on this beautiful journey; they feed my soul and uplift me in an indescribable way. My future looks so bright knowing I have the power to help heal others as I have helped myself.

Reflect on the relationships you've maintained throughout your life. At this time, which ones feed your soul more than others? What are some that used to feed you but don't as much anymore?

Day 48

"Mothers hold the children's hands for a while . . . their hearts forever."
Unknown

My journey to becoming a mother wasn't easy. I'd envisioned lots of beauty and a "floating on a cloud" type of feeling. My initial experiences were far from that. The reality was that I had to create this type of experience for myself, something I would learn during my spiritual awakening.

My oldest, Anthony, was my hurricane baby. In 2011, he was born four weeks early when a hurricane came to New Jersey, causing the change in pressure from the atmosphere to break my water. Needless to say, he was ready to arrive before I was mentally or emotionally aware of what was about to happen. Luckily, for a premature baby, he was healthy and perfect. On the other hand, I was clueless and viewed our new family of three as far from perfect.

I struggled. I cried. I was lost, silently drowning with my newborn because I didn't know how to ask for help. I'd always been the helper and the doer, never the one on the receiving end.

I didn't know how to be a mother, let alone feel the beautiful sentiments expressed by the quote above. I knew how to do my job in New York City with my to-do list and calendar. But this was new. My intuition was non-existent at this time, which meant I wasn't capable of trusting myself and understanding that I had the power within me to take care of my son.

When Anthony was under two weeks old, I made my husband drive me to purchase a new paper planner so I felt properly prepared to organize my new job title of "The Perfect Mom." I was tired and confused about how to be a mother. Was I doing enough? Did he feel my love? Was I enough?

I proceeded with my brain versus my heart when it came to caring for Anthony and our home. I thrived on lists and ensured that everything was accomplished.

Looking back on it with grace and love, I see that I did the best that I could. I wished I would have enjoyed more of the moments, but all I recall is a blur.

Flash-forward to the present, and reading this quote holds deep meaning and warms my heart and soul. I feel its meaning and know that I have become the mom that I always wanted to be.

Life goes in waves. It's helpful to recognize that's how it is supposed to be. No day is perfect, but within each day, I recognize that there are some perfect moments. The key is to be open and aware of their existence.

If I could go back to those first days as a mom, I would write in my planner, "The key to motherhood is to be present over perfect."

Yes. I now know that I was enough.

What's at the forefront for me right now, I realize, is raising my little boys to be men and fathers one day with love as my anchor, and a side of being present.

If you are a mother, reflect on your relationship with your child(ren). Was being present over perfect your outlook? If you're not a mother with children, are there people in your life that you mother?

Day 49

"Good Moms let you lick the beaters. Great Moms turn them off first."
Unknown

The relationship with your mom is your foundation for everything: your first relationship, first love, and first home. It's a very special connection built on trust, caring, listening, and understanding the needs of another. Often all before your mother cared for herself. Your mother gave you life. She carried your beautiful soul in her body, giving you an opportunity to exist.

My mother lived the motto "happiness is homemade" with perfection. Her main purpose and goal have always been to ensure her kids were happy and to keep the peace in our home. I inherited my creative genes from her.

Baking is my mom's specialty and passion, particularly cookies, and ensuring something homemade is always available for my boys is high on her priority list. As a young girl, I fondly enjoyed baking with her at Christmastime, for birthdays, and other occasions. We didn't buy desserts; it was important for us to create something with our hands as a pure sign of love for another.

Just like her, I have become quite a proficient baker. My passion in the kitchen always went towards the sweets, so when the diets had to change for my boys and me, it was initially quite a challenge.

No dairy, no gluten, minimal sugar? That is unheard of from

someone who enjoys the art of baking, but also the taste as well. With an open mind and an awareness of the reality that some of the foods we enjoyed in the past were harmful, I started to get creative. My job was to recreate key baked goods for my boys to enjoy that would satisfy their palette but also support their body in a healthy way. Naturally, my mom followed suit as gifting her grandchildren warm cookies is pure joy. She also perfectly depicts the quote, "Grandmas are Moms with lots of frosting," especially in our family where a passion for desserts is enjoyed across the generations.

This quote is quite funny to me. As a child, it was always a joy to have the opportunity to lick the beaters of my mom's masterpieces, as obviously being her helper had some delicious benefits and rewards. I also take pleasure in allowing my boys to lick the beaters as a treat. The smile on their face alone is priceless.

Reflect on a connection you share with your mother, and the feelings that come up for you. Is there a specific connection or memory that comes to mind? How does that impact or affect your life today?

Day 50

"Sisters are different flowers from the same garden."
Unknown

My sister, Andrea, is nineteen months older than me. When we were young, strangers would always inquire if we were twins. Now that I'm a parent raising two boys who are twenty months apart—who coincidentally people think are twins at times—I have a deeper appreciation for the special relationship of growing up so close in age.

As children, Andrea and I must have appeared to look the same on the outside, but we are quite distinct in many ways. This is a normal phenomenon; however, the truth is, I struggled that we weren't more similar.

The fact of life is we are not meant to be the same as our siblings or anyone else. Our souls are blessed to live their own unique journey and fulfill our own purposes in the world.

As we both grew, we became individuals: different flowers from the same garden. We have our own interests and have followed our own paths, but I know that if I ever needed anything she would be there to help or give advice, especially if it was related to technology or electronics.

Growing up we shared the same memories, since we both lived under the same roof with our parents. Family and traditions were valued with a lot of our rituals revolving around our Italian culture and food. I remember holiday baking with our mother, watching the Thanksgiving Day parade, hosting large Thanksgiving dinners, sharing recipes, birthdays, family vacations, waking up on Christmas morning. We were included in working toward a common goal of being hospitable and being present to family. Today, we have the same opportunity to take what we remember and use it as a foundation to create powerful memories with our own families.

"Sisters are like seashells, snowflakes, and precious works of art: each is a unique and beautiful treasure that can never be duplicated or replaced." Unknown

If you have a sibling, reflect on your own memories from what built your foundation when you were a child. How have those memories shaped how you celebrate or live now? What values have they influenced?

Day 51

"Do more things that make you forget to check your phone."
Unknown

We are all connected to our phones. While it can be beneficial to have instant access to information at all times, there are some disadvantages to it being readily available. Sometimes we're more concerned about what's happening on our phones than connecting with the people who are alive, and in person with us. Another thing is that it prevents your mind from fully shutting off, which is a great reason to implement a daily meditation practice. We'll discuss a meditation practice in a later section.

In September, I was invited to a first birthday party at my dear friend Frank's home, for his fourth child. My relationship with Frank is extra special and is truly priceless to me. Initially, he was the father of another boy in school, then he moved to exercise buddy, to my son's basketball coach, to potential business partner, to financial advisor, to divorce coach, and finally to "like a brother."

I was a little apprehensive to attend his party alone, but I was invited and, remembering to always say "yes" since you never know what the outcome will be, I went . . . and I had the BEST time. I was at the party for about three hours, even though I didn't know many people other than his immediate family, and everyone treated me with so much love, honor, and inclusion. It was uplifting and beyond special to be in the presence of others who genuinely valued me for exactly who I was. The party elevated my energy and made me aware that I was truly in a place with others who nurtured my soul.

I also noticed that I didn't check my phone once the entire time. Usually, I am worried about my boys contacting me or someone needing something, but my phone stayed away and it was glorious.

Frank has been a true gift to me and I'm so grateful to have connected with him at the soul level and in my heart on my journey. A psychic inquired if I had a brother from blood as she recognized a male who was "acting as a brother" on my journey. Without a doubt, that person is Frank—finding this quote post-realization basically sums up how valuable his relationship is to me: "If I could pick the best Brother, I would pick you." Unknown

Reflect on relationships in your life that are like siblings. How do these relationships enrich your life beyond your immediate family?

Day 52

"Pay attention to who you're with when you feel your best."
Unknown

When I was a child, our extended family for holidays and gatherings was quite small. My mother has one sister and my father is an only child. As a result, we had only two first cousins, with a few other second cousins from great aunts and uncles. So, our family has always been tight and close-knit.

In January 2020, before the lockdown, I visited my Aunt Grace and Uncle Frank alone to share with them about a trip I'd planned to Miami to become a certified prenatal yoga teacher. I felt a strong and intense pull of energy from the Universe for me to leave my family for nine days to attend this training, even though it was out of character for me. The training was beyond life-changing.

After leaving their home, I recognized how great I felt in their presence. My energy was uplifted; I felt free and truly myself as I interacted with them. As Pam and I reflected on my interactions and feelings, I wondered, "Why don't I spend more time with my aunt and uncle?" I am proud of myself for slowing down enough to be aware of the feeling and proclaiming that I wanted to feel more of this in the future, especially since this was the opposite of how I felt at my home. It was such a simple thing to do but it resulted in deep nourishment for my soul. Although I can't change my past, I can use it as a guide for the future to improve my daily interactions and experiences.

Flash-forward to the present where I'm still nourished by my interactions with my aunt and uncle. I am aware that we have a limited amount of energy in a day and so I consciously select my interactions based on what best feeds my soul. They often invite me for breakfast when I'm alone, and I bring my boys to their home for dinner, playtime with card games, and playing pool. The apple doesn't fall far from the tree, as my boys cherish the quality time with them as well.

Who are you with when you feel your best?

Day 53

"Some best moments of life are unplanned."
Priya P. Kanwal

I have always been a planner. I enjoy the control and structure of my calendar and to-do list. They help me have order. In the past, a gap in time felt uneasy to me. It allowed me to question, "What will I do now?" Open time allows opportunity for reflection, and to be alone with myself felt uncomfortable for me.

Overscheduling was a response to my anxiety: it became my coping mechanism.

What I've learned now, however, is that the beauty of life lies in the unplanned moments; they can present an adventurous opportunity or a surprise. They can help us build memories and create "time of our life" types of experiences. But only if we allow that open space to exist in our lives.

Now that my boys are active on several baseball teams, I treasure the times when practice or games are canceled. To me, it is like receiving the gift of time—something that is so valuable and yet we seem to always run out of. While I do enjoy watching my boys play a sport they truly love, I love the time with them more. That quality time allows us to connect on a deeper level. Remembering the time that we spent an entire weekend camping in a tent in the living room or how we binged on a particular television show—those are the childhood memories that touch their heart and soul and can change lives.

Unplanned moments are an opportunity to trust, let go, and allow the open space to be filled by opportunities from the Universe. They are true blessings from above, but only if we release, accept, and allow them to come our way.

Reflect on an unplanned moment from your past that is an enjoyable memory for you.

Day 54

"Believe in your heart that you are meant to live a life full of passion, purpose, magic, and miracles."
Roy Bennett

Living with a heart full of passion is my daily motivating factor and a mantra for my soul. In fact, "Live with passion" was the first wooden sign I purchased. Even at a young age, the deep meaning behind it was crucial to who I wanted to be.

Oxford Languages defines passion as "an intense desire or enthusiasm for something." Living with passion in your life connects and strengthens your second chakra, as I shared earlier. This area is responsible for creation and new life, and the energy for it originates at the sacral area.

Before my spiritual awakening and relationship with Pam, I lived everything with intense passion and energy. All aspects of my life received 100 percent of my energy, time, and focus—that is what a true perfectionist does.

Living this way was exhausting. I gave everything I had to others because I didn't understand that every situation doesn't deserve 100 percent of me. I needed to discern where to direct my passion and not give it equally to everything.

Giving myself grace and love as I navigated what amount of energy to expend in my life was a challenge. It's still a work in progress but has greatly improved my day-to-day energy level. Now I can offer the greatest amount of passion and dedication to the things that bring me the most joy.

I'm always grateful to Pam for her knowledge and guidance as I progress on my journey, a journey that now feels nourished, full of passion, purpose, and joy.

As Bill Butler states, "Passion is oxygen of the soul." We obviously cannot go on without its existence in our lives.

How do you live with passion?

Day 55

*"When I began to have a mad, passionate love affair
with my own life, the rest fell perfectly into place."*
Katrina Mayer

My Universe and life began to change once I changed how I viewed what was happening around me. As I shared yesterday in Day 54, Pam helped guide me to the fact that we have a specific amount of energy in a day to accomplish what needs to be done. Everything we do does not deserve the same amount of attention, passion, and effort to get the job done. Allowing more time for what sparks the most joy for you is critical. As we now know, what sparks the most joy connects to your heart and nourishes your soul.

This skill took time to perfect. Slowly I recognized that because I was preoccupied with completing random tasks from my to-do list, there were things I enjoyed that I wasn't making time for. Understanding that my to-do list is always never-ending was another great tip from Pam. This awareness helped me put into perspective the appropriate percentage of energy and effort to allocate to something. I also allowed myself to be "good enough" in areas that didn't spark as much joy to me.

When I began to utilize more of my energy for areas that connected with my truth and my soul, I started to love myself as I have loved other people and things. I gave my soul the attention it desperately needed to feel nourished, seen, and understood. A passion and love for Lisa exuded and freely flowed through everything that I did. It was a beautiful feeling and helped me realize I was on the right track for my own life.

Do you know how it feels to have a passionate love affair with your own life?

Day 56

"Meet people where they are, not where you would like them to be."
Unknown

My husband and I are co-parenting our two boys together. In the fall of 2021, we encountered some situations where our contrasting views left us with two completely different solutions. Since my spiritual awakening occurred, I have approached parenting and my life through a connection with the heart, with a focus on understanding how a decision will affect my boys' feelings and mental health. This spiritual way of life wasn't my norm; however, my motto going forward is to parent and educate my boys with spirituality as the foundation, as I feel it is in their best interest.

An exorbitant amount of time and energy was spent over a two-day period as we tried to hash out the topics. We didn't find a resolution until I physically drove to his house where my boys were that day to discuss the topics all together. It was efficient, worthwhile, and an effective use of time. Reflecting back, it was difficult to resolve as we view the world from completely different standpoints: I view it from a place of spirituality or place of consciousness, and it appears he views it from a mechanical perspective or place of unconsciousness.

It was apparent that his definition of balance as well as the idea of allowing time to just be was different from mine, or non-existent.

And it seemed the same way for overscheduling and fostering an awareness of feelings—we didn't have the same perspectives. I have lived from a place of both mechanics and spirituality, and I undoubtedly feel and believe that living and existing from a state of consciousness is the way to live the path of truth and connect with your soul.

I believe that all interactions are learning experiences for our future; I learned to let go, reflect, and process. I accepted that someone can only meet you at the depth in which they have already met themselves. I can respect that it has been my job the past couple of years as I've learned about spirituality and he hasn't had the same opportunities. As a result, our viewpoints differ. Going forward, this reminds me to respond with kindness and compassion in future difficult situations, granting him grace and myself plenty of opportunities to just breathe.

Have you struggled to connect with or relate to a person who doesn't have the same understanding and knowledge at their foundation? What are some of the struggles or feelings that have come up?

Day 57

"Intimacy is not purely physical; it's the act of connecting with someone so deeply, you feel like you can see into their soul."
Reshall Varsos

My younger self's understanding of intimacy was purely on a physical and bodily level. The truth is that my views about life and my surroundings were restricted; they existed only at the surface level. This contrasts with the present where I am living from the deep and approaching my life from a place of spirituality.

In the past, I wasn't comfortable living in or going into the deep with another—I also was not heavily exposed to others who interacted that way. I had a limited frame of reference. It can be scary to expose yourself and become vulnerable from fear of the response of another. But as I know from my spiritual awakening, living life from the deep is when life becomes exciting and real. It's when I became alive.

In fact, as a child under five, neighbors thought I was a mute because I never spoke around others whom I didn't know or have a comfort level with. My own insecurity and internal fears prevented me from speaking up, something that would take years to heal from. Plus, I had a very vocal older sister who would take the lead for me from a communication perspective. This helped with my fears, but it was not good for communicating my own personal truths to others.

Reflecting on my children when they were younger, similar patterns existed, where my oldest, Anthony, who was also more vocal, would speak for his younger brother, Michael. Thinking nothing unusual about this until recently, where Michael would later be diagnosed as a deaf child without the use of his hearing aids, the awareness about my life and lessons to be learned, came full circle, again. Is this a coincidence? I think not—it is a sign from the Universe.

Because of his hearing loss at a young age, Michael was given the opportunity to advocate for himself and use his voice to communicate his own truth. He struggles at times with this, but it is top of mind from those who love him most, and understanding that is the key to success for a child with his disability. What a gift to learn how to do at the age of seven! In contrast, as his mother, I didn't learn to use my voice and speak my truth until I was forty. It warms my heart to see how bright his future will be using his own powers.

Oxford Languages defines intimacy as "close familiarity or friendship; closeness." Through my awakening, I recognized that I truly value and connect with the power of deep conversations. The intimacy and connection with another soothes and nourishes my soul. A shared opportunity to relate with another in a way that is so personal, sincere, and true using the power of my voice.

What does intimacy look like and how does it play a role in your life?

Day 58

"Sexual energy is the primal and creative energy of the Universe."
Deepak Chopra

Sexual energy is a life force that exists in each of us and connects us to our soul and the Universe. It is you in the fullest light of who you are; and it is linked to your sexual desires and drives, your connection to others, your sense of self, and your creativity. The sacral chakra links the sexual energies at the second chakra.

"Tantra is primarily about uniting love, spirituality, and sexuality with awareness." Osho

In my previous relationships, spiritual intimacy wasn't very present. And I realized that I was hungry to experience this type of closeness. Yoga, breathwork, and daily meditation were already parts of my daily routine, so it made sense that I would feel drawn to Tantra.

Tantra is a key component of the Hindu and Buddhist religions. Those who practice Tantra believe that all life activities are woven together and are therefore sacred. Understanding how to practice Tantra can lead to love, happiness, connection, joy, and ecstasy.

Through the use of yoga, breathwork, and meditation, practitioners of Tantra enhance their mindfulness and awareness. The practice of Tantric sex often includes these spiritual techniques as a component of sexual activity. Tantra facilitates a shared spiritual intimacy between sexual partners, not just an orgasm, that results in the heart opening and creates a strong and powerful emotional and physical connection.

Tantra teaches us that all life is sexual energy—the drive forcing us to be our best self. Sexual transmutation transforms your sexual energy into physical, real-life success and thereby directs it into a higher purpose on your path. Also, it circulates your energy and reaches the seventh chakra at the crown, which helps you experience oneness or connection with the Universe.

Reflect on your sexual energy and spiritual intimacy with others.

Day 59

"In Taoist philosophy, 'yin' is the feminine principle, representing the forces of earth, while 'yang' is the masculine principle, representing spirit."
Marianne Williamson

In Day 58, I shared that sexual energy is a life force connecting your soul to the Universe. It is the driving force to live as your best self and results in sexual transmutation—the transformation of the sexual energy exchange flow between partners into real-life success, directed into a higher purpose on your path.

The masculine and feminine energies are two poles of duality, which means they are two opposites on a spectrum. Every person possesses both poles and a unique balance of masculine and feminine energies.

The yin and yang symbol originates from Taoist philosophy in Chinese culture. This symbol reminds us that our true path to harmony is one of balance, with neither side being superior to the other. The symbol depicts a balance between two opposites (black and white). There's a portion of the opposite element in each half and a constant chasing of each other to seek a new balance.

The black part of the symbol represents the yin energy, or feminine energy. Love, flow, feeling, intuition, negativity, and the moon are all connected with the feminine.

The white part of the symbol depicts the yang, or masculine energy. This energy represents support, grounding, direction, logic, positivity, and the sun.

The reality is that yin cannot exist without yang, nor can yang exist without yin, as the key to life is balance. These seemingly opposite energies are complementary and interconnected. They strengthen each other as they interact and, as a result, the whole is greater than its parts.

The differences between yin and yang demonstrate the contrasting makeup that the masculine and feminine have in their energies and motivations. When both parties are fully expressed (and therefore balanced) in their natural energies, this balance drives passion, connection, and a healthy relationship with the other. When parties are out of balance, this leads to disharmony, disconnection, and a lack of sexual intimacy.

My spiritual awakening opened my awareness to my own lack of balance between my masculine and feminine energies—I was more dominant in masculine energy. This became apparent when I moved out in the summer of 2020. To help balance the energies, I made several adjustments. I began to wear feminine, free-flowing white garments during my spiritual healings, and to give myself the love I gave to others. Instead of always being the problem solver or fixer, I started to ask others for assistance. I implemented a regular crafting practice and began to heavily rely on and trust my strong intuition. Through sound healing rituals, I connected with the power of the moon and, as an extension, myself.

Reflect on your own unique balance of yin and yang. How can you adjust the balance of energy in your life?

Day 60

"Life means little until you give it to someone else."
Unknown

Creation of new life can only exist through the energies of sexual intimacy, which is sourced from the sacral area. Committing to bring new life into your world is a magnificent wonder, blessing, and miracle.

As shared on Day 57, living from a state of consciousness is a new phenomenon and way of being for me. Thus, my own experiences creating, carrying, and delivering new life into this world through my two pregnancies weren't from a place of consciousness or awareness. I learned more about this in January 2020 while attending the Khalsa Way prenatal yoga teacher training held in Miami.

Khalsa Way is based on Kundalini yoga, with the premise of having a conscious pregnancy that would carry over to childhood. This includes building a loving community for the pregnant mamas, teaching postures to accommodate growing bellies, and learning breathing techniques to handle contractions, and meditations to remain focused. It's an opportunity to embrace the wondrous time that awaits the future gift to be welcomed into the world. Finally, it's about trusting the power of the mama's intuition; she has the force and confidence within her to care for her baby.

Pregnant mamas are treated like goddesses in Khalsa Way. Then once the baby arrives, that is the mama's only responsibility for forty days: to care for and connect with the baby and herself. Everything else can wait while she loves the baby; it's important to gather a tribe of helpers in advance to care for the home responsibilities so that the mama can rest and recover.

It is hard for me to relate to this glorious experience and treatment since my pregnancies were very mechanical and more of a "check the box exercise." I thought, "Well, I am married, time to have my children." But it is possible to have a conscious experience of pregnancy and birth, and I was over-the-moon excited to learn about this and share with others in order to raise awareness and change the narrative for future mamas and their babies.

While I cannot change my pregnancy experience and early years as a new mama, I can go forward and embrace with passion the phenomenon of creating new life for another. The fact that my body is built to grow a living, breathing, full-of-life soul to live as a human with his own lessons and opportunities for growth still amazes me. A woman's body is remarkable in every way and is a magnificent vessel for carrying new life. New life that will be embraced, cherished, and loved. As it should be.

If you have given life to another, reflect on your experiences. If you haven't, what are some other things you've birthed? Reflect on those.

I Am

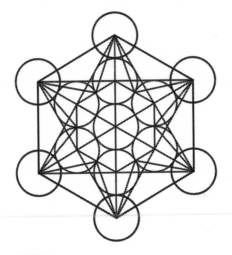

Power

I Am Power
DAYS 61–90

A strong, spiritual warrior with the will to succeed is a powerhouse. "I believed I could, and I did" is a powerful mantra that took years to come to fruition for me. It wasn't until I fully believed in my own strength and abilities.

Exuding a strong power center and having a "fire in the belly" quality is associated with the third chakra energy center, at the solar plexus area, located at the navel point. You will learn in this chapter that the third chakra sources the energy to be strong, charismatic, confident, and to live with courage.

As it relates to the third chakra, you will understand that:

- A healthy digestion and proper nutrition are key to keeping this area working effectively.
- Fire is the element associated with the solar plexus. Therefore, the energy behind possessing the intense "fire in the belly" concept is sourced from this area.
- Feeling like sunshine, with an optimistic and positive attitude, brings great light energy. Likewise, standing tall and possessing a spirit like that of a sunflower is a symbol of true faith and loyalty. Thus, consider implementing these as you approach your life.

- Rainbows represent opportunities in your life and the reality that eventually all storms run out of rain. Likewise, the world is full of unlimited opportunities for all who are brave and possess the strength and courage to pursue what they want.

- A daily practice of laughter is good for the heart, mind, and soul.

- Regardless of how insignificant your action might seem, you can always make a difference—even if you never find out. Having a strong sense of purpose and personal willpower is key to feeling fulfilled.

- Own yourself as you enter a room. Likewise, understand that there is power in being independent and beating your own drum.

- You constantly present your own brand to the world. Pay attention to your attitude and personality as they shape your image. Lastly, choose who you are becoming over everything.

- It is important to always recognize your big achievements and that your productivity is a direct result of your consistent activity.

- You have the power to prioritize your life and change its direction.

Tune In with the Adi Mantra
"Ong Namo Guru Dev Namo"

To center yourself in the higher self before practicing Kundalini yoga, chant the Adi Mantra three times.

"Ong Namo Guru Dev Namo" translates to "I bow to the Divine wisdom of all that is" and "I bow to the Divine teacher within."

HOW TO PRACTICE

- *Posture:* Sit in Easy Pose, with the spine erect.
- *Eye Position:* Eyes slightly closed, focused at the Third Eye, which is the point between the brows.
- *Mudra: Prayer Pose.* Place the palms of the hands flat together to neutralize the positive (right, or male) and negative (left, or female) sides of the body. Your thumbs should press against the sternum and your forearms will be parallel to the floor.
- Consciously begin to breathe. Gently inhale through your nose, feel the breath fill up your belly, fill up your lungs, and expand your rib cage. On the exhale from your nose, recognize the breath leaving your body. When ready to "tune in" with the Adi Mantra, inhale and exhale deeply from the nose and begin chanting the mantra three times.

Asanas

The asanas listed below focus on strengthening the energy center at the solar plexus area. It is recommended that you hold each posture for one to two minutes with a slight rest in between. Remember to stay within while holding the postures and while resting, keep your eyes closed, focusing on the Third Eye. This will allow you to focus on yourself and build your intuition, plus help you learn to trust your own power and ability.

- Sufi Grind
- Spinal Twist
- Bow Pose
- Triangle Pose

- Leg Lifts

Find a description of each posture in the Appendix on page 419.

Meditation
"Sat Siri Siri Akal"

This mantra strengthens courage and invokes radiant inner power. When we chant it, we confirm that we are timeless, deathless beings, known for giving victories in all aspects of life. With it, we declare that we are timeless, deathless beings.

- *Mantra:* "Sat siree, siree akaal, siree akaal, maahha akaal. Maahha akaal, sat naam, akaal moorat, wha-hay guroo."
- *Translation:* "The true great, great deathless, great deathless beyond, death. Beyond death, truth is his name, deathless form of God, experience of the Divine."

HOW TO PRACTICE

- *Posture:* it in Easy Pose, with the spine erect.
- *Eye Position:* Eyes closed, focused at the Third Eye, which is the point between the brows.
- *Mudra:* Gyan mudra, which is the seal of knowledge. To form, put the tip of the thumb together with the tip of the index finger.
- *Time:* Continue for three minutes. Build to seven minutes.
- *Helpful Tip:* Soundtracks are available to chant as you complete the meditation that can be found on any app that streams music. I like to chant this meditation along with the artist, Jai-Jagdeesh.

Deep Relaxation

- *Posture:* Lie on your back in Corpse Pose. With your eyes closed, place your arms at your sides, with palms facing up. Allow your body to rest, process, and absorb the movement of energy.
- *Time:* One to three minutes minimum.

Ending Prayer

To close your Kundalini practice, chant three long *Sat Naams*.

Sound Healing

Enjoy this ten-minute sound healing ensemble to further relax your mind and body. Consider listening during deep relaxation or at another time during your day when your body could benefit from and enjoy the beautiful healing gift of sound and vibrations.

Access this month's asana videos, meditation, sound healing audio, and more at www.LisaAnnese.com/i-am-light

Day 61

"Happiness for me is largely a matter of digestion."
Lin Yutang

Before my spiritual awakening, my day-to-day life revolved around the temperamental nature of my stomach. For as long as I can remember, I regularly experienced issues in my entire solar plexus area (mainly the stomach, small intestines, liver, and spleen). Pain, pressure, nausea, and inflammation were my norm in this third chakra energy center. I didn't know about chakras or have any knowledge that would eventually come from my yoga training. In 2016, I didn't realize that this journey would result in so many amazing things. Eventually though, I became aware that once I cleaned up my issues, the energy in this area would move freely at optimal levels. My triggers included poor diet—such as eating foods that were causing my body harm—external stress, and how I responded to situations.

As I previously shared, I took the functional approach to understand the reasons I was bloated, gaining weight, and unable to lose it despite my efforts. Food intolerances, SIBO, gut dysbiosis, and leaky gut caused inflammation in my intestines and limited my ability to absorb nutrients from my food. Eating products with gluten regularly caused brain fog, headaches, and confusion. Slowly I came to understand the mind-gut connection; the food I was eating was attacking my GI system, but it also was shaping how my brain viewed and responded to the world.

A healthy body starts in the gut and an effective digestive system. This is the center of your immunity and the nutrition your body requires. Prana in the form of food, water, and supplements offers nourishment and allows the human body to function at its ideal level. However, in order to reap these benefits, the organs supporting digestion must not be in chronic pain, as mine were.

As someone with a strong Italian cultural background, food is life and love. I'd married an Italian and carried this into my adulthood. I was thirty-six and all I wanted was to feel good. My clothes didn't fit and there was so much inflammation that every time my boys approached me, I braced myself.

Halloween was the day before I went to see the doctor, and I remember that I ate some Twix and Reese's because I knew the doctor would want me to change. And in fact, from then on, whatever the doctor told me to do, I followed to the letter. I needed relief. For example, I spoke with my family and learned how to take our favorite foods and make them appropriate to eat.

While it wasn't easy to change my diet and give up my favorite foods, I was desperate. I wanted to be a comforting and loving person, but the physical pain I experienced made it hard for me to enjoy playfulness with my boys. I began choosing to love my body by selecting food that would be better for me in the long run, rather than leaning into my cultural heritage. If my gut was at peace and happy, then I was happy; it was a domino reaction and impacted everything and everyone on my path.

Reflect on your own personal digestion. Is it a place of peace or pain for you?

Day 62

"The doctor of the future will no longer treat the human frame with drugs, but rather will cure and prevent disease with nutrition."
Thomas Edison

As I shared on Day 61, a healthy digestive system is key to the overall well-being of our mental, physical, and spiritual bodies. Our vitality and future depend on this system of organs working together for optimal health.

Before I understood that the food I chose to eat was in fact the medicine I needed to heal my digestion, I consistently relied on over-the-counter pain medications for headaches. I'd grab food on the go because I was so busy. I loved eating veggie stix, goldfish crackers, cookies, and especially salty snacks. Food offered comfort during stressful, difficult, and emotional times. I loved breads, bagels, carbs. Because I made cookies for my boys, I'd always have chocolate chips lying around to snack on. Now I make things that are gluten and dairy free and I use natural sugar like honey.

While my body never depended on regular doses of prescription medicines, I didn't understand or believe in the strength and power of my body, and especially that it was made to heal itself, via the immune system. Dr. Chris taught me this powerful truth.

Over time, Dr. Chris educated me on the importance of consuming whole foods. I learned about the dangers to the body when you consume processed food made from chemicals and ingredients I couldn't pronounce. He taught me a holistic approach for ailments: to rest when not feeling my best and support my immune system so it could remain powerful against pathogens. I found out that common household and beauty products contained toxins and I began to wake up to the fact that my body needed purity in all aspects of its care. Vinegar in a spray bottle became my everyday cleaner.

As I took everything I'd learned into consideration, I saw that it all came down to the food I chose to feed my body with on a daily basis. During the process of making these adjustments, it was important to me to learn how to make Christmas cookies that my boys could enjoy—I didn't want them to feel like they were missing out because I had to change our diets. As time went on, I sacrificed the food I'd loved because I loved my body. And I felt better than ever. That was all that mattered.

According to Louise Hay, "It's an act of loving ourselves to become aware of what we put into our mouths and how it makes us feel."

Reflect on your relationship with food and its ability to heal your body. What are your own personal food habits? Do you feel you're loving your body or harming it with your food habits?

Day 63

"She has fire in her soul and grace in her heart."
Unknown

In August 2021, I had my initial virtual consultation with Bryna, who is now my book publisher, to discuss the preliminary ideas about a book that I wanted to write. After I excitedly shared who I was, why I have the passion to write, and a little about my journey, she shared with me, "You have a fire and creativity in you—I do not want to ruin that fire."

The truth was that, yes, I felt that same fire and had confirmation from other sources that my solar plexus was on fire. Fire that nurtures and creates the oomph required to take brave steps and actions.

I'd also been contemplating a tattoo. I wanted something small that would signify my journey and reality that now it was just the three of us: my boys and me. I decided on a small triangle pointing upward. In the Day 14 meditation, I shared that my family structure went from a four-sided square to a three-sided triangle. Spiritually, a triangle represents the path to enlightenment, and using three triangles symbolized the elements. The triangle that points upwards indicates fire. I finally had the fire in me to take these chances. It became my favorite shape to represent my journey.

This is no coincidence. The term "fire in the belly" is often used to describe someone who's ready to act very energetically and passionately. It's also no coincidence that the element associated with the solar plexus, located at the belly, is fire. Fire represents the energy of the sun and illuminates your awareness of your own internal pilot light motivating you for continued success. You must be careful, however, to not overexert this energy or you may burn out from exhaustion.

Prior to moving out of my home, I began to write poetry. It was very soothing and healing and became a way to process and reflect on my emotions. Because it offered me a joy and comfort I'd never experienced before, I wanted to continue. I slowly graduated from writing for myself to becoming public on social media about Michael's hearing loss journey. Not only could I share my vulnerability, but it also helped me educate others about how challenges can be our greatest blessings. After regularly writing for a year, I felt I was ready to write on a broader scale, sharing my light for a larger audience. The Universe knew I was ready and I effortlessly connected with Bryna. The rest is history. The ease of the process helps me remember that when things are free-flowing, I am on the right path.

I am very proud of my efforts to reflect on my journey, sharing light with others. But my biggest motivating factor was to demonstrate to my boys that I turned a difficult time in our lives into something spectacular through my efforts to write a book for them.

Reflect on your own "fire in the belly" moments. Have you ever felt energy or warmth in your belly? How does this connect to your passion and your will to achieve your goals?

Day 64

"Stay close to people who feel like sunshine."
Unknown

This lovely quote has always been one of my favorites. Sunshine is light energy: bright, vibrant, and alive. Exposure to natural sunlight is also very beneficial to us humans—as the skin absorbs ultraviolet rays the body produces its own vitamin D3. This is why D3 is often referred to as the "sunshine vitamin." It keeps us healthy by building and strengthening our immune system.

In general, the energy to do things comes from the same place. A well-working energy area allows us to accomplish what we need to, just like sunshine. People who feel like sunshine are always brighter, always glowing, always smiling, always remaining in the light. Things might not be great, but they're always trying to return to the light rather than the dark. That's how we elevate and heal ourselves. We focus on the light. People who feel like sunshine are anchored in that same fire energy and driven by the third chakra energy center.

Every day, the sun rises again. A sunset represents an awareness that the past is indeed behind us and that the present day awaits with its upcoming sunrise. It's a new opportunity for learning and growth, a chance to be better than we were the day before, and to try again until we reach our goals and dreams.

I love the quote, "When your world moves too fast and you lose yourself in the chaos, introduce yourself to each color of the sunset." It reminds us to look at gloomy moments during our busy day and pause to really absorb what happened. To examine and absorb the different colors of the situation, step by step. Slowing down to dissect it into pieces can help us recognize that all in life is not lost. The more we can understand it, the more we can process it and bounce back.

I am continually mesmerized by the sheer beauty of the sun. I enjoy the daily surprises that the sunrise brings each morning—often the most beautiful time of day is when the world still sleeps. And at the end of the day, sunsets are like a new painting every night, with my favorites free-flowing with pink. A true blessing and gift from God.

Who feels like sunshine to you? Are you making an effort to regularly include them in your life? If not, what's one way you could connect with them today?

Day 65

"Her spirit was like a sunflower. Even on those darkest days
she could stand tall and find the light."

Unknown

In 2020, a friend shared with me that I was like a sunflower. They said, "Your feathers are too bright for most people to appreciate." Intrigued by this statement and clearly flattered, I wanted to understand the deeper symbolism beyond the beautiful exterior of this flower.

Oxford Languages defines a sunflower as "a tall North American plant of the daisy family, with very large golden-rayed flowers. Sunflowers are cultivated for their edible seeds, which are an important source of oil for cooking."

Spiritually, sunflowers symbolize faith, hope, peace, and adoration for all. They're a symbol of true faith and loyalty to something much bigger and brighter than themselves. In Latin, their name is Helianthus annuus, which combines two Greek words: helios as sun and anthos as flower. Thus, the literal translation is "flower of the sun."

Sunflowers truly resemble how we view the shape of the sun, especially the way in which the blooms always face towards the sunshine. Many cultures also value them for their ability to protect and to seek enlightenment and truth. So deep. So powerful.

This has become the flower that symbolizes my journey and path to truth. For you, in times of darkness, remember to be like the sunflower: turn your face towards the light, stand strong and tall, and always be true to yourself.

Buy yourself some sunflowers to brighten your day. Let them remind you of the sun and to always live your truth.

Day 66

"If you want the rainbow, you gotta put up with the rain."
Dolly Parton

We all have the power to shape our lives and existence from both a short- and long-term perspective. Life isn't meant to be viewed as good versus bad or positive versus negative. Rather, we should develop an awareness of and acceptance that all living, existing things are made of energy. In turn, our actions represent the movement of energy.

Therefore, what matters most is how we consciously choose to use the energy that we possess. What we do with our given energy makes a difference for ourselves, our children, and those who are around us.

Remember that challenges are our greatest blessings; plus, there's always a silver lining if you choose to view your life through that lens.

Rainbows are a beautiful phenomenon and are only possible after it rains. They're a gift from God for our eyes to enjoy and our hearts to recognize the beauty and reward of weathering the storm. As Maya Angelou said, "Every storm runs out of rain." Rainbows represent hope, peace, promise, equality, and new beginnings. My boys and I are always on the lookout for rainbows post-storm.

Writing this book for you to enjoy is my rainbow. My spiritual awakening and journey to live the path of truth was not easy. I consciously chose to be the light. As such, I feel inspired to use my energy to help others who may be struggling and to create an awareness about living with more spirituality. The key is that I did not let my darkness destroy me—I used it as a springboard to catapult my energy higher than I ever thought possible. To me, that is a life well lived.

Reflect on your own rainbow opportunities.

Day 67

"The butterfly is only beautiful because the caterpillar is brave."

T.m.t

Moving out of the home I built with my family took courage; it was an intense internal struggle driven by the feelings in my heart. My soul knew that the next step on my path was to start over on my own. Logically, this decision made no sense. As I shared with my husband, "This is not a head decision, it is a heart decision." Energy coming from my core gave me the power to act. This moment in my life confirmed for me an Anaïs Nin quote that I love: "Life shrinks or expands in proportion to one's courage." My life completely deepened and widened as I found the courage to speak my truth.

Everyone notices the butterfly or the final result of our hard work, but rarely do we pay attention to the inner struggle or the hard work of the brave caterpillar. The same creature first had the courage to be brave, to face its fears and own internal challenges, but in this state, it was often unnoticed or unrecognized until it transformed into the externally beautiful butterfly. It's the power of beauty versus that of being brave.

Oxford Languages defines brave as "ready to face and endure danger or pain; showing courage; to endure or face unpleasant conditions or behavior without showing fear."

Being brave and having courage strengthens and balances the energies of the solar plexus, which increases positivity, self-worth, and the "fire in the belly" energy you need to manifest your goals.

According to Brené Brown, "Courage originally meant to speak one's mind while telling all one's heart. Over time, this definition changed and today courage is more synonymous with being heroic."

The root of the word courage is "cor," which is the Latin word for heart. Courage cannot be bought; it develops internally at the soul level as you believe in your own internal power to allow yourself to experience discomfort and make a heartfelt decision. Courage is acting with confidence in the face of fear.

Reflect on your own internal struggle with courage and being brave.

Day 68

"Aerodynamically, the bumble bee shouldn't be able to fly,
but the bumble bee doesn't know it, so it goes on flying anyway."
Mary Kay

The bee is my spirit animal. She is so small, yet vital to our very existence. I intuitively connected with this creature as I was brainstorming ideas for my new business venture. The words, "Be radiant ...be true...be you" kept buzzing in my head, and then I saw a bee in my vicinity. A perfect match for my style and brand!

Once I announced this to the Universe, bees began to visit me at all of my outdoor classes and events. It was synchronicity at its best and a sign that I was on the right track.

The bee has the will—and thus finds the way—to accomplish her purpose of buzzing from flower to flower, pollinating as she goes, and making honey at the hive. The bee has her job and uses all of her will to accomplish it, despite the fact that there are limiting factors.

"Anyone who thinks they are too small to make a difference, has never met the honeybee." Unknown

Some key takeaways about the bee for you to consider:

- Bees are everyday miracle workers—despite being so small, the honeybee accomplishes so much. A reminder that we all can do anything.

- Bees thrive in a community and focus on teamwork. A reminder to use your talents to help humanity and your personal contributions to help grow the community.
- Bees are strong and have consistent goals. A reminder of the power of consistency over time.
- Bees are productive. Twenty-four hours is never enough time to accomplish everything. We talk about people having a "worker bee ethic," where they bring a sense of pride to their work. However, it's still important to understand the need for balance between work and play. This is a constant struggle for me.
- Bees are passionate and committed. And as I shared in the last chapter, I live for passion! This passion fuels my dreams and helps them come true.

Without the presence of bees in the world, we wouldn't be able to survive as a species.

Having a strong sense of purpose for yourself can motivate you on a daily basis and is a sign of a strong solar plexus. Connecting with the symbolism of the bee helped to guide me to my own purpose and to recognize that the world is full of unlimited possibilities and opportunities.

Remember a time when you accomplished something despite limiting factors. Was there a moment where your strong belief or will helped you accomplish something that you thought was beyond your capability?

Day 69

"The most lost day in life is the day we don't laugh."
Charlie Chaplin

In early 2020, during my darkest moments, I recognized that I had stopped laughing and having fun. As previously shared, I was confused about the state of my marriage and had allowed a sense of doom and gloom to take over everything. I began to ask myself lots of questions. Why am I not laughing? Why don't I make time to add things in my life that allow me to laugh, let loose, and have a good time anymore?

For me, laughter is the sound of joy. It indicates that something amuses or entertains you.

Remember the phrase, "Laughter is the best medicine"? If you can laugh in both good times and bad, it cues your body to not take everything so seriously. Laughter decreases stress hormones and triggers the release of endorphins—the body's natural feel-good chemicals. This promotes an overall sense of well-being, strengthens the immune system, and temporarily relieves pain.

The truth is that laughter has the power to carry you. It's good for the heart, mind, and soul. Life is seriously more fun when you laugh, joke, and connect with others through banter. Laughing strengthens the solar plexus where your energy is sourced from.

My oldest, Anthony, has the best laugh. He is my jokester and the one who always reminds me of laughter's benefits. His pre-K teacher first made me aware of the uniqueness of my son's jovial laugh, full of innocence and spirit. She shared with me that she wanted to record his laugh so she could play it back when she was having a bad day. It warmed my heart that my son had the ability to spread joy for others so naturally. I was saddened that I hadn't slowed down to recognize it myself, but grateful to have the awareness. My role model and teacher reminded me that life is a gift to enjoy.

During the pandemic, I introduced Anthony to the television series, *Friends*. I loved going back in time and enjoying one of my favorite shows. It was fun to relive old memories while making new ones as I shared laughter and joy with my son.

My spiritual awakening reminded me that smiling so hard that my cheeks hurt and laughing to the point of crying is my definition of a worthwhile and enjoyable moment where I allow myself to feel carefree and enjoy the sound of my body full of joy. Making time for these moments to exist in my world is priceless—and necessary for maintenance and survival.

How do you define laughter in your life? How does it change your state of existence and shift your outlook?

Day 70

"The woman you're becoming will cost you people, relationships, spaces, and material things. Choose her over everything."
Unknown

In July 2020, shortly after I moved out of my home, I began to feel how my separation was affecting how others viewed me. People who I'd developed a relationship with because of my husband either didn't know how to maintain our connection or were uncomfortable doing so. This was confusing to me. I didn't understand why a relationship between myself and the other person had to change when it was the relationship between myself and my husband that was shifting. Despite my perspective, this did in fact happen to me. It wasn't verbally communicated, but I felt it through a change in the energy exchange. Energy does not lie: it is our truth. So, I knew it was real.

Shortly after I noticed this in some of my relationships, I encountered this quote. And then it all made sense. My separation was going to cost me people whom I'd previously valued. My separation also cost me my house and material possessions that I would no longer have access to. None of these items mattered anymore as they represented my first life—a life that was lived mostly for others, not for myself. A life that was living for my ego rather than for my heart and spirit.

The strength, power, and energy from my solar plexus gave me the confidence to speak my truth and completely change my life.

My first life was dead; the Lisa before my spiritual awakening no longer existed. I was now living my second life from a place of spirit and deeply connected to my feelings. I chose her over everything.

It was challenging to accept that some relationships I valued would never be the same. It took time to heal and process. Overall, my saving grace was to remember to choose people that choose you. Always.

Reflect on a time you chose yourself over everything else. What feelings arose during this experience?

Day 71

"A woman who is OK being alone is a powerful woman."
Unknown

My birthday is the only day of the year that tells me to do something: March 4th. This is a very powerful birthday; it is an action verb and one that became my mantra: "March forth on March 4th."

Oxford Languages defines powerful as "having great power or strength," "having a strong effect on people's feelings or thoughts," and "having control and influence over people and events."

A strong and balanced solar plexus generates the energy to have the strength and courage to be alone and independent. The truth is that all I ever wanted was to be respected, appreciated, and loved for who I sincerely am. Choosing to be alone and move out wasn't on my "to-do list" or set of goals for my life at forty years old. However, it became a necessity for my survival and rebirth.

The day I moved out of my home was my lowest "rock bottom" moment; however, I accepted it with grace and dignity. I acknowledged the quote, "If your path demands you to walk through hell, walk as if you own the place." Well, I owned my path and walked through my level of "hell" while holding a flashlight to ensure that I knew how to get out. I was born to "March forth." It's my mantra. I am a warrior whose purpose is to share God's Divine love and light. There is no other way for me.

Reflect on a time when you had to face something alone. Did you feel powerful or did other feelings arise?

Day 72

"I used to walk into a room full of people and wonder if they like me. Now I look around and wonder if I like them."

Unknown

Before my spiritual awakening, I was insecure and unsure of myself. I always maintained the mentality of "beating to my own drum" in how I functioned when alone, but I often changed when it came to social situations. I desperately wanted to be accepted by others, to fit in and for everyone to like me, especially people I didn't know. Walking into a room of people brought about fear of the unknown and sparked questions: Who would be there? Will I know anybody? Will I fit in? Will I feel comfortable?

Reflecting back on how I approached my past life, I've wondered, "Why did I care if strangers liked me?" I didn't know them and would probably never see them again. They had no deep or lasting impact on my present or future life.

The answer to this question is that, in the past, the energy at my solar plexus wasn't strong or balanced. As a result, the power and strength that should derive from that area didn't function properly. It's only now, after my spiritual awakening, that I can have this awareness.

Now I don't agonize over walking into a room worried about who will be present. I walk in with confidence and my head held up high because I feel secure and believe in myself, my abilities, and offerings. I've accepted that the true people and energies who are meant to be in my life will always gravitate back to me.

I embody this quote by Maryam Hasnaa, "Read the room, but don't match the energy of the room. Own your space and set the tone for yourself."

Always be true to who you are.

How do you feel when you walk into a room full of unknown people? Have those feelings changed over time or at different points in your life?

Day 73

"Now, every time I witness a strong person, I want to know: what darkness did you conquer in your story? Mountains do not rise without earthquakes."
Katherine MacKenett

I always possessed a strong willpower and a determined and ambitious outlook toward my life. Oxford Languages defines strongwilled as one who is "determined to do as one wants even if other people advise against it." I've always been driven by being the best and doing what others say can't be done. It's my motto and comes from a fire driven by the energies of the solar plexus.

At times, my strong willpower was to my own detriment, especially when I focused on the end result of whatever I was striving for. I didn't recognize the pain or imbalance that it caused in my life.

For me, this way of life stems from childhood where I never felt I was good enough for others around me, including my family. My response was to study and work hard to prove that, "Yes, I am good enough and deserve the same recognition for my efforts."

A great example is when I passed all four parts of the CPA exam, something that was uncommon at the time. My father downplayed my achievements and months of studying with, "I didn't think you could do it." It was the opposite reaction I hoped for—I wanted him to be proud and excited for me for accomplishing a huge goal.

All these years later, I still recall that moment because it hurt and was so painful. Reflecting back on it, I know that I am a rock star for my efforts and I no longer need to receive the external gratification that I hungered for in the past. The truth is that we are all enough. Now I finally recognize how I killed myself for an end result that didn't even matter. With my new spiritual view of life, I have the ability to recognize and distinguish what really matters at the end of the day. That is where I will prioritize my energy: in love and compassion for myself.

What are some experiences where you knew that your third chakra had to be strong enough to provide the energy to endure a difficult time? How did those moments make you feel?

Day 74

*"Optimism is the faith that leads to achievement.
Nothing can be done without hope and confidence."*
Helen Keller

Possessing an optimistic and positive attitude is the mindset needed for any new goal, venture, or endeavor. Optimism is defined by Oxford Languages as "hopefulness and confidence about the future or the successful outcome of something." Experiencing confidence in your abilities and living with a "Yes, I can!" outlook is a stepping-stone on your path to success. When you can live with optimism during challenging times, you strengthen the energies derived from the solar plexus.

Although it was hard to separate from my husband when I chose to move out, I was optimistic that everything would unfold as it was supposed to. I was following the path of my heart and soul; I didn't have to climb the entire staircase to know that I would be OK in the end. All I needed was to take one step at a time using the power of my faith and hope that I could change the blueprint of my future.

That initial step opened my eyes to a new reality where I could breathe freely. There was room to process and reflect on the first of many steps on my own journey of truth.

Lisa Annese

How has living with optimism impacted your path?

Day 75

*"Charisma is a spark in people that money can't buy.
It's an invisible energy with visible effects."*
Marianne Williamson

Charisma is one of my absolute favorite qualities. It is a unique distinguishing characteristic that makes you stand apart from others.

Oxford Languages defines charisma as "compelling attractiveness or charm that can inspire devotion in others," and "a divinely conferred power or talent."

I've always possessed a strong charismatic style; it is the light that exudes from me when I shine for others. Expressing my charisma has consistently been a natural and innate attribute of mine, especially when I am living from my highest self and doing what I love with joy.

From a young age I had a fear of public speaking. I worried about making a mistake and clearly not performing perfectly to my high standards. Inevitably, I would come across as flustered because I spoke faster than my mind could process. I couldn't wait to spit out the words and be done.

All that changed in 2006 when I became a campus recruiter and my daily responsibilities suddenly included presentations for others. I became a human brand for my firm.

I loved my role as a recruiter and was comfortable in front of others, but still maintained an internal uneasiness. And then my boss at the time shared that there was something about my presence that set me apart from my peers—my charisma. He told me that I could walk into a room or onto a stage and not say a word, but still make an impact. Likewise, even when I would communicate, I didn't have to say much to get the point across. Sometimes, less equals more when you need to make a difference and a lasting impression.

Another great piece of advice my boss shared with me was, "Nobody knows what you are going to say; so, if you forget something, just add it to the end or forget about it." This was ingenious because it removed my fear of perfection from the picture. Today, I still carry these very impactful words with me. In fact, I shared this guidance with my son who has the same fears around speaking to others.

When you feel charismatic, how does this differentiate you from others? What changes when you're not feeling charismatic?

Day 76

"You are your own brand, so brand yourself, beautifully!"
Dawn Davis

In Day 75, I shared how I became a walking brand for the accounting firm I worked for. Dressed as a "human billboard" and wearing the firm's branded colors, I walked the walk and talked the talk. My job was to sell the firm and the ways in which our firm differed from other firms. I believed that the people at my firm were what made us different, and I was our number one cheerleader. I promoted their work environment, lifestyle, job responsibilities, and top employer status beautifully and with ease. I loved the enthusiasm and passion I shared for my firm and am grateful that I could use my skills positively on a daily basis.

The truth is that we are all walking billboards for our own lives. We have the opportunity to sell ourselves or our unique "brand" every day to everyone who crosses our paths. Living and acting with consistency in style, form, and personal attributes is key to presenting yourself as a strong brand. You become someone who's memorable, trustworthy, and reliable. By promoting yourself with a strong sense of enthusiasm and self-awareness, you strengthen the energy at the solar plexus. Ergo, when you connect with Lisa, you know I will always show up, give you 100 percent of my time and attention along with a bubbly personality. I'll shine my light to make sure you know how to shine yours as well.

"A brand is simply trust." Steve Jobs

Reflect on the attributes of your brand that make you beautiful. If you haven't thought of yourself as a brand before, what would it be?

Day 77

"I am comfortable in my own skin, no matter how far it's stretched. Ha, ha."
Dolly Parton

For the past forty years, self-image has always been a struggle for me. Before my spiritual awakening, I viewed my external image very poorly. I wasn't good enough. I constantly compared myself to others, and I connected my worth to the number on the scale. This terrible, negative internal self-talk was degrading and demeaning. And it was completely self-motivated. Reflecting back on this time, I can see that I didn't love myself the way I deserved to be loved.

This negative, poor self-image was rooted in the fact that I was overweight as a child and struggled for years with my image. Food was something I constantly had to monitor as my body was different compared to other young girls my age. Even after losing weight and achieving a healthy BMI, I never viewed myself as good enough. I also attached the idea of beauty to achieving a certain weight. Without that, I didn't allow myself to be seen as beautiful. Now, it seems crazy to think I put so much on a predetermined target, especially one that's such a poor and insignificant indicator of value. Still to this day, I know I have my limitations.

Oxford Languages defines self-image as "the opinion or idea you have of yourself, especially of your appearance or abilities to have a positive/negative self-image." Having an awareness of your identity and the self-image that you consistently present to the world is a sign of living your truth and strengthens the energy at the solar plexus.

Increasing the self-love I have for myself was a battle. In fact, it was one of the last areas that I "allowed" myself to heal because deep down inside, I struggled with the fact that I actually deserved the same love that I gave to others.

Presently, I have a stronger and more positive view of my external self-image. As I go with the flow, I understand that bodies change, especially with age, and I allow myself the necessary love and grace as I manage the unavoidable stresses related to my divorce and regular day-to-day activities. I am comfortable, inside and out, with the beautiful Lisa I have become. The woman who is a single mom with two young boys and is doing the best she can every day to live on the path of truth for the highest good.

Reflect on your self-image. If you feel in a good place with your self image, how does that change how you interact with the world? On the other hand, if you're thinking your pants are too tight, how does that change how you show up?

Day 78

*"When you believe in a thing, believe in it all the way,
implicitly and unquestionably."*
Walt Disney

My oldest son, Anthony, has been intrigued and impressed by the magic and works of Walt Disney for several years. From the wonder of the different theme parks, movies, characters, television programs, and the history of the creator himself, my son is beyond obsessed. He is a human encyclopedia of facts and information.

I fully support this, especially since the Disney empire is quite exquisite and provides us with entertainment and family enjoyment. As Disney himself said, "It all started with a mouse. If you can dream it, you can do it."

Dream big, believe big, and believe in yourself are the key themes that Walt Disney teaches us; coincidentally, they also indicate a person with a strong solar plexus as the energy is sourced from this area.

Believing in yourself and all the stages of this belief doesn't happen overnight. Your truth, your power, and your efforts go from a dream state to planning state to implementation state to slowly building your own empire. It takes effort, willpower, determination, and faith in yourself at the base and foundation. All these key pieces are ingredients in a recipe to create success.

Believing that you can create something out of nothing takes immense energy and faith. If Walt Disney can take an idea so small and, in turn, build it into a magnificent empire, so can you.

Reflect on things you've believed in that were created by your faith. Do you have a time where you relied on your faith in difficult situations? How did it help?

Day 79

*"It's not what we do once in a while that shapes our lives.
It's what we do consistently."*
Tony Robbins

The objective of the Kundalini yoga teacher training course I attended was to help me become a teacher, and it was also designed for me to develop my own, consistent daily practice, which is referred to as a "daily sadhana." This was accomplished by giving us various forty-day practices to complete on our own outside of the training weekends, which included a kriya (a set of postures) and meditation. The idea was to practice daily, based on a schedule that worked for me. Ideally, this would happen before the sun rises. It was an opportunity to create a healthy habit, discipline my body, generate energy, strengthen my intuition, and improve my health.

Our life is based on our daily habits; when we learn to change our habits, the world around us begins to change. Being regular and steady, over time, will create results. But we must have patience and grace with ourselves as time passes. We won't see results immediately—there is no express elevator to our dreams. Everything takes time.

According to the lessons learned during my Kundalini teacher training experiences, when you practice a particular kriya or meditation daily, it will affect your habits in various ways:

- Practice forty days straight to break any negative habits that may be blocking you.
- Practice ninety days straight to establish a new habit in your conscious and subconscious minds.
- Practice 120 days straight to confirm the new habit into consciousness created by the kriya.

My daily sadhana has changed based on the reality of my life and daily commitments; it is a fact that I only have a limited amount of time to practice. However, what has worked consistently for me is twenty to thirty minutes of yoga postures and meditation. That's what I recommend you commit to, for 180 days. For me, this is a manageable habit and the effects last throughout my day.

In what ways has being consistent affected your life? How about when you were inconsistent?

Day 80

"Who you are tomorrow begins with what you do today."
Tim Fargo

My to-do lists keep me organized, structured, and are an effective way for me to manage the thoughts that my mind processes on a daily basis. Remember earlier when I shared about how I had my husband buy a planner right after my baby was born? I know that I consistently work best with one paper to-do list and a large appointment calendar. And I believe that daily actions and accomplishments from today will shape the future to come. Using this system for myself has helped me feel more in control of the outcome of my day and, of course, helped me stay on track. Having ownership and control over managing my day strengthens the solar plexus.

Through my spiritual awakening, I have learned that I work best writing things down and prioritizing as I go to ensure that I'm aligned with my goals. Being able to see the big picture from a weekly or monthly perspective is critical for me to visualize assignments, appointments, and, therefore, expectations. I've also minimized my rigidity and obsession with completing everything in one day. This allows me to go with the flow, maintain balance, and understand there is always tomorrow.

"Ask yourself if what you're doing today is getting you closer to where you want to be tomorrow." Unknown

Reflect on how effectively you manage your responsibilities. What can you implement to get you closer to where you want to be? If you're not sure yet where you want to head, can you set a goal for yourself to spend some time thinking about that?

Day 81

"The tragedy of life is not death but what we let die inside of us while we live."
Norman Cousins

It is your right to fulfill the wants, desires, and dreams of your soul through the burning fire energy in the belly. That is how you will make a difference for those around you and yourself. Following that fire to act—despite the fear of what it may generate—is when and where the magic happens.

Letting the unlived accomplishments and truths die is the real tragedy as you never know how your actions may influence and impact the people you love. It's a reminder to always choose yes when approached with an opportunity and to be open to whatever opportunities come out of it.

Early on, I wasn't fully focused on my sound healing practitioner training. A month prior I had received my real estate license, which was something I'd been inspired to pursue for many years. A good friend of mine was a broker and as I was about to move out of my home, pursuing this career seemed in my best interests. It would offer security and benefit my future.

I was torn between two worlds: the stability of acting as a real estate agent was reflective of the "Old Lisa" prior to my spiritual awakening. I took the approach of "I should do this." But "New Lisa" was training to become a sound healer, post-spiritual awakening, and taking the approach of "I want to do this." It was a new area that intrigued me at my heart and soul.

There were so many avenues for my time and spirit but only so much energy and capacity for me to focus my efforts. Kathy, my sound teacher, shared with me, "You are a light beam and a healer. You are doing the world a disservice by not fully pursuing this path, living as a healer to help others." I loved her bluntness and appreciated her sharing these truths.

So, there it is. That's how I switched gears and started to focus on my new path. It was an unknown area and I had no familiarity with it, but I learned to trust and have faith that the Universe brought it to me for a reason. I am beyond grateful for taking a chance and not allowing the fire to die inside me. I trusted the truth of my soul and knew what I wanted.

Don't let things die inside of you. What are some of the things you've buried? What are those things living inside of you that you can bring to life and take action on?

Day 82

"Abundance follows people in their purpose."
Teal Swan

All souls have a true purpose: it's your God-given talent deep within your heart. Trusting your own path and purpose is always the right direction for you to naturally bring more free-flowing happiness and abundance into your life. Abundance is defined by Oxford Languages as "plentifulness of the good things of life; prosperity."

As I shared on Day 30, when your spirit is living from a place of purpose you can trust in a higher power and have faith in your own intuition for direction and guidance. Life is lighter; it flows more naturally and with ease. You become calm, full of joy, love, and happiness, with an overall sense that you are fulfilling your time living as you should be. According to my teachers, your soul's purpose and destiny can be found in your own spiritual name, which is tattooed on your forehead. Purpose is also referred to as living your "dharma." Choosing to live with purpose strengthens the solar plexus.

I am finally living my life through my purpose every day. Having a love and passion for helping and healing others is a natural extension of who I am. Thus, there is no distinction between "Lisa at work" and "Lisa at home." Having this healing ability fills me with joy to help others on their own path to healing.

**What is your purpose? If you're
not living your purpose, what is
preventing you from living that way?**

Day 83

"Don't worry about what others are doing. March to the beat of your own drum. Define what a happy, successful life means to you and live it."
Regina Williams

Living from a strong sense of independence and personal power connects you to the strong energies at your solar plexus.

Thus, "marching to the beat of your own drum" signifies a person who moves freely, is self-reliant, and is confident in their own actions and expression of their personality.

Marching to the beat of my own drum has been a characteristic of mine since I was younger. Albeit, I recognize that this way of being is stronger and more prevalent when I am deeply connected with the truth at my heart and soul where my spirits are aligned. It brings about an intense feeling of being alive. This offers even more reason to live solely for what is best suited for you.

Sadly, my spiritual awakening revealed to me that I did not beat to the rhythm of my own internal drum and vibration during my marriage. I lowered my vibration to be in sync with my spouse. Our connection was not a true connection.

Ironically, as a sound healer, I have become extremely intrigued by different percussion drums and have implemented them into my practice. I began with a table drum for my son, Michael, and have since expanded to the shaman drum, hand pan, and ocean drum. Each makes their own unique vibrations and has different effects on the listener. Playing these, I am free-flowing with my own move-ment to the sounds placing me in my own meditative state.

I believe it's no coincidence (and a sign from the Universe) that I would connect so deeply with the most spiritual instruments of rhythm that were originally played by the Divine feminine women who were worshipped for the true goddesses that they are.

According to the late Layne Redmond, "One of the most pow-erful aspects of drumming . . . is that it changes people's conscious-ness. Through rhythmic repetition of ritual sounds, the body, the brain, and the nervous system are energized and transformed."

For my boys and I, beating drums has connected us in a way I never realized we were missing. It's become a way to build and play music. Playing with drums is deeply personal and requires us to be in our own rhythm and feel all the feels necessary. It can be a unique individual expression and it also has the power to effortlessly syn-chronize our little triangle family with grace.

It's a reminder to always be brave enough to walk to the beat and rhythm of your own happiness, which never goes out of style.

How do you beat to the rhythm of your own life? What feelings do these acts bring out for you?

Day 84

"Attitude and personality are as important as experience and ability."
Brian Tracy

On Day 83, I shared how living an independent and personal life-style and marching to the beat of your own drum indicates a person who moves freely, is self-reliant, and possesses a strong personal power. This internal awareness to care for and honor your actions and expression of your core personality connects with the strong energies at the solar plexus.

Allowing your true personality to shine through—despite difficult or challenging circumstances, situations, or people—is a true gift and blessing to give to yourself. Oxford Languages defines personality as "the combination of characteristics or qualities that form an individual's distinctive character;"

Your personality opens doors and attracts others into your energy field. However, your attitude is what will keep you in the door and/or propel your energy to higher fields of opportunities. This is a perfect expression of the idea that "your attitude determines your altitude."

In September 2021, the spirit eagle was tattooed on my fore-head during two reiki energy healing treatments given to me by my dear friend, Nicole. Previously, I shared about the spirit bee, another flying animal that I was intuitively connected to; however, the presence of the spirit eagle further moved me with its deep significance.

The eagle is symbolic of the importance of honesty and truthful principles. This compelled me deeply as I am living my own path of truth, so in a sense, I have the energy of the spirit eagle to prove it—he is within me as my guide. The eagle epitomizes the saying, "The truth will set you free" and reminds you that when you live in truth, you have the power to soar higher than you ever imagined.

Eagles also have the ability to fly higher than almost any other bird; they convey the powers and messages of spirit and serve as our connection to the Divine. They also signify freedom and independence and are a reminder that freedom starts in the mind. Hope, power, resilience, foresight, and psychic awareness are also key qualities of the eagle. These qualities are the gifts of a strong intuition and offer a potential and increased awareness to fulfill your purpose while on Earth.

In summary, the eagle's symbolism and traits portray something we can all aspire to on our own path of spirituality. I'll return to the eagle later.

Reflect on your own path of how your attitude determines your altitude. How has your attitude impacted you?

Day 85

*"Big achievements come one small advantage at a time,
one step at a time, one day at a time."*
Jim Rohn

Achievements are to be recognized and felt deep within your soul and celebrated for their fabulousness. They result from consistent effort, dedication, and personal power, all sourced from the energies at the solar plexus.

The biggest surprise to my healing journey has been my new love for writing. In April 2020, I began to write poetry to help manage the rocky waves of my life. I had no idea that a month later I would announce to my husband my need to separate and move out of our home. What started with one piece evolved into roughly fifty pieces that were written for my eyes only. Each piece reflected the confusing state of my life. They helped me feel, reflect, process, and release the magnitude of emotions floating around me during that time.

However, in August 2020, I felt a calling to write publicly about Michael's hearing loss diagnosis. I became vulnerable for the first time on social media to promote awareness and to help others who may have similar experiences. I wanted to share the consistent underlying theme that challenges are our greatest blessings.

In October 2020, the editor of our local magazine, Franklin Lakes Living Magazine, contacted me to be the featured family for the March 2021 issue. I was surprised, shocked, and blessed to share our story with others and shine light on information about deaf awareness. And I was also excited to highlight my achievements and community efforts. My hope was that my ability to handle challenges with a positive and uplifting outlook could help motivate the magazine's readers.

I agreed with a grateful heart, fully knowing that a majority of the people in town didn't know I was also handling a private divorce. My family of three became the first featured non-traditional family, highlighting a strong, single mom who did whatever she had to do to help her boys with grace and dignity.

It was a huge achievement to be honored for living my life the only way I knew how and to be recognized because someone felt that my light could help others on their own paths. I understand that this acknowledgment didn't happen overnight. It was from gradual, determined steps, day by day, until finally someone noticed I could help and be of service for the greater good.

The featured family article a year after my fortieth birthday was a time when I recognized there was an energy shift, and that the way I was living was no longer serving my highest good. In a way, it was like the Universe was rewarding me for my past pain and saying, "Wow, Lisa can help others. It is time for her to shine for others so they can heal too."

Reflect on your past achievements: how do you feel when you think about them?

Day 86

"She believed she could, so she did."
Unknown

It took me roughly twenty years to believe in myself and the words above. I first came across this quote in 2001, on a green, fabric-wrapped frame with brown letters at the Hallmark store. At the time, I hated the color green, but I loved the quote—so I purchased it and it proudly sat on my desk from that day forward through all my moves in life. I was always a dreamer who wanted to open her own business, but I was scared. The outcome of whatever I did needed to succeed with perfection and flying colors. I was afraid of all the risks and vulnerability that came with opening a business.

For my fortieth birthday in 2020, close friends of mine gifted me this quote on a keychain as well as other yoga-inspired items and a small mind bowl—my first sound bowl. It touched my heart as they knew where my passions were and wanted to gift me something special that I would treasure.

Earlier, I shared that I created an LLC for my business in September 2020, Prem Livjot, named after my spiritual name. I intended to offer spiritual healing services of Kundalini yoga and sound healing. My initial offerings were virtual due to the pandemic, but in the Spring of 2021, I taught outdoors at the homes of friends.

On November 1, 2021, I signed a one-year lease for my very own healing center. It's a 300 square foot space with lots of light and positive energy located at 362 Main Street. If you add the address, the numbers 3+6+2 = 11. The number 11 is the most spiritual, in my opinion, and the timing of signing the lease on 11/1, meant that all signs pointed to this as my next step. When I walk up the stairs, I feel the same sense of "I am home" and "I feel safe," just like I did at my previous yoga studio.

The clarity of my path solidified with the power of the vibration of the name "Michael." My son, Michael, is the reason I became a sound healer. When I work with clients, I'm aware that Archangel Michael is present at the healings and this fuels my fire to help others. And finally, my real estate broker, Michael, completed my paperwork and finalized the last aspect of my dream.

I believe in miracles, the power of synchronicity, and trusting the Universe that it was the right time for me to fly. All I can say is, I believed I could, and I finally did. These are very deep, powerful words that are only possible because of my strong, internal personal power and the strength of my solar plexus.

The keys to my healing center are proudly secured and are a daily reminder of how far I have come on my journey of designing a life for myself and my boys.

Reflect on moments you believed in the strength of your internal power. How did it make you feel?

Day 87

"Activity leads to productivity."
Jim Rohn

On Day 86, I shared how I rented a small space to be used as my very own healing center. The fire that began to burn inside me after signing the paperwork is quite remarkable. It was an energy that I recognized from my early twenties. It was of someone who was entrepreneurial, young, and hopeful about future dreams to build something of their very own. It was there all along, fulfilling no purpose—waiting for this moment to make an appearance.

When I shared these feelings with Dr. Chris, he expressed, "Well, isn't it a wonderful feeling to be productive?" My immediate response was, "YES!" Because that is what was missing all these years. I hadn't felt productive toward a goal of my very own which would form my own personal and professional development. I had lacked being busy and productive for the right reasons: to grow Lisa into the person who she was meant to live as. That is why I had been extremely active volunteering at school. My body was craving the feelings that ooze out of you when you feel accomplished and productive.

Luckily, I now have the opportunity to live my second life. One that is full of truth, passion, light, love, and happiness with a side of productivity.

How do you feel when you are productive?

Day 88

"And the day came when the risk to remain tight in a bud
was more painful than the risk it took to blossom."
Anaïs Nin

This quote is very close to my heart as it mirrors how I felt about my life-changing decision to leave my husband. I included this quote in the magazine article about my boys and me, and I shared it just a few days ago. The quote spoke to me so deeply. It was a huge risk to leave my husband. I didn't have it all planned out and I didn't know if I'd end up better or worse. I was pretty complacent and, from the outside, it looked like I lived a perfect life.

Blooming as a person only happened with extensive healing, a healing that could only be done by myself, on my terms, and in my own time. I accepted that the only way out was in—so I went in and was blessed to have a tool belt of tools. My only job was to heal and de-stress my body.

"Get busy living or get busy dying. Remember, Red, hope is a good thing. Maybe the best of things and no good thing ever dies." Andy Dufresne, *The Shawshank Redemption*

This mantra was spoken by Andy to his friend Red and gave Andy the hope and motivation to escape prison and start a new life for himself in Mexico. Andy also encouraged Red to do the same:

to take a chance at a different life and to take risks. At first, Red wasn't so sure about following the unknown path, but he trusted his friend and decided to follow him and create a new life for himself. This unknown chance was the risk he needed to take in order to blossom, in essence to live his second life.

What risks have you taken which allowed you to blossom?

Day 89

"If you don't go after what you want, you'll never have it. If you don't ask, the answer is always no. If you don't step forward, you're always in the same place."
Nora Roberts

You have the power to shape your future and destiny; you are the driver of this beautiful thing called life. Take chances and risks, despite the fear.

Have you allowed yourself to stay positive and question, "What if it turns out way better than I could have ever imagined?"

Ignore the negative thoughts and doubts in your mind telling you to play it safe. If we all lived life in the shallow end, then we would never have the opportunity to experience the magic of real living from the powerful deep end.

According to C. JoyBell C., "Don't be afraid of your fears. They're not there to scare you. They're there to let you know that something is worth it."

My yoga teacher training program was transformational in so many ways: from the knowledge perspective to my spiritual awakening, but also the strong connections from others in the class. These connections with others are shaping my future as we support each other in sharing our spiritual gifts with the world around us. We work together to help, heal, and serve others.

I shared on Day 47 about my dear friend and soul sister, Nicole. We are both aware that the time has come to share our healing gifts with the world. It's our turn to be the guides and offer tools to help others heal their bodies from the inside out.

But in doing this we are swimming in the unchartered waters of the deep in an area of the ocean that we haven't experienced before. It's scary, but we have each other for encouragement and to give each other the confidence and power needed to set the fears aside and dive in, as that is what we are being called to do. We can do this because the energy and power behind our efforts is sourced from the solar plexus.

The key is to visualize and focus on the end result—the deep feelings at the heart that are surrounded by love, as that is the path that will take you home.

Reflect on a time you went after something you wanted and overcame your fears. Was the outcome worth it? How did that experience make you feel?

Day 90

*"Starting tomorrow, what are you going to do that
will make a change in your life's direction?"*
Jim Rohn

On the day I finalized my real estate transaction for my own healing
center, my real estate broker, Mike, sent me this quote via a video of
Jim Rohn. I'd previously shared with Mike about writing this book
and my own reflection on quotes to help others deepen their own
spirituality.

He didn't have any more information than that, but he intuitively sent me quotes that were beyond perfect for this section that
I am currently writing about, "I am Power!"

It wasn't a coincidence, but rather a deep sign to trust in the
powers around us. Before that day, I wasn't familiar with Jim Rohn,
but I am grateful that Mike shared different people's works with me,
all of which had deeper meanings. Their work allows you to reflect
that there is more than what's visible at the surface; allowing yourself
to dig deeper opens up a new world of possibilities and amazement.

Mike is a very entrepreneurial and hard-working professional,
with an energy and intense drive similar to mine before having children. The only difference is that he exudes an intense passion for
his work.

When I was younger, I didn't feel the same level of passion for
my work. I performed with an intense energy because that is how

I approached everything. The difference all these years later is that now passion fuels my work to help others. Having this true passion fills me with joy unlike any other. It's a sign that my life's work will be fulfilling and uplifting for myself and others whom I have the pleasure of connecting with. Signs from the Universe will lead us the right way on our path and the power to change our direction is sourced from the strong energies at the solar plexus.

Lastly, always remember: "Just where you are—that's the place to start." Pema Chodron

What will you do tomorrow that will make a change in your life's direction?

I Am

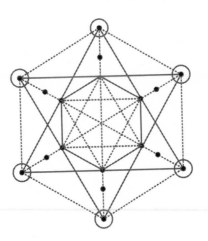

Love

I Am Love
DAYS 91–120

Feeling a true love for myself was the last area of my body that needed to be healed. A challenge indeed, as I did not feel I deserved the same amount of love that I often gave to others in abundance. Recognize that in order to really give love to others, you must first learn how to love yourself.

The fourth chakra is the balance point between the lower and upper chakras and is considered the focal point of love and compassion in the human body, located at the heart center. This point marks the awareness of a higher consciousness and a transition from "me to we," where the energy that flows here moves beyond the personal to the consideration of others. We often take for granted the fact that our heart is the pump that powers our entire body, and air is the element that filters through our lungs. Both functions occur without any effort of our own, keeping us alive.

As it relates to the fourth chakra, you will understand that:

- Self-love, self-care, and true appreciation for yourself should always be your top priority, both during the good and bad times.
- We all have a unique way we prefer to give and receive love, as depicted in Gary Chapman's book, *The 5 Love*

Languages: The Secret to Love that Lasts. The true key to love is built on a foundation of understanding.

- In life, there are two paths that can be followed: that of your spirit and love, or that of your ego and fear.
- When you follow the path of your heart, it will always bring you back home.
- Feeling safe to be authentic strengthens your connection with others.
- You often lose yourself doing the things you love and it is important to have a love for learning.
- Acceptance is critical because you are enough, exactly as you are.
- It is important to interact with kindness, smiling, and hugs as they connect directly at the heart center.
- Saying "thank you" is the only prayer you will ever need as living with gratitude and appreciation fills your heart with love.
- It is valuable to say something beautiful to others and to be grateful for those in our lives who make us happy.
- It is important to take time to make your soul happy.
- Living with grace is healthy and loving to your soul and body.
- Forgiveness sets your soul free from past experiences.

Tune In with the Adi Mantra
"Ong Namo Guru Dev Namo"

To center yourself in the higher self before practicing Kundalini yoga, chant the Adi Mantra three times.

"*Ong Namo Guru Dev Namo*" translates to "I bow to the Divine wisdom of all that is" and "I bow to the Divine teacher within."

HOW TO PRACTICE

- *Posture:* Sit in Easy Pose, with the spine erect.
- *Eye Position:* Eyes slightly closed, focused at the Third Eye, which is the point between the brows.
- *Mudra: Prayer Pose.* Place the palms of the hands flat together to neutralize the positive (right, or male) and negative (left, or female) sides of the body. Your thumbs should press against the sternum and your forearms will be parallel to the floor.
- Consciously begin to breathe. Gently inhale through your nose, feel the breath fill up your belly, fill up your lungs, and expand your rib cage. On the exhale from your nose, recognize the breath leaving your body. When ready to "tune in" with the Adi Mantra, inhale and exhale deeply from the nose and begin chanting the mantra three times.

Asanas

The asanas listed below focus on strengthening the energy center at the heart center. It is recommended that you hold each posture for one to two minutes with a slight rest in between. Remember to stay within while holding the postures and while resting, keep your eyes closed, focusing on the Third Eye, the point between the brows. This will allow you to focus on yourself and build your intuition, plus learn to trust your own power and ability.

- Bear Grip
- Yoga Mudra

- Baby Pose
- Yoga March
- Windmill

Find a description of each posture in the Appendix on page 420.

Meditation

"Ad Guray Nameh"

This mantra meditation is for projection and protection from the heart center, giving you an enchanting and magnetic personality. Also known as the "Mangala Charn" mantra, it is often chanted after you tune in with the Adi Mantra for additional protection. It surrounds your magnetic field with protective light.

Mantra: (pronunciation guide)

- "Aad guray nameh
- Jugaad guray nameh
- Sat guray nameh
- Siree guroo dayv-ay nameh"

Translation:

- "I bow to the primal wisdom
- I bow to the wisdom true through the ages
- I bow to the true wisdom
- I bow to the great, unseen wisdom"

HOW TO PRACTICE

- *Posture:* Sit in Easy Pose, with the spine erect and a slight neck lock.

- *Eye Position:* Eyes closed, focused at the Third Eye, which is the point between the brows.
- *Mudra:* Place the palms together at the heart center in Prayer Pose. The thumbs are crossed.
- *How to practice:* Inhale at the heart center to begin. Chant the first line as the arms move up and out to a 45-degree angle. Inhale as the hands move back to the heart center. Repeat the same sequence for the remaining three lines to complete the mantra. The full extension of the arms is timed to the chant. As you change, you're projecting your words out. Your motive is to open the heart.
- *Time:* Continue for three minutes. Build to eleven minutes.
- *Helpful Tip:* Soundtracks are available to chant as you complete the meditation that can be found on any app that streams music. I like to chant this meditation along with the artist, Simrit.

Deep Relaxation

- *Posture:* Lie on your back in Corpse Pose. With your eyes closed, place your arms at your sides, with palms facing up. Allow your body to rest, process, and absorb the movement of energy.
- *Time:* One to three minutes minimum.

Ending Prayer

To close your Kundalini practice, chant three long *Sat Naams*.

Sound Healing

Enjoy this ten-minute sound healing ensemble to further relax your mind and body. Consider listening during deep relaxation or at another time during your day when your body could benefit from and enjoy the beautiful healing gift of sound and vibrations.

Access this month's asana videos, meditation, sound healing audio, and more at www.LisaAnnese.com/i-am-light

Day 91

"The yoga pose is not the goal. Becoming flexible or standing on your hands is not the goal. The goal is to create space where you were once stuck. To unveil layers of protection you've built around your heart. To appreciate your body and become aware of the mind and the noise it creates. To make peace with who you are. The goal is to love . . . you. Shift your focus and your heart will grow."
Rachel Brathen

In January 2020, I flew to Miami to attend the Khalsa Way prenatal yoga teacher training program. The desire to attend this course came from an immense energy and pull from my heart. I yearned to leave my comfort zone and receive training in an area of yoga that was intriguing to me, plus one that I felt could make a difference for other women. I recall approaching the Miami airport from the air and had this vision and download that my life would forever change after that trip—and boy has it sure changed!

Women helping women. That was whom I had the privilege of spending my training with. I had the honor to meet over fifty spiritually like-minded women who had the same goals in mind: to love, help, and serve.

This beautiful quote was posted on a bulletin board in the studio. It was an absolutely lovely and unique description of "what is yoga" depicted in a truthful fashion—with the prime goal to give yourself all the love that you need and deserve. The love that has been missing from your world. The love that you often give to others but forget to give yourself.

Well, it is time for you to allow yourself to love you like you have never loved yourself before! To get to the core at your heart center as that is where the truth of your spirit lies. Uncover an awareness of, appreciation for, and gratitude toward your body and temple for supporting your spirit for all it has done for you up until today.

My personal truth is that I never gave myself self-love or the true appreciation that I deserved. My love for others was plentiful and constant, not understanding that I needed love too. I always looked externally for love, not recognizing that the magic secret to healing my fourth chakra, located at the heart center, was to focus on my own self-care and love.

Throughout my spiritual awakening, healing my heart was the final area to be healed and the last piece of the puzzle. I still have unpleasant moments and days and self-darkness, but now I have access to tools that allow for faster recovery. I can snap out of it quicker than I have in the past.

It seems ironic, but why do we choose to love and give to others more than we love ourselves? It is a change in mindset and understanding that has the opportunity to transform your world beyond your beliefs—at least that is what happened for me.

How will you love yourself differently today?

Day 92

*"Love has nothing to do with what you are expecting to get,
only with what you are expecting to give, which is everything."*
Katharine Hepburn

Part of my spiritual awakening was my growing awareness of the fact that there are five love languages, as written and defined by Gary Chapman in his book, *The 5 Love Languages: The Secret to Love that Lasts*. Those languages are: "words of affirmation, quality time, receiving gifts, acts of service, and physical touch." Thus, if you understand your partner's love language—how they feel and perceive love—then you can connect on a deeper level with them, and they'll feel the love that is being expressed in a "language" they can understand.

After reading the book, I recognized that my love language is to give gifts and perform acts of service to those who are dear to my heart, never expecting anything in return. However, I prefer to receive love in the form of deep conversations and experiences. The reality is that you can have different love languages for receiving versus giving love. I'll discuss this more on Day 100. Giving unconditionally warms my core and it gives me great pride and joy to know that my thoughtfulness is appreciated by those I love. I always give my all as that is my destiny and purpose, to share God's Divine love as my one-pointed devotion.

Reflect on "The Five Love Languages" listed above. Out of those five, how do you prefer to show your love? How do you prefer to receive love?

Day 93

"'What is love?'
"'The absence of fear,' said the master.
"'What is it we fear?'
"'Love,' said the master."
Unknown

Oxford Languages defines love as "an intense feeling of deep affection; a great interest and pleasure in something; and a person or thing that one loves." Furthermore, fear is defined as "an unpleasant emotion caused by the belief that someone or something is dangerous, likely to cause pain, or a threat."

We can experience a never-ending cycle of love versus fear and then fear versus love. This will continue until we break the cycle and understand that, as spirits, we are all born with the innate power and ability to love each other and ourselves. Also, we do not want to experience any pain; we fear getting hurt from love. But how can we fear that something we're innately born with will hurt us?

It is really our ego, or our view of ourselves, which is afraid of getting hurt. Following your own spiritual journey you will discover your unique truth, which will allow you to make choices based on the voice of your own spirit and soul.

A large part of my spiritual awakening was the awareness that I never really felt loved the way I needed or wanted to be loved. This was a large motivating factor for separating from my husband.

On New Year's Eve, heading into 2020, we took the boys to Disney World. We were in a beautiful hotel room and everything was "as it should be." I woke up to fireworks going off and considered waking the boys and my husband, but I didn't. Sitting there, I realized that it all looked real, but actually, my definition of what I had wanted from love wasn't real. I knew it at that moment. It reminded me of when Carrie Bradshaw goes to Paris in *Sex and the City* and everything looks real, but it isn't real, despite seeming dreamy. I wanted real love similar to when she says, "I'm looking for love. Real love. Ridiculous, inconvenient, consuming, can't-live-without-each-other love."

My goal is to feel a never-ending cycle of "real love" from myself and my partner. This wish would never come true had I stayed in my marriage. Thus, I chose the opportunity to one day experience "real love" versus staying with fear and my ego. I was craving a partner who wasn't yet identified.

When it comes to decisions about love, do you follow the path of your spirit and choose love or tend to follow your ego and choose fear? How does it make you feel to choose love over fear?

Day 94

"Love doesn't make the world go round.
Love is what makes the ride worthwhile."
Franklin P. Jones

Living with love for yourself and others makes your day happier and
has a domino effect, impacting the world around you. Our "crazy
ride" becomes more worthwhile when you couple love with having
a sense of purpose, fulfillment, and with deeper meaning. Sourcing
your decisions and actions from the heart center and
focusing on how a situation will make you and others feel is crucial
beyond words. Remember the words of Maya Angelou, who said,
"People will forget what you said, people will forget what you did,
but people will never forget how you made them feel."

Having a sense of love in you makes everything brighter. Things
may not be great, but you have love as a foundation. It is an indescribable feeling to experience love flowing freely in your body when you
are operating from your heart's center. Your body feels warm, satisfied, and full of love. A glorious feeling sourced from your soul.

As shared on Day 35, before my spiritual awakening I lived
from my head, not my heart. I seriously ignored my emotions and
feelings; my life was basically a mental checklist as I progressed
through my years of living. I didn't experience life with deep meaning or question anything beyond the surface level. Until I focused
on love and my heart.

Lisa Annese

Moving out of my home was a difficult decision, made from my heart. My soul just did not feel right where I was. That's why I kept explaining that it was a heart decision, not a head decision. When in doubt, always follow the love from your heart, as it will bring you back home. As it did for me.

Reflect on how you feel when you make love a priority in your life.

Day 95

"The heart is the household divinity which, discharging its function, nourishes, cherishes, quickens the whole body, and is indeed the foundation of life, the source of all action."
William Harvey

Your heart is the pump which powers your body, keeping it physically alive. It supplies oxygen-carrying blood and nutrients to every cell, nerve, muscle, and vital organ in your body. It is roughly the size of a clenched fist and located in your chest between your lungs, slightly to the left of center, protected by the rib cage.

Life cannot exist without the heart and thus it's the root of life for all of us. Even though the heart's literal function is just to pump blood, the energy associated with feelings of love deep within the soul is sourced from this area at the fourth chakra.

As shared on Day 94, "People will never forget how you made them feel," so yes, let's make sure that everyone you meet feels your love. In Winnie the Pooh, Piglet says, "Pooh, how do you spell love?" Pooh responds, "You don't spell love, Piglet . . . you feel it." Share love with ease and hand it out freely as if it were free—because it is! There is always an unlimited supply of love to give.

For me, I always feel fulfilled when I share my love and light with everyone. Being kind to someone brightens my day and brightens their day. Even with the most mundane things, you can share your light.

As an example, I'd built relationships with the people at my local UPS store and when the article about our family (that I mentioned earlier) came out, the girl in the store was so excited to see me. She said to me, "I'd never have known you had all these hard things you were going through! You're always smiling and happy." Because we had built a relationship around mundane things, we had that foundation for sharing love and energy. It was like two strings connecting me with another deep within the soul at the heart center. It is an infinite energy exchange of love as I simultaneously feel the same love that I extend to another.

How do you share your love with others and how does that make you feel?

Day 96

"We breathe in what the trees breathe out, and they breathe in what we breathe out. Forever overwhelmed by the beauty of God's design."
Sabrina Barich

Maintaining healthy lungs also strengthens the fourth chakra. As shared on Day 21, the life force energy or prana is crucial to our existence. According to Swami Vivekananda, "Prana is the driving power of the world, and can be seen in every manifestation of life."

We also have a set number of breaths before our physical body dies. Learning how to consciously breathe to manage our life and vitality is crucial.

Trees are the lungs of the world. Coincidentally, the side profile of a lung shares a striking resemblance to the profile of a tree as the bronchial tubes of the lung appear to be similar to the limbs of a tree as they branch from the trunk.

As humans, our connection to nature runs deep—the reality is that without trees, our lungs wouldn't be able to receive the oxygen we need to breathe. Thus, our existence depends on each other for survival.

Likewise, air is the element that associates and connects with the fourth chakra. It is a constant among all of us. We are all breathing the same air—it puts us on the same playing field.

As an element, air reminds us to trust our faith; the reality is that nobody can see air, but we know it is there. We trust that air will be available to give us the necessary prana and energy needed for the continuation of our survival.

Air is often forgotten and taken for granted, but it is truly powerful and integral to our lives. To me, it is fascinating how consciously managing your breath, with something that cannot be seen, can change a mood, situation, outlook, and your future, all for your highest good.

A true love affair can occur with the air. A love affair that is rich and vast, as Laini Taylor shared, "Love is a luxury. No. Love is an element. An element like air to breathe, earth to stand on."

We often take for granted our need and love for air. Reflect on other basic things in your life that are often overlooked and taken for granted.

Day 97

"I'll never regret the love I gave anyone, even if it wasn't reciprocated, love always comes back full circle, that love is coming back to me in some shape or form. Keep putting love into the universe, cause it's coming back with interest."
Tonto Dikeh

It is a karma that whatever we put out into the Universe will come back to us. Oxford Languages defines karma as "the sum of a person's actions in this and previous states of existence, viewed as deciding their fate in future existences."

Understand that when you constantly lead and serve from your heart, it will always be returned in your favor with the power of Divine timing. It may not be immediately or within that situation, but trust that all the goodness that you share with others will make its way back to you.

Through my spiritual journey, I connected with the different geometric figures and patterns of the mandala, which represents the Universe in Buddhist symbolism. Likewise, the mandala, which translates to "circle" in Sanskrit, is a sacred symbol used for meditation, healing, and art therapy for both adults and children.

Initially, I was attracted to the mandala's unique beauty and balance between the symmetry of the designs—which was very appealing to the eyes. However, after further research, I wasn't surprised to learn that the deeper meaning behind these figures represents your spiritual journey, starting from the outside and then moving to the inner core, weaving through the layers.

On my own personal journey, healing happened from the outside first, but interwoven with the inner changes, like the mandala. To me, the mandala represents how everything in life is connected: me to others, others to me and the broader Universe. I possess faith in and goodness from my heart to always live from my highest self by choosing to follow the path of love. Love is always the answer, despite the question or situation.

Reflect on a time love was returned to you in a greater form.

Day 98

"Safety is not the absence of threat, it is the presence of connection."
Dr. Gabor Maté

On Day 17, I discussed the importance of healing the inner child and feeling peaceful, secure, and safe in the root area. Answering the most basic questions that are at the heart and center of your inner child: Am I good? Am I safe? Am I loved?

Even as an adult these similar themes weave throughout your daily life: the need to be seen, recognized, felt, and understood are at the core of our desire for a strong connection with another at the heart center. When you have a deep connection with another human or with something that brings your soul great joy and passion, you are engaged and interested. You feel an overall sense of safety which ultimately results in a deep feeling of love. These deep connections help your soul feel safe enough to be authentic and to share with the world fully without the fear of judgment or disapproval.

When connection is lacking, we no longer feel safe to fully communicate or truly express ourselves. This is what I had experienced for the majority of my marriage but was not aware of until my spiritual awakening, when my way of life, interests, and daily activities began to change.

As shared previously, in 2018 I attended regular Kundalini yoga classes where I practiced wearing white clothing, covered my head with a turban and chanted in a different language. I felt amazing and free; I'd finally found my tribe of people. Wearing the white clothes, I felt a different aura. However, since my husband and I did not connect from an emotional perspective, I was not comfortable sharing anything about it with him for fear of judgment.

My Kundalini practice had become divinely sacred and meaningful to me; I didn't want his lack of understanding to tarnish the deep love that was filling my soul.

I was blossoming, becoming aware, and following my heart for the very first time. However, without a true connection, I was no longer living with authenticity in my home. It was like I was two different people. It was a huge energy shift to act one way around my husband and another way outside of my home. This way of life was lonely, exhausting, and confusing for my soul.

It is important to note that living with authenticity doesn't need to only happen around those with whom we are connected. It should happen regardless of our surroundings when we are feeling secure and stable at our root center. However, when a situation presents itself, as it had with me, my goal was to protect my true soul at all costs. This would save me from further hurt and pain. But the harsh reality was that my pain wouldn't cease until I removed myself from what was causing my feelings of isolation and being judged.

Reflect on your connection with others. Do you feel safe to be authentic? Why or why not? How does it impact you when you feel safe to be authentic versus not?

Day 99

"We lose ourselves in the things we love; we find ourselves there, too."
Kristin Martz

As a young adult, I jumped around from different jobs within my career every two years or so. I believed there was something wrong with me for not feeling satisfied or content with my "job" at that moment, so I kept searching for what was "missing" that would eventually fill that void.

On Day 38, we looked at the question, "What will make me happy?" As a young adult, choosing something based on my happiness was not top of mind for me. In my opinion, choosing what will make you happy goes hand in hand with doing something we love, because happiness ultimately equates with feelings of love.

The truth was that I wasn't truly happy because instead of finding a "job," I needed to discover my purpose. That was the missing piece for me. Ironically, when I was at my lowest, I connected with my spirituality, through the practice of Kundalini yoga, which became the door to my purpose. Through that door, I discovered a love that never existed before, my truth, and I became lost in the beautiful possibilities that my life had to offer. In turn, my purpose came into the light: to help and heal others using the power of spiritual healing tools.

I seamlessly love and help others as a natural extension of who I am. It is not a job, but a way of life for me. Often as I perform my healings, my spirit is in a deep meditative state, a sign that I have indeed gotten lost within myself. I recognize that this is exactly where I need to be—in a love like no other with myself.

Remember to love what you do, do what you love, and you will never work a day in your life.

What are some of the things where you can lose yourself while doing them? How does this make you feel?

Day 100

"True love is born from understanding."
Buddha

It isn't possible to truly love something we don't understand. What we understand, we don't fear; thus, what we don't fear, we possess the ability to truly love.

Oxford Languages defines understanding as "the ability to understand something; comprehension;" and "sympathetically aware of other people's feelings; tolerant and forgiving."

Through my healing process, I developed the realization that I was never properly loved the way I needed to feel loved. It took me more than four years of therapy, my rising Phoenix moment of time, and forty-one years of my life to recognize this truth.

It was hard to see that what was missing from my life was the sense of experiencing real love during my forty-one years of life. This dense truth was difficult to process and, reflecting back on my life, left me feeling extremely sad and empty. I believe this happened because I was never really understood past the surface level, and perhaps those around me weren't aware of my feelings. It was a harsh reality to see that this goddess whose one-pointed devotion is to share God's Divine love and light for others lacked the same love she gave to others.

To feel loved is like receiving the prizes from the greatest treasure chest or the pot of gold at the end of the rainbow. However, the feeling of love does not materialistically fill your soul; rather, it spiritually completes your soul. Thus, the love is realer than real and truer than true. It is the only type of love that is meant for me and others living on the path of truth.

As I shared on Day 92, my spiritual awakening was my awareness that there are five love languages, as written and defined by Gary Chapman: "words of affirmation, quality time, receiving gifts, acts of service, and personal touch." After reading his book, I recognized that I like to receive love through deep conversations and quality time experiences with like-minded people whom I connect with. That's what had been missing and why I lacked the feeling of love and disconnection.

Now that I am aware of the truth of how I desire to feel loved and understood, it is like I possess the map to my life and I am on my own personal hunt to find the love that has been missing and that I truly deserve. I also believe in the power of Divine timing and that everything happens in due time so our souls can experience the lessons they were sent to learn on our specific life journey. I am right on time for my next assignment: to feel loved for who I am.

> **Being aware of someone's love language can be life-changing. Being aware of someone's love language is crucial to someone's relationship. Have the past few days since we discussed it on Day 92 made a difference in your relationships? And if it hasn't, or you haven't incorporated it, how could you be more aware of your interactions with others?**

Day 101

"People who were raised on love see the world differently from people raised on survival."
Unknown

Before my spiritual awakening, I was like an actress or an entertainer who performed based on the acceptance and approval of others. Since I lacked a strong sense of internal self, I didn't trust myself to know the way to go, so I relied on others to determine my direction and next moves. I was like air, ever-changing and dependent on what or who else was around.

Wanting to feel accepted and included have been common themes in my life since early childhood; I always felt that I was an outsider looking into situations. As I shared on Day 98, at times I didn't feel safe or secure at my foundation because I lacked a true connection from the heart center. Ironically, the above deep quote complements the way I handled my life: my goal was daily survival. I didn't have the ability to thrive without unconditional love as my anchor.

I wasn't guided by the internal love and light in my heart, nor did I believe that I was enough. Because I'd achieved so much, it appeared that I breezed through life effortlessly. But at the foundation of those achievements was lots of doubt, uneasiness, and hard effort. I lived and operated my life through the lens of others. If it worked for them, then it had to be good for me too. However,

I didn't recognize that this pattern wasn't the answer to real-life living for me—it was the answer to living as a survivor.

Emotionally, I possessed a fear that in order to be loved I had to conform to others, and so choosing my own path and way wouldn't be enough. As a result, I was never fully myself for fear that I would not be loved for who I was.

The feeling of not being enough was uncovered in therapy with Pam when I was thirty-eight years old. It's tragic to me that I lived prior to that time with the feeling that no matter what I did, it was not good enough, and that I thought I must always do more in order to feel seen and recognized.

Being aware of these patterns, I now have the opportunity to break the cycle and raise my boys to follow the power of their own spirit. I can help them recognize that following the light and love in their hearts is the path to happiness. And I can make sure that they understand the reality that they are already enough with no strings attached. I can love them unconditionally.

**Reflect on your awareness of life:
were you raised on love or survival?
How did this make you feel?**

Day 102

*"To be beautiful means to be yourself. You don't need to
be accepted by others. You need to accept yourself."*
Thich Nhat Hanh

On Day 101, I shared that before my spiritual awakening I so desperately wanted to feel accepted and included by others. I lacked
the love for myself to follow the desires of my own heart in turn for
those of others, thinking that was the way to go for me.

Oxford Languages defines acceptance as "the action of consent-
ing to receive or undertake something offered; the action or process
of being received as adequate or suitable, typically to be admitted
into a group."

I now recognize that to accept yourself is to give a sense of security and love to the most important person you know . . . you. It
means you will allow yourself to be who you are and do what you
choose without letting the opinions of others tarnish the desires of
your very own spirit.

It is so interesting how we often choose to favor the opinions
and voices of others versus ourselves. Why do we doubt ourselves?
Why do we not love ourselves and trust our true instincts? In the
end, we are the ones who know the way: the only acceptance that is
needed is from our heart and soul. As shared by Dr. Steve Maraboli,
"When I accept myself, I am freed from the burden of needing you
to accept me."

How do you feel when you choose to fully accept yourself and your choices?

Day 103

*"Today me will live in the moment, unless it's unpleasant.
In which case me will eat a cookie."*
Cookie Monster

Some days life is hard and we just need a cookie to feel better. A cookie could be anything that soothes your soul and helps to support you emotionally. Accepting this reality and giving yourself the self-love you need in the moment without judgment is healthy, natural, and a perfect sign of self-love.

As I shared earlier, I was overweight as a child. In fact, I struggled with weight my entire life. It was hard on my soul and difficult when other children would call me names and judge me because of my exterior appearance.

Once I lost weight and learned how to properly dress, care, and maintain my body, I became externally beautiful in a way I didn't recognize. However, deep down inside, my soul still identified with the fat girl I was as a child.

As such, my relationship with poor food choices became detrimental to me as it provoked negative internal self-talk with my soul, which was beyond healthy for me mentally and emotionally.

Properly loving yourself is to accept that having one cookie is not going to put you in a deep spiral of obesity, but it may offer you the comfort you need to emotionally process the temporary discomfort that is happening around you.

I also understand now that, in my past, this poor self-recognition took a toll on my self-esteem and created an overall belief that I wasn't good enough. However, with spiritual healing and awareness, I now know that I am enough. As Maya Angelou shared, "You alone are enough. You have nothing to prove to anyone."

When you are experiencing something unpleasant, what helps to soothe your soul?

Day 104

"A love for learning has a lot to do with learning that we're loved."
Fred Rogers

The celebrated Mr. Rogers has been a staple for many young children, known for his pure love and care for educating with kindness and love for the young.

As a child, I fondly remember watching *Mr. Rogers' Neighborhood*, and when my boys were younger, they had watched *Daniel Tigers' Neighborhood*, which was based on Mr. Rogers' teachings.

You can feel the love when Mr. Rogers would communicate his teachings and learning lessons for his viewers. A common theme from both of these programs was a love for learning because he'd created a space where you felt safe to make mistakes and to learn as you grow.

From a very young age, my oldest, Anthony, always had an immense love for learning something new. Anthony was constantly eager to learn more and apply to his own world because of his very fast processing speed. Plus, he longed to share and teach others because it brought him joy and excitement to educate those he loved about his teachings.

In fact, as a two-year-old, his teacher at the time sent me a beautiful card at the conclusion of the year explaining how special and eager Anthony was and that he would do "big things" in his future.

His passion for learning was so immense and it was my duty to provide him an array of opportunities to broaden his knowledge.

Wow. To read that about my child made me feel proud because I always knew there was something special about Anthony. Of course, the underlying belief is that he has thrived so strongly because he is filled with love.

How has a love for learning impacted your life? If learning hasn't been a love for you, what has? Where did you find a love?

Day 105

"Kindness is the language which the deaf can hear and the blind can see."
Mark Twain

This sweet quote touched my heart so dearly since my son is hard of hearing. But the truth behind this quote is so real as kindness is the universal language that everyone understands. Specifically for my son, Michael, who happens to be the sweetest and kindest angel of a little boy I know. I know Michael cannot hear and understand everything that is said to him, but he definitely can feel and understand when someone is kind to him. Personally, for me, kindness rules everything.

Oxford Languages defines kindness as "the quality of being friendly, generous and considerate." It is the only thing that costs nothing for the giver but both parties receive results tenfold in the form of the intangible—goodwill.

Treating others with kindness is an opportunity to give something of yourself out of the goodness of your heart. It takes presence, care, and respect to treat others with kindness. And these are free to all. Nobody is ever too busy to be kind.

One of the kindest and most gracious people I have ever connected with is the technician who assists me annually with my breast MRI at a women's specific breast care facility. I am at high risk from breast cancer so I am monitored regularly to ensure all is good with my health. After having this procedure done at other facilities, I have had the most enjoyable time at this small, women's specific facility as their service is top-notch. More specifically, the technician who prepares my IV and is with me for the entire process is extremely attentive, sweet, caring, and kind. She understands that women who have this procedure performed may be scared and uncomfortable and so she goes above and beyond to show her love to all. She's a very beautiful and memorable person who treats people exactly how she would like to be treated if the situation was reversed.

According to Proverbs 16:24, "Kind words are like honey, sweet to the soul and healthy for the body." There's a grand opportunity for us to make like the bees and "bee kind" to all we know because everyone is struggling with something that you don't know about.

How do you feel when someone is kind to you versus unkind?

Day 106

*"When someone helps you when they're struggling too,
that's not help, that's love."*
Unknown

As shared on Day 92, I recognized that my love language is to give to others through service and gifts. Always the helper since a child, it is completely fitting for me and consistent with my soul to love others this way. Likewise, by helping others, I am overjoyed and filled with love for myself during and after the act has been completed.

This quote about love for helping others reminds me of a time I helped my dear friend, Lorrie: a woman with a heart of gold and most beautiful soul who has a special place in her heart for helping others as well.

As I've shared several times, my life was transformed after attending a yoga training in Miami. This nine-day experience in Miami completely changed my soul and understanding of my place in the world. A recognition that while I was away, my soul felt free, empowered, and true for the very first time; I returned confused, sad, and unsure of how to handle my new reality.

The day after my trip, our school was hosting a family Mass and reception in honor of Catholic Schools week and Lorrie was in charge of the refreshments. She hadn't previously led an event at our school and so she called me for assistance. Normally, without hesitation, I am the first to give a helping hand. However, this time was different; I was not the same person and all I wanted to do was stay home and cry. Then, I recalled a statement that was shared by one of the spiritual teachers, Gurmukh, on my trip, "As a teacher, your greatest gift is serving others. Even if you are troubled, find someone who is more troubled than you to help and you will be overcome with joy."

I took a deep breath, and I knew that my duty was to help and serve with love. I used the energy of my sadness and channeled it into doing something that was good for the school and helpful for my friend. That was the only way out of the misery I was feeling—and just like my teacher explained, helping my dear friend filled me with the joy that was desperately missing and helped to heal my very own soul as well.

Reflect on a time when someone who was also struggling helped you, giving you the love that you desperately needed.

Day 107

"If you want to change the world, go home and love your family."
Mother Teresa

This beautiful quote was hanging on a canvas in the mud room at the house I shared with my husband. I loved this so much as I deeply believe in the power and the long-term effects of these words.

Family is everything. Growing up in an Italian home, life revolved around our immediate and extended family with grandparents, aunts, and uncles. We were always together and aware of what was happening in each other's lives. Being there for each other was love.

When I eventually had my own family, it was important that my boys felt my love for them every day. I wanted not just to be there and exist for them, but to feel connected to their individual souls on a deeper level. To love and support their unique personalities, curiosity for the world, and the spark that would set their world on fire.

I often sit back in awe reflecting on how beautiful each of my boys are in wonder, as they are indeed my little wonders, or as Oxford Languages defines, "someone or something that feels admiration or amazement for another."

For example, my oldest does everything so fast: talks, works, eats, you name it, he completes all aspects of his life first, at top speed, and well. However, my youngest does everything slowly. He takes his time and enjoys the experience; he really soaks up the feelings that are happening in a moment. This pattern has been apparent since birth and a pleasure for me to remark and reflect on. Both styles are lovely, and I encourage them each to remain who they are, not changing a thing.

Personally, having two beautiful sons with such contrasting styles is my own personal blessing and lesson as I always lived my life in the fast lane. I didn't understand the value of slowing down to enjoy the ride in the slow lane until my spiritual awakening.

My youngest shows me that there is another way to live and to appreciate the beauty of life as it is presented. You don't always have to look for what comes next, but instead absorb all that is happening in the present as that is all that truly exists.

How can you love and appreciate your family a little harder today?

Day 108

"It's not what's under the Christmas tree that matters, it's who's around it."
Charlie Brown

In 2007, I had my first apartment and very own Christmas tree. Growing up in a loving home where Christmas was heavily celebrated with decorations galore, I was up for the challenge to decorate my space. I chose to decorate everything with love and perfection in mind and, at that time, that was white and silver with an angel topper.

Fast-forward to 2020 where my definition of perfection seriously changed. I recognized that in the past, decorating for Christmas was always a combination of love and complexity. Every year I'd make fifteen types of cookies instead of just one or two. Everything had to be over the top. I had the mindset that I could never have too many decorations; however, with my spiritual awakening, I was now motivated by peace, simplicity, and the philosophy that less is more.

I traded a 7.5 foot tree for a 3.5 foot tree to fit our small apartment lifestyle; I purchased it in July as it was extremely important for the boys and I to not only maintain but also create new Christmas traditions at our new home.

Downsizing our tree, just like our lives, was not an easy task as the tree holds our family history decorated through the ages. The best ornaments are those from my boys' childhood and our family vacations: the ones handmade with glitter and the annual photo collages. All of these keep our rich memory alive and remind us of the times that were most important. This is a true connection at the heart center: a connection bringing love, warmth, happiness, and richness with the awareness and importance that all that matters is who is around our tree. This represents the true meaning of the holiday season: love.

Our first Christmas in our new home was designed by and full of spirit from my boys. Perfection wasn't white lights. It became rainbow-colored lights galore with a glow up "Santa Stop Here" star topper and a rotating disco ball. I gave my boys ownership and allowed them to be creative; they beamed with pride and happiness to have a home decorated for Christmas as they envisioned: full of magic, wonder, and joy. I absolutely loved the final product because it is alive with their spirit. That to me is what Christmas is all about. This year, I didn't do too much—and I really enjoyed the holiday!

As I reflect on my past in silence during meditation, I have recognized that Christmas was never about the presents, but the love that we share for each other. It is simple, pure, and full of peace. It's a feeling of freedom and the belief that all is well when we live with love from our true heart's center.

What feelings are represented from your experiences with the holiday season?

Day 109

"The people whose first instinct is to smile when you make eye contact with them are some of Earth's greatest treasures."
Unknown

My first instinct is always to smile at people. Smiling connects with the heart and strengthens the fourth chakra. A smile is inviting and welcoming. It's the door to connection with another's heart.

Smiling is positive, and as a natural drug it's good for your health. It can reduce stress, help heart health, and boost your immune system by decreasing cortisol in the body. Smiling produces endorphins and serotonin, which are the "feel-good" chemicals. They elevate and improve your mood, making you feel happier.

Picture the classic, yellow smiling emoji. It is the universal sign used to express positive feelings like happiness, gratitude, and affection. Even just seeing the image of the emoji has the power to uplift and put a smile on your face.

People who smile are happy: smiling creates a chain reaction of happiness with another as people tend to mirror the facial expressions they see. I know for myself that I feel a better energy alignment and comfort level when I'm in the presence of someone whose facial expressions are positive rather than dull or lifeless.

I remember when I was working as a campus recruiter my boss would refer to me as "smiley." Thinking back to this time, I generally loved what I was doing, thus that filled me with happiness. Upon meeting with another person, I always welcome and connect with them with a very cheery, bubbly, and inviting demeanor—never forgetting my big smile.

As Mother Teresa shares, "Let us always meet each other with a smile, for the smile is the beginning of love."

Is smiling your go-to connection with another? If not, what is your go-to connection?

Day 110

"Sometimes a hug is the answer, even when the question is not known."

m.s.

Hugging is a form of communication and expression of love through physical connection. Physical touch is also one of the love languages that was shared on Day 92. Either by hugging, holding hands, or another form of touch, the giver and receiver develop a strong emotional connection through the physical. For those who like to receive love this way, it fills their emotional tank and, as a result, they feel more secure with the other.

During a difficult emotional time, sometimes there are no words that can be shared—you just need to be held to feel understood, loved, and to know that you are not alone.

I didn't grow up in a home where physical connection was regularly expressed. So, for me, it isn't always natural to connect physically with another unless I feel the connection deep within my heart, which is a by-product of words of affirmation and deep conversations.

As shared by Gary Chapman, "Babies who are held, stroked, and kissed develop a healthier emotional life than those who are left for long periods of time without physical contact."

Before my spiritual awakening, I was not aware that hugging your child in times of difficulties was a better way to connect with them and soothe their pain.

Unfortunately, yelling to fix a problem was my solution, which solved nobody's problems. However, choosing to connect, understand, and hug someone lets them know that you are there for them, you care, and you love them. Now that I know that truth, it is my go-to way to help my boys and the response is life-changing. We all understand that we're going to have a conversation and maybe discuss something difficult, but first we're going to connect and they'll know they are safe and loved. Only then will we have the hard conversation.

When people hug for twenty seconds or more, oxytocin—often called the love hormone—is released, which creates a stronger bond and connection between the huggers. This release has been shown to slow down heart rate and reduce stress and anxiety.

The same is true for dogs. Our dog, Roco, absolutely loves to be close to us and can always be found on my lap or at my feet while I am working. We both benefit from this closeness and bond. And due to his small size of under ten pounds, he is easily transportable and loves receiving hugs from us. If I am experiencing something stressful or catch myself doing too much, I often hug him for a while and I feel all my uneasiness melt away.

How has a hug or other form of physical connection impacted you during a difficult situation? At the end of the day, is there another way you work in order to feel safe in a situation?

Day 111

"A dog is the only thing on Earth that loves you more than he loves himself."
Josh Billings

In March of 2021, our toy poodle, Roco, joined our family. At the time, he was a two-pound baby of curly apricot fur with the biggest brown eyes that melted my heart. I just knew the first time I held him that he was meant for us.

He's a true example that one's love doesn't equal the size of their hearts: now nine pounds, Roco has the biggest heart and love in the tiniest package. He completed our family and filled our hearts with love in a way we did not know was missing.

Growing up, I had a major fear of dogs. I had no familiarity with them and was uncomfortable in their presence. However, my youngest, Michael, has had a love for dogs since birth. It is a pure and genuine love, full of joy and sweetness unlike anything I had ever witnessed before. His love for wanting a puppy was so immense and we never would have gotten one if I had stayed married to his father. In fact, the day we brought Roco home, Michael shared that it was the best day of his life because his dreams had come true. My heart melted because I went outside of my comfort zone to give my son a gift that changed the rest of us for the better and made our family whole.

The initial intention to bring Roco into our family was for Michael; I didn't expect the immense love that Roco would fill my heart with. He is my little buddy who's helped me prioritize what's truly important in my life. Plus, he is constantly at my side to give me wet kisses, warmth, and hugs. The reality is that I will never be alone as I have Roco to give me all the unconditional love that I will need.

Often what is missing can be found when you are not looking for it. As shared by Mr. Bridwell in the *Clifford the Big Red Dog* movie, "The thing about animals is that the best time to find them is when you're not looking for them."

Do you have a favorite pet animal in your life that gives you unconditional love? If so, reflect on the feelings that arise from that relationship. Or, if you were to have a pet in your future, what feelings do you think would arise for you?

Day 112

"Make every day a personal day of Thanksgiving."
Unknown

From the time I was a child, my family always hosted Thanksgiving. In 2018, the tradition was passed on from my mother to me and I had my first opportunity to finally "own" a holiday of my own and share the family experiences I'd learned but implemented with my unique personal vision and flair. I've always loved the role of hostess and so I accepted the challenge with bells on and we decorated our family Christmas tree! It was the first time for us to celebrate this way, but I have pride and passion with lots of spirit.

With my spiritual awakening, my awareness of Thanksgiving has changed from a one-day-of-the-year celebration to a daily occurrence. Now, Thanksgiving has a very deep and special meaning for me in my heart and soul. I've learned the power of being thankful and that offering an expression of gratitude elevates my energy to a higher level.

I recognize that we all need to view Thanksgiving as an every-day occurrence. Likewise, it's no coincidence that the Thanksgiving traditions were passed on so that my boys and I could host our loving family. It was an opportunity to come together and share, to reflect on and appreciate the goodness that exists all around us.

The opportunity to prepare, cook, and serve a delicious Thanksgiving dinner meal for my family is not about the food, but about the love we share through the whole process of celebrating the most grateful holiday there is. The reality that we have so much to appreciate when we fill our hearts with love is indescribable. This is the greatest gift from my parents to me and now to future generations through my boys.

While we may not recognize all the good that happens in one day, there is always something that we can reflect on and say thank you for. We can acknowledge our appreciation and gratefulness for its occurrence in our life that day.

"If the only prayer you said in your whole life was, 'Thank You,' that would suffice." Meister Eckhart

What are you thankful for today?

Day 113

"At the table of Christ, are you serving or eating?"
Katherine Hamer

Early on during my sound healing training, my teacher, Kathy, who recognized my immense desire to serve others, asked me, "At the table of Christ, are you serving or eating?" Naturally, my immediate response was, "Of course, I am serving."

The preference to serve was ingrained into me as a child. Early on at holidays or family functions, I always helped the adults in the kitchen: preparing food, clearing the table, washing dishes, etc. Whatever needed to be done, I was ready and willing to take ownership of it.

When you choose to serve others, you are doing something primarily for the benefit of another person or group. It is a demonstration of love without expecting anything in return.

As I shared on Day 6, I felt the need to connect more with God and the church as I was confused about my life's direction and future. I started to attend the daily Mass and something about that act uplifted me and gave me the light that was desperately needed during my time of darkness.

At the end of 2019, I decided to serve the community by becoming a lector at Mass. I had enjoyed the community and feelings that church brought me and wanted to share with others. As a lector, I am part of the Mass and responsible for several readings from the Bible. I absolutely love my role as lector, especially as I enjoy public speaking and appreciate the opportunity to share sacred passages— passages that provide deep reflection and spiritual guidance—with others.

The church had been my place of peace and saving grace during my darkest moments, and now I revel with joy that I can serve others in a different capacity with the motive of shining my light for others to see.

Christmas Eve 2021 was the first time in thirteen years that I would wake up alone on Christmas morning, since my boys would be with their dad. In full acceptance of my reality, but feeling a tad sad, I turned to the church and offered to serve as a lector for both the evening and day Masses so I could feel uplifted and give to others during a time when I needed to feel loved as well. It was a true blessing and testament to the phrase, "In giving we receive."

Reflect on your own personal truth: at the table of Christ, are you serving or eating? If Christianity doesn't resonate for you, then when you're surrounded by others, are you the one who's giving or receiving?

Day 114

"When you see something beautiful in someone, tell them. It may take a second to say, but for them it could last a lifetime."

Unknown

I am a firm believer in saying something that will make people feel good, because too often they are not being told it by others.

It is important for me to want to make a difference for others. It comes naturally and is genuine. Oftentimes I give compliments to friends and strangers alike. My only motivation is to share happiness by speaking the truth because it is like second nature to me.

You never know how saying something kind or beautiful to another can make or break their day. Plus, it generates a ripple effect in that person's day and the people they may come in contact with. It is another example of how we are all connected.

A by-product of the divorce process was a shift in hormones caused by stress. This hormonal change wreaked havoc on my body, but the biggest change for me was hair loss. This was very hard because I have always been known for my long, voluminous hair and I had extreme difficulties with this. I felt incredibly insecure about how my hair looked to other people.

At one of my lowest moments about this loss, I was attending a party feeling my hair was not at its best. At the party I met and connected with Jen, who is a hairdresser. In our first interaction she exclaimed, "Your hair is so beautiful!" This was the confidence

I needed at that moment to snap me back to the reality that, yes, my hair is beautiful. All is not lost and I can accept that this is all happening the way it is supposed to happen. I am grateful for Jen's kindness and the truth that I needed to hear at that moment as that comment totally changed my outlook about myself on that day.

It is all about the positive vibes we put out into the Universe. By doing something to spark joy or happiness for another, you become a happier person. Giving random compliments will change your life, and more importantly, it may change someone else's as well.

Do you recall a time when someone changed your day by sharing something beautiful about yourself with you?

Day 115

"Take time to do what makes your soul happy."
Unknown

This quote has traveled with me through my mental health journey with my therapist and beyond. I was first exposed to its glory and magnitude in the form of a beautiful wall tapestry in Pam's office. It was a constant reminder and reflection of what really matters at the end of the day: "Is my soul happy?"

During our sessions, Pam would often point to these deep words as a check in for me to reflect back to my own truth about how I was operating in my world.

As my therapy journey continued and my spiritual awakening was beginning, I turned an unused bedroom in the house I shared with my husband into "my room." It was a place for me to do yoga and meditate. It was also a sanctuary where I could contain the beautiful and special things that I loved. I bought this same tapestry to cover my wall as a reflection of what is really important to my life. As I moved out of our home, the quote followed me to a wall in my new bedroom in my apartment. Again, it serves as my reminder to ensure that, above all things, the truth of my soul was happy.

This quote has been with me for four years or so and I can honestly say, every day, I am living closer to this feeling. It's a great benefit to have visual reminders in your life as they become ingrained and eventually part of your consciousness. The reminders can change the way you operate and flow in your world.

How will you make your soul happy today? What are some visual reminders you can incorporate to remind yourself?

Day 116

"Let us be grateful to the people who make us happy; they are the charming gardeners who make our souls blossom."

Marcel Proust

I love the beauty of this quote which reminds me of my dear friend, Jean, who was the secretary at my boys' school. She is a beautiful ray of sunshine: a person full of life, energy, and love for the children and adults at the school.

I devoted a majority of my free time to support the volunteer efforts at my boys' school. For seven years, I was heavily involved in activities for my children; from class mom to event chair to treasurer and, eventually, president of the parent board. I was happily busy devoting my time to a greater cause as I knew all my efforts directly supported my children. Plus, my skills from the professional world could add value and impact to the volunteer efforts. At the time it offered me connection, community, and a sense of purpose. I started when my oldest was three, and the work met needs that I wasn't getting fulfilled elsewhere.

I regularly spent time at my boys' school during the day, assisting in various activities and lending a hand wherever needed. In fact, when my sons were really young, other students thought I worked for the school because I was always there! Giving back to the school filled me in a way that was needed at that time and served a purpose that will forever be cherished in my heart. Because I was regularly inside of the school, my friendship with, and love for, Jean began to grow as an indirect benefit of my volunteer responsibilities.

The feelings were mutual for Jean and when I showed her this quote, she felt it reminded her of my relationship with her as well! That's when you know two souls are destined to be friends and care for each other so deeply. Having close friends are like the flowers of life; we are the lucky ones who can act as gardeners to ensure that the friendships are maintained, nourished, and cherished in a way that reflects the beautiful gifts that they are. As Helen Keller said, "We are never really happy until we try to brighten the lives of others."

Reflect on a relationship with a close friend who makes you happy and makes your soul blossom. How does this relationship make you feel?

Day 117

"Grace means that all of your mistakes now serve a purpose besides shame."
Unknown

I love living with grace. Oxford Languages defines grace as "simple elegance or refinement of moving; and an attractively polite manner of behaving."

On the other hand, shame is a painful emotion brought on by embarrassment or humiliation related to something being perceived as wrong (which is really just a learning experience).

As a natural perfectionist, I lived with shame for my entire life when I did something that I believed was not right. I carried that shame with me and allowed it to ruin my day. My spiritual awakening brought me the awareness that mistakes are really just learning opportunities. I could accept that nobody is perfect and give myself the grace and love needed to learn from and process for the future.

Living with grace is far healthier and loving to your soul and body. Simply stated, living in grace allows you to elegantly walk with love.

Unfortunately, my oldest carries the same shame with him when he does something that he believes is wrong. He is even harder on himself than I was as a child. Luckily, since I understand the pain that this can bring, I have the opportunity to share my experiences with him from a place of love versus a place of wrongdoing.

It is a blessing to recognize how I can help my boys recover from and process difficult emotions at a young age. This will help them to always walk their own unique paths with dignity, grace, and love.

How has living with grace helped you to process shame?

Day 118

"To forgive is to set a prisoner free and discover that the prisoner was you."
Lewis B. Smedes

Forgiveness doesn't make things right; it just sets us free.

According to Oxford Languages, to forgive is to "stop feeling angry or resentful toward someone for an offense, flaw, or mistake."

Forgiveness was a big area of healing for me. I was holding onto ill feelings for years and didn't realize how painful and detrimental it was to my soul.

There was pain from my inner child. There was also pain from not feeling loved the way I needed to be loved, feeling like I did not belong because I was not understood, and pain from being excluded. These are only a few, but they were all heavy items that were weighing down on my spirit.

I had to make peace and forgive my soul for past experiences in order to be set free; the reality was that I was the true prisoner. And I could set myself free from past triggers. Triggers that would recreate the same feelings in the present if they weren't healed.

When you truly allow yourself to release feelings of anger and resentment, it results in a projection of love. According to Jon Krakauer, "When you forgive, you love. And when you love, God's light shines upon you."

Switching the mindset to focus on the lesson rather than the pain is the key to unlock yourself as a prisoner and become free. It is a growth opportunity for your mind, heart, and soul.

What or whom can you forgive from the past that could help you heal for your future?

Day 119

"I love myself enough to say no to things that no longer serve me."
Unknown

Giving yourself the love that you need strengthens and heals the heart chakra. Oxford Languages defines self-love as "regard for one's own well-being and happiness; considered as desirable." When we live from our highest good, we have the ability to recognize and decipher what no longer is serving us. This gives us the freedom and opportunity to release those things and make room for new energies to enter. These new energies can serve our highest self.

My journey to self-love was a battle. It took forty years to recognize that it was missing from my life and to understand why it was so important and necessary. A large part of learning self-love included forgiveness for myself, which I discussed in Day 118.

I learned how to tell the little girl inside that, "I am proud of me." No more waiting for recognition externally or for words of encouragement or appreciation. I had to understand that I was enough and I have the power to give myself all the love that has been missing.

I needed to find forgiveness for my marriage and the fact that there were karmic lessons for this lifetime that had to be accomplished. My marriage helped me grow and it was time to accept that in order to love myself the way I needed to, I had to move on.

As I've shared, I struggled with feeling worthy and deserving of the love I give to others. As a Pisces, I am naturally selfless. I often forget to make the time and effort to give myself the same love I offer others.

Processing the importance of self-love was a journey in itself and I'm grateful for the lessons I've learned. Now I understand that once I learned how to properly love myself, I would have the opportunity to truly love and connect with a male counterpart or "my person" who was meant for me.

How is your lack of self-love holding you back in your life and/or how has its existence helped you?

Day 120

*"If you knew the secret of life, you too would
choose no other companion but love."*

Rumi

The fourth chakra is very powerful as it is the balance of the lower
and upper chakras, plus the focal point of love and compassion in
our energy system.

At this chakra, our consciousness has an awakening, a recognition and awareness of going from "me to we." The energy that flows
from this center is directed beyond personal survival of the lower
chakras to consideration of others. As a result, romantic love for a
companion and counterpart is sourced from this area.

In September 2021, I had tarot cards read by a local medium,
where a majority of my reading revolved around my relationships.
The most intriguing and impactful information shared was that I
would meet my person: a person with whom I would share a deep
spiritual, mental, emotional, and physical connection.

This was important to me as I had accepted the reality that
I have been alone for my entire life, even during my marriage. I
became aware that once I learned how to heal myself through
self-love, forgiveness, and balancing the different areas of my life, I
would divinely be ready to meet my male partner.

The key takeaway for me has been unlearning how I had
approached love from a romantic perspective in the past and healing

myself before trying to give my love to another. In the past, I would think, "I'll have a boyfriend and things will be great." Now, however, I feel complete, and thus I'm not looking for a male to complete the parts of me that weren't healed before. I can approach relationships from the perspective that I'm a whole person and he should also be a whole person. Today, I have a totally different understanding of what I need and want.

As I shared on Day 58, sexual energy is a life force that exists in all of us. It connects you to your soul and the Universe and is also the drive that forces you to be your best self when you direct your sexual energy into a higher purpose on your path. You do this by circulating your energy to reach the seventh chakra at the crown and thus experiencing oneness or a connection with the Universe.

Likewise, as I shared on Day 59, in order to effectively live for our highest good and remain in balance, our lives are meant to be shared deeply with another as a complement of male and female energies, as depicted in the yin yang symbol.

The lessons learned from the medium were deep and real. Unbeknown to me, I did not recognize how writing this book would heal years of unhealed emotions as I traveled up the chakra system, sharing my reflections about topics that are near and dear to my heart. I don't believe it's a coincidence that big movements in my life are matching up with areas in my book as I write about them either. Life-changing healing occurs all in Divine timing.

Reflect on your journey of "me to we." How has it made you feel and/ or want to feel if you are still on your journey to becoming a "we"?

I Am

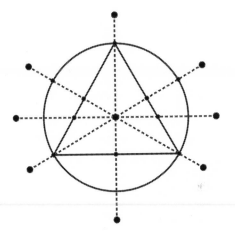

Intuitive

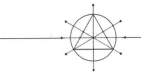

I Am Intuitive
DAYS 121–150

Trust your own innate superpower of intuition and follow your gut instincts. Understand that you already possess all you need deep within yourself to control the direction of your life and trusting yourself is its own superpower. We've had these powers from the start, but we have to rediscover them. I mean this both from the Third Eye, but also from the literal gut/solar plexus. A consistent and regular meditation practice strengthened my intuition and I realized that this characteristic has been within me all along. As your keen awareness grows, your intuition can further develop and evolve.

The energy to be intuitive is sourced from a strong and open Third Eye, which is located at the point between the brows, at the sixth chakra. With consistent practice in cultivating this area, you will sustain a pure and peaceful mind and have the ability to hear and understand a voice that has no words. You will gain wisdom and be wise with your words. You'll understand that the silence will make your mind feel lighter. This chakra is also an area known for higher intelligence, openness, concentration, self-initiation, and determination.

As it relates to the sixth chakra, you will understand that:

- Light is the element associated with this energy center, which develops and evolves with a consistent meditation practice that works specifically for you, providing tools to navigate your unique life.

- The eyes are the entrance to see into your soul, and with the Third Eye, you have the ability to see energetically. This provides perception beyond ordinary sight.

- Prayer is a time for asking questions; meditation is a time for receiving the answers, but you must be quiet enough to hear and understand your answer.

- There are powerful healing benefits for your body when you allow sound waves and frequencies to move energy and alter your consciousness.

- Extraordinary visionaries are clairvoyants: clairvoyance is a psychic ability that will expand your spiritual awareness. You have the ability to cultivate this skill.

- It is far better to maintain an attitude of gratitude rather than complaints. This results in more positive effects. For example, shifting your mindset changes the effect of stress on your body.

- Nothing in life is a coincidence. Everything is a message from a higher power and with a developed intuition, you can interpret it.

- The dragonfly is known as the light of God and is the spirit animal of this energy center.

- It is important to pay attention to your dreams and utilize your imagination to change your life.

- Your mind benefits when you try something new.

Tune In with the Adi Mantra
"Ong Namo Guru Dev Namo"

To center yourself in the higher self before practicing Kundalini yoga, chant the Adi Mantra three times.

"*Ong Namo Guru Dev Namo*" translates to "I bow to the Divine wisdom of all that is" and "I bow to the Divine teacher within."

HOW TO PRACTICE

- *Posture:* Sit in Easy Pose, with the spine erect.
- *Eye Position:* Eyes slightly closed, focused at the Third Eye, which is the point between the brows.
- *Mudra: Prayer Pose.* Place the palms of the hands flat together to neutralize the positive (right, or male) and negative (left, or female) sides of the body. Your thumbs should press against the sternum and your forearms will be parallel to the floor.
- Consciously begin to breathe. Gently inhale through your nose, feel the breath fill up your belly, fill up your lungs, and expand your rib cage. On the exhale from your nose, recognize the breath leaving your body. When ready to "tune in" with the Adi Mantra, inhale and exhale deeply from the nose and begin chanting the mantra three times.

Asanas

The asanas listed below focus on strengthening the energy center at the Third Eye. It is recommended that you hold each posture for one to two minutes with a slight rest in between. Remember to stay within while holding the postures and while resting, keep your eyes closed, focusing on the Third Eye, the point between the brows. This will allow you to focus on yourself and build your intuition, plus learn to trust your own power and ability.

- Shoulder Shrugs
- Yoga Mudra
- Sitting Bends
- Front Bend
- Rock Pose

Find a description of each posture in the Appendix on page 421.

Meditation
"Kirtan Kriya"

This mantra meditation represents the cycle of creation. From the infinite comes life. From life comes death or change. From death comes the rebirth of consciousness. From rebirth comes the joy of the Infinite through which compassion leads back to life.

- *Mantra: "Saa, Taa, Naa, Maa"*
- *Translation:*
- *Saa*: Infinity, beginning
- *Taa*: Life, existence
- *Naa*: Death, transformation
- *Maa*: Rebirth

HOW TO PRACTICE

- *Posture:* Sit in Easy Pose, with the spine erect.
- *Eye Position:* Eyes closed, focused at the Third Eye, which is the point between the brows.
- *Mudra:* The elbows are straight, with your arms resting on your legs, just as with most of the other mudras. While chanting, your hands start in Gyan Mudra. Each finger touches in turn, the tip of the thumb with a firm but gentle pressure. The mudra is as follows for each sound:
- *Saa:* the index finger touches the thumb
- *Taa:* the middle finger touches the thumb
- *Naa:* the ring finger touches the thumb
- *Maa:* the pinkie finger touches the thumb
- *Visualization:* As you practice and chant each sound, visualize an inflow of energy in an "L" form from the top of your head at the crown and out through the Third Eye.
- *Voice:* This mantra is chanted in the three languages of consciousness:
- Aloud: as the voice of the human
- Whisper: as the voice of the lover
- Silent: as the voice of the divine
- *How to practice:* Chant aloud for two minutes with the appropriate mudras with each sound. Follow with a whisper for two minutes. Next, be silent for three minutes. Follow with a whisper for two minutes. Conclude with chanting aloud for two minutes. Close the meditation with a deep inhale and suspend the breath as long as is comfortable (up to one minute); then complete with one minute of absolute stillness and silence. Finally, stretch the hands up as far as possible and

spread the fingers wide. Stretch the spine and take several deep breaths. Relax.

- *Time:* Eleven minutes.
- *Helpful Tip:* Soundtracks are available to chant as you complete the meditation that can be found on any app that streams music. I like to chant this meditation along with the artist, Nirinjan Kaur.

Deep Relaxation

- *Posture:* Lie on your back in Corpse Pose. With your eyes closed, place your arms at your sides, with palms facing up. Allow your body to rest, process, and absorb the movement of energy.
- *Time:* One to three minutes minimum.

Ending Prayer

To close your Kundalini practice, chant three long *Sat Naams*.

Sound Healing

Enjoy this ten-minute sound healing ensemble to further relax your mind and body. Consider listening during deep relaxation or at another time during your day when your body could benefit from and enjoy the beautiful healing gift of sound and vibrations.

> **Access this month's asana videos, meditation, sound healing audio, and more at www.LisaAnnese.com/i-am-light**

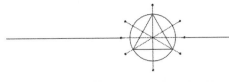

Day 121

"For there is always light. If only we're brave enough to see it.
If only we're brave enough to be it."
Amanda Gorman

As I shared on Day 1 of these meditations, we all have our own spark of divine light (paraphrasing Pope Frances). Likewise, we are all beams of light; all of our experiences and connections act as an energy exchange connecting us and each other to the power of the Divine.

Consequently, light is also the element associated with the sixth chakra. The sixth chakra is located at the Third Eye, which is the point between the eyebrows.

Your light further develops and evolves as you regularly and consistently meditate. Light serves as a symbol of life, happiness, prosperity, and positivity. On the contrary, darkness is associated with chaos, death, and the underworld. It's important to understand that light can only exist because of the darkness.

"Be the light" is a simple mantra I regularly share and use when people who are hurting and in need of guidance come to me. I share my light with them in order to uplift their spirits and help them with their own direction, so they can learn to see again.

To be the light is to remain strong and brave even at your lowest point. By being the light, we become a human lighthouse, guiding others on their own way. This is possible because the ability to be light is always present and accessible for those who believe.

By shining this light, you elevate your spirits, and your own personal light shines even stronger and will remain even when you have left this plane. As James Garrison says, "The light remains— there are some who bring a light so great to the world that even after they have gone the light remains."

My son, Michael, is my light. He helps me view the world with a sense of wonder, simplicity, and presence. In his future, I see him doing magnificent things for others in the deaf and hard of hearing world. He is a marvel and I am so honored that he chose me to be his mother.

Michael's spiritual name is Deg Jotdev, which means the angelic and fearless lion who personifies graciousness and hospitality throughout his life as he connects to God's light. It's no coincidence that we both have 'jot' in our spiritual names. It means 'light' in Gurmukhi, the language used by the Sikh culture. He stems from me as his mother, but together our light will shine bright to help and heal those we love around us. It is our purpose and right; and I am honored that we can walk this beautiful awakening together.

Recall a time you were the light for another to see. How did that make you feel?

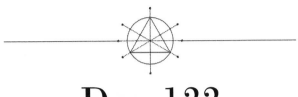

Day 122

"She wore her truth in her eyes, molded stones of love and tragedy, freckled constellations of pleasures and pain from a life's true story."

Atticus

On Day 121, I shared that light is the element associated with the sixth chakra. This makes sense because the role of the human eye is to detect light and send signals along the optic nerve to the brain. The eye is an organ of the visual system, which is also located at this same energy center. It is a complex organ with several parts, with each contributing to your ability to see.

The eyes tell a story of our lives and past travels. The good, the bad, and the ugly. It's fascinating how such a small organ holds so much beauty, truth, and depth. The eyes are also known as the entrance to see directly into one's soul.

Eye contact is a type of body language that speaks louder than words. Keeping good eye contact with the person you are talking to shows that you are engaged, paying attention, and being as authentic as possible. Likewise, poor eye contact could be a sign of disinterest, discomfort, or lack of truth.

A requirement for my Kundalini teacher training program was to attend White Tantric Yoga with my fellow trainees. White Tantric Yoga is a more than eight-hour long class full of multiple meditations done in pairs as a group. The intention is to break through subconscious blocks that our minds and bodies carry.

These blocks weigh us down.

Unless stated otherwise, the meditations are performed as you stare into the eyes of your assigned partner; it's an intense and deep experience that allows you to connect deeply with another as you generate energy and increase awareness.

To be honest, prior to attending White Tantric, I was most afraid of staring into the eyes of another person for an extended period of time. I was concerned about not knowing what to expect and was scared about the overall experience. However, once I began the meditations, I eased into the expectation, relaxed, and became more comfortable. I quickly learned that there was nothing to be afraid of and began to look forward to the deep healing that the meditations intended.

Reflect on a time when the eyes of another spoke louder than the words spoken. How did this affect your response?

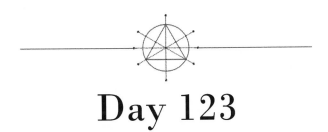

Day 123

"I have three eyes. Two to look. One to see."
Bellamor

The Third Eye can see energetically and is the focal point for providing perception beyond ordinary sight. As I mentioned earlier, it is located between the brows.

When the Third Eye is strong and developed, this leads you to believe in your own powers and self, thereby giving you a strong sense of intuition.

For me, I believe the intensity of my yoga teacher training caused my Third Eye to finally open. I think this is because it taught us how to have our own daily practice of Kundalini and meditations. I became open and present to the world around me in ways I never had dreamed possible or experienced before in the past.

I began to notice that when my eyes were closed and I focused on my Third Eye, I could see waves of indigo energy swirling in the darkness. I wasn't seeing them with my two eyes. I was clearly able, however, to energetically see a new world and realm that existed beyond my physical body.

At different points in time, the colors I would see have changed and the changes all connected with areas of my chakra system that were activated at that moment. From turquoise for my fifth chakra, to pink and bright light from my crown, I have gloriously been exposed to a belief in something greater than what my physical eyes have seen in the past.

This allows me to believe that my powers are immense and my abilities are stronger than I could ever mentally comprehend.

This results in an intense feeling that I can now see energetically. This feeling leads me along my path and journey. It helps me follow what is best for my highest good. I believe that I possess these powers and trust in myself to lead the way on my own path.

I remember a vivid example in February 2020. I was shopping for wall decorations to hang in Michael's new bedroom and as I walked around HomeGoods, I had a vision that Michael loves to play the board game, Monopoly. So, I said to myself, "Well, yes, how cool would it be if I could find him a picture of something that depicts that game in his room?" I made a mental note to search online for this type of picture.

About two minutes later, as I continued to walk around the store, a picture of Monopoly was hanging on the wall! Well, I was blown away that something I had just thought about came to life without any additional effort on my part. I knew that the picture was perfect and exactly what my son would love!

Once I got over the initial excitement, I recognized that this wasn't a coincidence. My Third Eye was open and strong enough to understand that there was a picture in that store my son would love. That is why I received the download about Monopoly and when I saw it, I knew it was the right decision for me.

The Third Eye has immense abilities for those who are open to believe and receive that which exists beyond the physical world.

What coincidences in your life can you now see as moments of connection with the Divine?

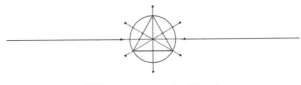

Day 124

"The reason you have a hard time trusting your intuition is because you are still convinced that some outside authority knows better than you."

Maryam Hasnaa

Oxford Languages defines intuition as "the ability to understand something immediately, without the need for conscious reasoning; a thing that one knows or considers likely from instinctive feeling rather than conscious reasoning."

In my Kundalini yoga classes, a majority of the postures and breathing techniques are performed with the eyes closed. Rather than using your seeing eyes, you're focused on the Third Eye. As I shared on Day 123, when the Third Eye is strong and developed, this leads you to believe in your own powers and self, and thereby strengthens your sense of intuition.

The underlying theme and mantra of Kundalini is "Sat Naam" or "Truth is my identity." This means living your unique truth, the truth that comes from within, and can only happen when you trust and believe in yourself. It's the truth that you know and understand deep down inside. This confidence and ability to trust deeply in your own intuitive powers is the result of a developed Third Eye.

Pisces have an innate intuitive gift. However, it wasn't until my spiritual awakening that I became aware of this ability and had the wherewithal to understand what I was energetically feeling or experiencing. Slowly, with regular meditation and more frequent choices to live as a more spiritual being, I began to trust my own powers and the direction of my life.

As I shared earlier, I never trusted myself with even the simplest of decisions. I always had to have someone agree with me in order to feel confident in my choice.

Before my spiritual awakening, my outside authority was my parents. As a child and young adult learning to explore my world and planning my future, everything passed through their gates of approval. I trusted that they knew what was best for me. This worked well until my mid-twenties when I recognized that some decisions I had made weren't for my highest good, despite the fact that they were approved by others.

Reflecting back, I now understand that my soul was sent here to learn specific lessons. I've accomplished this learning through a magnitude of healing and by trusting what was best for my soul, despite outside authorities. But in my mid-twenties, life was pretty dark because I felt I was trapped by decisions younger me had made. My intuition was not developed enough to understand that there was another way and I had the power to go into the light.

How has your intuition impacted your current life or how do you hope for it to impact your future?

Day 125

"No meditation, no life. Know meditation, know life."
Osho

As I previously shared, 2016 was the beginning of my "take charge" initiative to heal my body with functional medicine and uncover the root cause of what was bothering me and why I couldn't lose weight. My functional doctor had recommended a holistic plan for healing, which included a daily meditation practice. I sporadically listened to guided meditations using free apps, but I didn't really do it for my benefit; I did it so I could report to my doctor that I did what he requested. Really, I was just checking the boxes to accomplish what was recommended and remain an A+ patient.

Not until I started to regularly practice Kundalini yoga did I really understand, value, and appreciate the time spent in meditation. Oxford Languages defines meditate as "to think deeply or focus one's mind for a period of time, in silence or with the aid of chanting, for religious or spiritual purposes or as a method of relaxation." To be honest, early on during my Kundalini journey, I struggled with staying still long enough to meditate. It was challenging for me and I mentally recall having difficulties with a short, seven-minute meditation.

Fast-forward to my teacher training and the White Tantric Yoga experience that I shared on Day 122. The training was an eight-hour day with six or more meditations . . . and some of them were sixty minutes long. That's sixty minutes of focused eye contact, deliberate hand movements, and chanting at the same time. It was grueling. However, at the end of the day, even though it was a tough experience, it deeply connected with my soul. It was also proof that I can do anything when I focus my attention on something specific, such as eliminating the stream of chaotic thoughts that may be clouding my mind and causing stress.

Now I value and cherish my time spent in meditation. It's an opportunity to spend time with my soul. It gives me peace, presence, and the healing benefits that I am craving. It's an opportunity to strengthen my intuition and to understand my life and who I really am at my core.

Do you have a consistent meditation practice? How does it make you feel? If you don't have a consistent practice, what is holding you back from starting one?

Day 126

"Mantra meditation is not magic, but the results can be magical."
Unknown

On Day 125, I introduced the concept of meditation using my own personal experiences. I talked about how consistent practice taught me the ability to sustain longer moments in a meditative state and thus reap the benefits of peace, presence, and healing for my soul. It was an opportunity to spend time with my soul, strengthen my intuition, and understand the true essence of my life.

A consistent meditation practice gives you the tools to manage your life, both emotionally and physically. You gain a new perspective and the building blocks to manage your stress, increase self-awareness, and reduce negative emotions. You also increase your imagination, creativity, patience, and tolerance. Spiritually, meditation creates inner stillness and peace, fosters less reactivity, and cultivates a sense of inner bliss.

Anyone can practice meditation. You can use any location and don't have to buy equipment or incur expenses. In meditation, you focus your attention on something specific, which helps eliminate the chaos of thoughts that may be clouding your mind and causing stress. In a sense, you're giving your mind a break so that when you finish meditation, you have a refreshed outlook on managing your life.

For example, you could do a silent meditation with your eyes closed or a walking meditation where you consciously focus on how you are feeling in that moment. You could also meditate during many other types of activities that you enjoy. The key is to consciously pay attention to that activity and forget about all the chatter in your mind. It doesn't always have to happen on a yoga mat. You may not have the ability to go lock yourself into a room—this is real life, and you can add to your day little by little. You could even try meditating while you brush your teeth! The bottom line is that you have to learn how to adapt to difficult situations that come your way.

For me, my preferred method to meditate is through chanting mantras. On Day 23, I shared how chanting resonates deeply with the truth of my soul in a way I had never experienced before. It was definitely the answer to what had been missing from my life and it allowed a flood of love and joy to flow through my body. Chanting mantras fills me with such immense light that, after a session, I feel that my physical body is magically illuminated in all directions. It is definitely the chosen path for me and a way for me to consistently remain in the light and serve as a guide for others.

As a sound healer, the meditations I host for others use the power of sound vibrations to heal. Sound vibrations connect with every cell in your body, leaving you feeling refreshed and rejuvenated. Attendees participate on their own journey with sound as it relaxes the body, calms the mind, and moves energies from the subconscious and through the body. As a result, it helps them live from their highest good.

What is your preferred meditation method? If you are new to meditation, what are you already doing that can be turned into a meditation?

Day 127

"When the mind is pure, joy follows like a shadow that never leaves."
Buddha

Oxford Languages defines pure as "without any extraneous and unnecessary elements." Having a mind that can be described as "pure" is one of the many positive results of a consistent meditation practice.

In April 2020, before I proclaimed to my husband that I wanted to separate, a friend described me as "pure and refreshing." They were beautiful adjectives that nobody had ever used to describe me before. I let those kind and truthful words sink into my core and then, for the first time, believed them to be true for my character. I actually felt "pure" because, for the first time, my mind was "pure."

Before my spiritual awakening, my mind was scattered, cluttered, and cloudy. I was constantly jumping around to different items, never focusing on the present, and always ready to do the next thing on my list. All for the satisfaction of crossing it off with my pen or pencil.

Accomplishing things is great. As we discussed on Day 85, accomplishment is a sign of a strong solar plexus. However, we shouldn't sacrifice our minds and peace in order to accomplish items on our to-do list. Unfortunately, that approach was my motto. I never focused on just one place for an extended time.

Prior to meditation, "stressed" was the definition of me. Meditation was the magic answer to help me slow down and recognize that my body feels amazing in a peaceful state. It's much better than feeling stressful in a chaotic and scattered state. I became a better mother and was more appreciative, grateful, and joyful. Plus, I was more pleasant to be around when I meditated.

As reflected in this unknown quote, "Meditation isn't about trying to clear the noise of your mind. It's about reminding yourself that the noise isn't your identity. This clears the mind."

Has your mind ever felt pure, without extraneous elements? What can you do for yourself to help you feel this way?

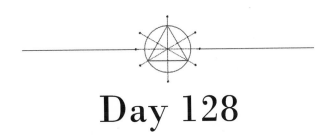

Day 128

"Prayer is the asking; meditation is the receiving."
Unkown

The spiritual leader at the teacher training I attended in Miami said something similar to this quote and it stuck with me deeply because of my connection with the church.

Prayer's goal is to ask God for help and the goal of meditation is to be still enough to receive His answers.

I always share with my classes that I receive all my answers to problems, questions, or things that I am struggling with while on the mat in meditation. It is the place that I feel secure. The mat offers an opportunity for me to let go and be open to the gifts of peace and calmness rather than struggling with the chaos of my mind.

Reflect on the truth in this quote from Ma Jaya Sati Bhagavati, "Quiet the mind and the soul shall speak." This is exactly what you will experience in meditation: a voice that you can't hear, but you can feel energetically. This will be felt in your whole body, delivering a sense of tranquility, a relief, and an answer to alleviate your struggles.

Once you consciously choose to make the time to have a consistent healing practice that includes meditation, your world will begin to change. This further strengthens your intuition and your awareness that life exists in dimensions beyond the physical. As a result, you'll develop an increased awareness of the voices around you that you are feeling energetically.

I recall struggling with a miscommunication among friends because someone felt they were purposely excluded from a get-to-gether, but that wasn't the case. However, my friend was so angry and hurt because of this misunderstanding and it led me to a deep fear that this would trickle down and affect another friendship, which was deeply important to me.

This fear became intense and was driven by the egoism in my mind. The only relief became meditation. It centered and cleared my mind so I could receive the thought, "Choose people who choose you." This is a brilliant nugget of truth applicable to this particular situation, but also to countless others in the future. It was a gift of wisdom that keeps giving, and a blessing indeed, to heal and calm my soul.

Have you ever been quiet enough to receive the answer to your question? How did it make you feel? If you don't feel like you've heard an answer before, what might be preventing you from that?

Day 129

"If yoga is stairs to meditation, sound is an elevator."
Yogi Shelly (Michelle Berlin)

Yoga is the stairs to meditation in that it creates a slow, steady build-up with the end result of meditation. However, the power of sound vibrations relaxing and calming the body and mind is like an elevator. You can achieve the results faster and with a deeper impact.

The basis behind every Kundalini class is to prepare the body for meditation, as meditation is the ultimate gift, goal, and result of Kundalini. It's critical to prepare the body in a certain way to generate and elevate your energy through movement. This happens alongside the calming and energizing effects of the various breathing techniques as well as deep relaxation, often with a gong bath. Finally, once all those have been achieved, there is meditation for the mind.

On the other hand, participating in a sound meditation to heal the body is a whole body experience in itself. I utilize ancient sound healing instruments, including Tibetan singing bowls, different size gongs, crystal bowls, chimes, drums, mantras, and more to create a sound healing experience that will vibrate and connect with every cell in your body, leaving you feeling refreshed and rejuvenated. As the sound healer, I do all the work; the participant's job is to arrive with an open mind and the ability to just lie still and relax. It is the most beautiful gift that you can give yourself to heal your body and mind and release what is no longer serving you.

A sound meditation has an overall full-body calming effect, especially if you are new to practicing it. You may come with a preconception or fear about meditation because you don't understand the benefits or dynamics behind it. I know that I had that belief. As I shared on Day 125, this is why it took me several years after hearing this recommendation from my functional doctor for me to actually consider a regular practice. However, the beauty of the sound doing the work is that it can distract you from thinking about the idea of what is being accomplished, possibly the fact that you cannot do it. As a result, you might consider a different type of meditation once you experience the benefits from sound.

Describe your own personal experiences and feelings as you listen to the sound healing recordings in this book. Have you been able to allow your mind to be still for the full time frame?

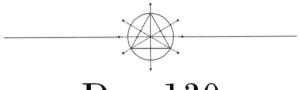

Day 130

"Future medicine will be the medicine of frequencies."
Albert Einstein

On Day 129, I shared about the power of sound vibrations and their ability to calm and relax you as they transport your mind and body into a meditative state.

Oxford Languages defines frequency as "the rate at which a vibration occurs that constitutes a wave either as in a material (as in sound waves), or an electromagnetic field (as in radio waves and light), usually measured per second." In other words, sound waves are also sound frequencies that vibrate to heal the body at the cellular level.

My sound healing instruments, like the singing bowls and gong, harmonize and allow deep relaxation on both sides of the brain because sound frequencies can influence your brainwaves. The bowls bring a wave of energy like the flow of a gentle stream, while the gong is more intense like the flow of the rapids. These sound waves can alter consciousness and help treat issues like migraines, anxiety, depression, and other ailments or pains in the body. They move energy that the body is holding onto, stimulate stress relief on all levels, and eliminate toxins from the body.

According to my teacher, Kathy, when a singing bowl is played, the process of entrainment occurs. Entrainment is defined as "the tendency for two bodies or organisms in the material world to pulse in a synchronized rhythm so as they vibrate in harmony." As a result, in my sound healing practice, the bowl harmonizes all aspects of physical, emotional, mental, and spiritual bodies of the group or individual who is receiving a healing. The science behind why sound healing works is incredible. "This [vibration] coaxes and encourages the cells, tissues, blood, and other physical and non-physical matter back to a state of ease and alignment. Energy that has been stored and therefore released during the process is converted; commonly expressed in the form of heat, tears, coughing, thoughts, dreams, etc."

As I wrote on Day 81, I was called to pursue sound healing to help my son's hearing loss. I trusted my intuition despite lacking clarity with respect to how sound healing would fit into my life. I just knew that this was the path to my soul. During my sound healing training with Kathy, I learned that the ting shaws (which look like small cymbals on leather straps) are used in Tibet to cure hearing loss. It was like time stopped in that moment and a bell went off notifying me that this is why I am on this path. I had found my answers.

My son wears hearing aids as he is considered deaf without them, as I shared earlier. He wouldn't be able to function without using them. However, I am hopeful that all the work with sound and his exposure to sound healing will keep his loss from progressing further.

How do you feel about the idea that the future of medicine is from a more holistic viewpoint? What holistic practices are already part of your life?

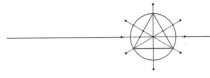

Day 131

"You should sit in meditation for twenty minutes a day,
unless you're too busy, then you should sit for an hour."
Old Zen saying

This quote always makes me laugh about the sheer irony of and implication for those of us who try to do everything under the sun in one day—those of us who are too busy to take time away from our lives to focus on our own personal growth and healing.

I would definitely have fallen into that category as I didn't initially understand the benefits that meditation would offer me. Thus, I wasn't going to carve time out of my schedule for that. The irony is that taking a pause to meditate will actually provide the clarity and energy boost needed to effectively execute with excellence the remainder of your responsibilities and plans that you hope to accomplish.

As Nipsey Hussle put it, "Sometimes you have to take two steps back to take ten forward." I can 100 percent agree with this philosophy as it appears pausing to meditate is a setback, but it is exactly what your mind and soul are craving in order to work effectively to support your needs and desires.

My go-to meditation is always the Kirtan Kriya, the recommended meditation for this chapter. The Kirtan Kriya is a perfect eleven-minute meditation with various mudra placements and changes in voice tone with the mantras, so that my mind is being asked to perform different sequences every few minutes. I love its simplicity and its end result—a perfectly meditative state.

Have you ever found yourself "too busy" to take time to focus on your healing? How did that make you feel?

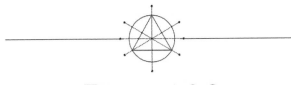

Day 132

*"Never discredit your gut instinct. You are not paranoid. Your body can pick up
on bad vibrations. If something deep inside of you says something is not right
about a person or situation, trust it."*

Unknown

Trusting your gut instincts is another phrase for trusting your intuition. This feeling deep inside is like a warning sign from your body that tells your soul that something, someone, or a situation is not supportive of your highest good. Your intuition arises as a very personal feeling in your body. It's a feeling unique to you and your situation; usually it's a physical reaction you have to the world around and inside of you. These can also be the warning signs or "red flags" that you know are there but want to ignore. Sometimes you don't want to believe the truth because deep down inside you really want something to work out.

Going against your gut instincts even though you know that the red flags are there isn't necessarily a bad thing. Pursuing what's not meant for you provides helpful experiences and lessons. These lessons can benefit and teach you something deep and valuable. Something that will stay with you forever on your journey.

Understand as well that your intuition knows something better is waiting for you—something that will support your highest good if you have the courage to believe and trust in the power of the Universe. The longer you hold onto something that is not for you, the longer you have to wait for what is meant for you.

Reflecting on my past, before my spiritual awakening, I didn't always trust my gut instincts when it came to dating men. I always wanted to feel loved by others because deep down inside I wasn't giving myself the love I desperately needed. I ignored all the red flags and dated the wrong types of men. Today, I can look back with gratitude for and pride in myself for how far I have come on my journey. In order to have a deep and healthy relationship with another, I now understand that I need to properly love myself first before loving someone else. And, once the lessons have been learned, everything will happen in Divine timing. I don't need to worry as God is always on time.

Reflect on a time when you didn't trust your gut instincts and it caused a painful reaction. How does your gut instinct physically manifest in your body?

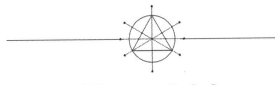

Day 133

*"Education is not the learning of facts.
Rather it's the training of the mind to think."*
Albert Einstein

Connection with the mind and achieving a higher intelligence is achieved through a strong sixth chakra.

My oldest, Anthony, lights up when he shares knowledge. There are all kinds of fascinating tidbits of random significance that he is attracted to. He feels safe to share his learnings from school with me; it is simultaneously remarkable and exquisite for me because I don't recall ever coming home from school so excited to share on a daily basis. His mind is constantly working and he has the ability to piece things together eloquently.

Anthony loves to read and is beyond fascinated at the world around him. His beautiful mind in motion is glorious. It's a blessing to see and, as his mother, I am excited for his own future, which will be beautiful and bright because I know he will fulfill his purpose.

Since he was a baby, Anthony was always a gifted learner. I recall the first time we took him pumpkin picking. He had just turned two and instead of picking just one pumpkin, he decided to organize all the pumpkins around him by size. Even with the simplest of tasks, his mind was always working and taking something to the next step. It's a beautiful memory and speaks to his intelligence.

As shared previously, Anthony does everything quickly because his processing speed is through the roof. This speed allows his beautiful mind to learn, absorb, and move onto the next piece of information. He thoroughly enjoys learning at school and is constantly engaged—it's a perfect environment for his style.

Anthony's spiritual name is Raj Pavan. This very regal name means "the noble lion who embodies sacred prana, the pure breath of life, when he connects with God's divine flow of wisdom." When Anthony is learning and has the opportunity to share, he operates at his best. In these moments, he is in the flow of life. He is in his purpose.

As a mother of two boys who recently learned her purpose at forty years old, I am overjoyed that I have an awareness of their purpose while they are still children. What a blessing to recognize a path with their direction and to understand that following their purpose and truth will be the key to a lifetime of joy and happiness for them.

I am honored to walk this path with them. For Anthony, it is simple: to continue the path of learning using his mind and higher intelligence, but also to spread the teachings for others to hear.

Reflect on your own mind and higher intelligence. What do you enjoy about learning and building on your knowledge base?

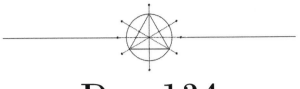

Day 134

"It's a highly effective practice to cut down on the amount of complaining you do. Literally, one complaint closes 30% of your intuitive faculties like an iron gate."

Guru Jagat

Before my spiritual awakening, I often complained about things that bothered me or that I didn't agree with. I'd also often complain if something didn't seem fair or it made me feel less than my best. I didn't live my life through the eyes of spirit focused on myself; instead, I viewed myself as being the victim and constantly pointed fingers at others for my mistakes.

Although I am not proud of this approach, I can reflect back with grace and recognize that I didn't have any prior knowledge or experience to help me approach life from a place of spirit rather than my ego.

I generally maintained a positive and happy exterior with others, but I would complain in private or reflect to myself all the negativity that I was experiencing. As a child and young adult, my sister and I were very different and often had conflict. This was a big stressor for me, especially since we didn't agree on anything. Sometimes I would express my stress, but a majority of the time I kept it private.

Instead of learning how to let go of what was no longer serving me or approach it with a different mindset, I held on to the stress. This harmed my body.

Complaining rewires your brain for negativity, which has detrimental effects on your body. The rewiring clouds your mind and things become blurry; this weakens the Third Eye and diminishes your intuitive powers. Complaining also causes the body to release the stress hormone cortisol, which impairs your immune system and makes you more susceptible to diseases.

Complaining also has a mirror effect on others around us. Remember the saying, "Misery loves company"? Frequently, we can feel the negative effects of someone who is complaining just by being in close proximity to them. Avoiding people who constantly complain is key to saving yourself in these situations.

Instead, focus on healthier solutions with a more positive approach to the stressors in your life, so that chronic complaining isn't detrimental to your health in the long-term.

Cultivating an attitude of gratitude allows you to shift your attention to something you are grateful for instead of focusing on the negative, thus reducing the release of cortisol. Another approach is to engage in a positive solution for your complaint. This creates a shift in your mindset and can change the impact of stress on your brain.

How has complaining affected your body? How does it make you feel? What solutions have you used to calm these effects on your body?

Day 135

"It's not a coincidence, it's a message. Trust it."
Unknown

When the energy at the sixth chakra is balanced, the Third Eye begins to open.

Developing this region allows us to energetically feel the truth that surrounds us and to recognize that nothing is a coincidence. With a strong intuition, you will see that they are all messages from a higher power. It's an opportunity to trust something you believe is true, without having concrete evidence. Plus, it's a way to experience your interconnectedness with the world around you and to feel a deep connection with the Universe.

Noticing a sequence of numbers and patterns was how I first became aware that my Third Eye was opening. I'd constantly see "1:11" or "11:11" and it was huge for me. It was as if angels were messaging me to look at the clock at that exact moment. Reflecting back on those moments, I was either doing something that was good for my highest good or not good for my highest good. The consistent sign was the number that my angels wanted me to recognize; the moment would alert me that I should keep doing or stop doing a particular action.

Later, I learned that the number 11 is a master number which signifies intuition, insight, and Enlightenment. It's an example of synchronicity often linked to chance or coincidence.

Seeing 11:11 can be a call to reflect on your purpose in life, return to balance, and reap the life lessons presented to you.

I believe that nothing is a coincidence. It's all part of the Divine plan and timing. You can take the opportunity to read the signs presented to you and to receive the Universe's guidance.

Have you ever pondered the deep significance and impact of a coincidence in your life?

Day 136

"The best advice I ever came across on the subject of
concentration is: wherever you are, be there."
Jim Rohn

Oxford Languages defines concentration as "the action or power of focusing one's attention or mental effort." When your sixth chakra is strong, the mind has the ability to focus and concentrate.

Before my spiritual awakening, concentration wasn't my strong suit. I was known for bouncing around between different topics or activities. I was always a hard worker, so the job always got done despite the costs to me. When I was twenty-two, I recall defending my ways by declaring, "If I had ADD, I would never have passed all four parts of the CPA exam."

Concentration is beneficial to the mind and body. It can free the mind from annoying thoughts that distract from the task at hand. When you're focused, you tend to complete faster and with a higher-quality final product than when your mind is scattered. Lastly, a person's intelligence level is tied to their ability to concentrate.

My son, Michael, has the best concentration and focus when he is dedicated to a task. This is most evident on the pitcher's mound when he's playing baseball.

Despite Michael's hearing loss, he was determined to be a pitcher. He trained for a year at private lessons, which resulted in superior performance, greater ability, and significant results. He has proven that despite a smaller build and disability, he can accomplish anything with the right concentration and determination.

I honestly believe that his hearing loss allows him to focus while he's under pressure on the mound with all eyes watching him. As his mother, it is a glorious sight to see his hard work and efforts come to fruition, but the most important piece for me is his strong ability to concentrate. His success drives his concentration. The disability that blocks his hearing helps him focus and concentrate by blocking out the surrounding sound.

**Reflect on your ability to concentrate.
Do you find certain situations are
better for you than others?**

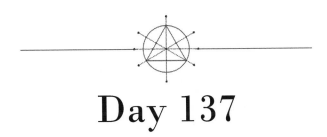

Day 137

"Taking initiative is a form of self-empowerment."
Stephen R. Covey

A strong sixth chakra gives you the energy and power in your mind to self-initiate or to be a self-starter. It's empowering to take charge and pursue what you know is best for your highest good.

When you take the initiative to work without supervision, you're often considered a self-starter. Self-starters usually possess certain key skills like motivation to take action, confidence in trusting their intuition, ambition when setting goals, and the resilience to overcome difficult situations.

This type of worker reminds me of my dear friend, Kim, whom I recently had dinner with. Kim and I met on the first day of college and have been friends for more than twenty years. She's a beautiful soul who has been through it all with me; we share deep young adult memories as well as the challenges of motherhood and beyond. This year, we even got our first tattoos together! It's been a true blessing to remain connected to her throughout the years and is a true testament to the power of friendship. She is also my most stylish fashionista friend—always full of sparkle, shine, and a side of leopard.

Kim has worked part-time in her church for a few years. It gives her a sense of purpose and supports a purpose she's deeply connected

319

to. As an English major in college, Kim has a true passion for creative writing. She creatively harnesses this passion and implements it at her job; her responsibilities include communicating messages about the church to parishioners. As Kim passionately shared her writings in the weekly newsletter with me, she was glowing with pride and joy. She loves being able to write about something that speaks so deeply to her, and she also appreciates receiving positive feedback from her readers. Their feedback affirms that she is also connecting with others with her writing. Kim also shared with me that her pastor had left the church; now she is basically working alone to accomplish all her tasks. She is a true self-starter with a strong initiative. Kim understands the task at hand and can execute it beautifully with a side of flair as she is oh-so-special and a true spirit at heart.

Do you associate yourself with being a self-starter? Why or why not? Would you like to implement this style in the future?

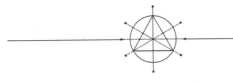

Day 138

"When you find your why, you don't hit snooze no more!
You find a way to make it happen."
Eric Thomas

Do you often hit the snooze button in the morning or are you ready to seize your day full of life and determination?

Living with determination in your life as it relates to your responsibilities is sourced from the energy of a strong sixth chakra. Determination can include setting goals and having high expectations. People who are determined often have their own definition of personal success as well as an understanding of their own abilities. Determination helps you develop strategies to meet your goals, work hard to accomplish tasks, and remain flexible and adaptable.

Everything about this quote and way of living reminds me of my dear friend and bestie, Amanda. Amanda and I met at the library in our town when her youngest and my oldest were just shy of one year old. We've felt connected since our first meeting. Amanda was full of sunshine, friendly, and beyond sweet. I've deeply valued the ease of our relationship knowing that Amanda will always be there with a smile and understanding ear even when I'm at my lowest. And I'll do the same for her. Once her mom shared with me about our friendship, "Everyone is looking for someone." They are such beautiful and true words, and I am honored to be her "someone."

Amanda recently completed six years as an unpaid volunteer on our town's board of education. She began this role when her youngest was only three; responsibilities included nightly meetings and regular committee meetings, and she did this while also balancing a full-time job and family. Amanda constantly displays determination in accomplishing her goals and responsibilities. It is remarkable what she can accomplish because she is reliable and fully committed. When she shares her list of daily tasks with me, her famous line is always, "Somehow it always gets done." Yes, of course it does, because Amanda is full of determination!

In what areas of your life do you display determination?

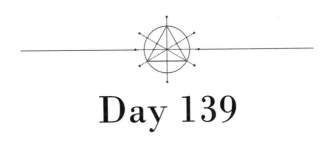

Day 139

"Honesty and openness are always the foundation of insightful dialogue."
bell hooks

Oxford Languages defines openness as "lack of restriction; accessibility and lack of secrecy or concealment." The ability to be open is sourced from a strong sixth chakra.

Openness in a relationship with another is a beautiful and free thing. You feel safe and secure that no matter what is communicated, you are free to share. Nothing is off limits. Openness is understood as the ability to reveal one's feelings, thoughts, needs, and fears.

I am beyond blessed to feel open to communicate and share everything and anything with my dear friend, Linda. Our boys are the same age, which makes it very easy for family get-togethers as everyone has a friend.

Linda is also my confidante. I share my relationship struggles with her and she's always available with an ear to listen and a heart to provide love and support for anything I may need. She's a true blessing with two beautiful sisters of her own; I often joke about being adopted into her sisterhood as their bond is so tight and remarkable.

I can always count on Linda to be there for the good times and the bad. No questions asked—she has my back and I have hers. From moving during the pandemic, to watching my boys when I don't trust another, to just listening to difficult experiences (albeit temporary), I am beyond grateful for her openness and love. Linda's a true friend to be counted on.

Reflect on a relationship you may have with another where you can truly be open and honest.

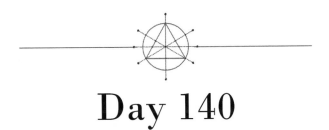

Day 140

"A mind beyond judgment watches and understands."
Buddha

When I was working in human resources, I took the Myers-Briggs personality test. This test is an introspective self-report question-naire that indicates different psychological preferences in how people perceive the world and make decisions.

As I learned from the Myers-Briggs, one of the four categories describes how you like to live your outer life: "Do you prefer a more structured and decided lifestyle, as in a 'judging' personality type; or a more flexible and adaptable lifestyle, as in a 'perceiving' personality type.

It was no surprise to me at this time to find out that I perceived the world as a judger. I was in my twenties and the test results showed I did so to the highest extent. Having a flexible viewpoint of the world was not in my vocabulary as a perceiver. I only knew how to operate one way and it was from my structured perspective.

Knowing what I now know about spirituality and living as a healer and yoga teacher, I recognize that back then I lived the opposite of how I now view the world and myself. As this quote from an unknown source states, "If you are being judgmental, that is non-yogic." In my twenties, yoga was not my lifestyle. I aspired to it, but never slowed down enough to really value all of its benefits. For taking care of my body, I focused on lifting weights instead because I could see a tangible result with them.

Not surprisingly, I married someone who was also judgmental. However, as I recognized my need to live more spiritually during my awakening, my mind began to change. As a result, my exterior views of the world also began to shift as I became more perceiving. With this new outlook, I am more conscious and understanding of others and open to their views. I allow them to co-exist with mine.

Now I consciously choose to respect others' views and decisions as everyone is fighting their own battle that we don't know about. So, to judge another without knowing the full picture does not appear to be a wise decision.

Do you view your outside life from a place of judgment or perception? How does that make you feel?

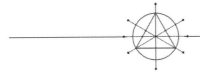

Day 141

"Yesterday I was clever, so I wanted to change the world.
Today I am wise, so I am changing myself."
Rumi

The sixth chakra is the center of wisdom. No one has the right to change another person; we don't own or control another's actions. The only thing that we have the power to change is ourselves, and we can turn to our sixth chakra for guidance.

We can lead by example, but that's by no means an expectation that our actions will force another to change. We all lead our own unique, beautiful, spiritual lives, and sometimes others will change and other times they will not.

Before my spiritual awakening, I always wanted to fix things. I'd get involved and try to control the outcome of everything. Living this way was exhausting. Now, it is so much easier to go with the flow and focus on the one thing I do have power over, myself!

Focusing on what is best for me—allowing everyone the opportunity to lead their own lives through the power of spirit—has been less stressful and minimizes the expectations I place on others.

I recall back in 2019, when I was contemplating the prenatal yoga training in Miami, I shared some concerns with one of my fellow teacher trainers. I was worried about how my husband would manage my boys for nine days in my absence.

Her words were simple and straightforward, "You can't control anyone else." Even though I'd always been the "control freak" in every situation, I had to learn the power of letting go of what was going to happen at home. Without this, I couldn't focus on learning from the training and bettering myself. I had to acknowledge and accept that everything didn't fall on my shoulders and my husband would figure it out, just like I had done every day for our boys.

It was a beautiful wake-up call for me to stop, connect with my spirit, and breathe. I could breathe in the awareness that I cannot control the outcome of everything, nor should I want that responsibility. Instead, I could focus on myself and accept the blessings that awaited me.

Reflect on a situation where you recognized it was best to focus on yourself versus fix something out of your control. How did it make you feel?

Day 142

"Genius is clairvoyant."
Abel Stevens

When the Third Eye is open, you can clearly see the past, present, and future. Individuals with this extraordinary vision are known as clairvoyants. Oxford Languages defines clairvoyant as "a person who claims to have a supernatural ability to perceive events in the future or beyond normal sensory contact." It is a French word that means, "clear seeing." This psychic ability is also referred to as the intuitive "Sixth Sense." For example, you may have a subtle perception of energy in the form of light, colors, pictures, images, or movement. Clairvoyance expands your spiritual awareness. For me, I feel the energy movement around me and it often helps me draw conclusions about what will happen in the present or future.

The summer of 2020 was the first time I really paid attention to the opening of my Third Eye. It was during a group mantra meditation. My eyes were closed, rolled upwards, focused on my Third Eye. However, after a few minutes, I started to see waves of purple/indigo light; this color is associated with the Third Eye. Recognizing this color in my vision was fascinating; I was truly seeing with my Third Eye as my "seeing eyes" were completely shut. Since that initial moment of recognition, whenever I am in a meditative state, I can see colors via my Third Eye, even though my two "seeing eyes" are closed.

With respect to seeing into the future, I have had visions of my boys implementing their purpose as portrayed in their spiritual names. As previously shared, I can see Anthony using his wisdom to educate others and Michael using his light to help others with hearing loss. It fills me with such joy and gratitude that their gifts will be a blessing to help others around them, just as I plan to live my life helping others.

Accepting, trusting, and believing in my clairvoyant abilities took time, but I do believe in the power and truth behind this inner knowledge. It serves as a guide and tool along my path. These skills were developed and cultivated during a consistent meditation practice.

Have you previously experienced any clairvoyant abilities? How did it make you feel?

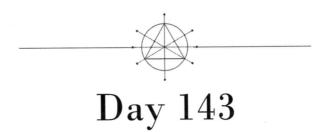

Day 143

"A smart person knows what to say. A wise person knows whether or not to say it."
Unknown

Cultivating and strengthening your wisdom is a result of a strong sixth chakra and awareness at the Third Eye. Oxford Languages defines wisdom as "the quality of having experience, knowledge and good judgment; the quality of being wise."

Before my spiritual awakening, it was important to me that others shared my perspectives, regardless of how it would be received. Sometimes I wasn't even in the right company for it to be perceived or understood, but that didn't matter. I would often get frustrated and angry when I shared something heartfelt or important and it wasn't received as I'd expected. The result was that I'd feel worse than before.

At my therapy sessions with Pam, she would often remind me of Buddha's quote and the importance that our words pass through three gates: "If you propose to speak, always ask yourself: Is it true? Is it necessary? Is it kind?" It took time for me to master this deep quote and understand that in order to preserve my energy, I must choose my words wisely.

Recently I had a chance to practice this knowledge with a situation at my boys' school. I had made the decision to step down as president of the parent organization and resign from the board at the conclusion of the school year in 2021. My life and responsibilities were transforming and it was time for new parents to have an opportunity to lead. As a result, things began to change at school in ways that I did not agree with.

One day a request came through for parents to pay for something that was previously free; I felt it was asking too much and could be viewed as them taking advantage of me. However, I evaluated my options and recognized that it cost me less energy and frustration to just pay what was requested instead of questioning and sharing that this was not standard from the past. By reflecting on Buddha's quote, I saw that it wasn't necessary for me to share that I disagreed with the proposal.

It was a wise decision and one that I was very proud of—I made the choice that was best for me and chose to preserve my energy for something that would better serve my highest good. I didn't expend my energy on something that wouldn't result in a favorable outcome and that could possibly lead to more frustration.

I was proud of myself for understanding what was worth my energy and what was not, regardless of whether or not I was right.

Reflect on a time you chose to preserve your energy versus speaking what you felt was right.

Day 144

"Dragonflies are reminders that we are loved. We can reflect the light in powerful ways, if we choose to do so."

Unknown

The spiritual meaning of the dragonfly is "the light of God." Therefore, it is fair to say that this spiritual insect connects deeply with the sixth chakra and intuition since light is the element associated with this chakra. The dragonfly symbolizes rebirth, immortality, change, transformation, adaptation, self-realization, and spiritual awakening. It also moves with elegance and grace as it understands the deeper meaning of life.

The dragonfly is a beautiful spirit animal to represent intuition, which indicates that more exists beneath the surface of life beyond the physical. The timing of a dragonfly showing up in your life is not coincidental; it reminds you to bring more light and joy into your life and is a calling to transform and evolve.

In July 2021, I was struggling with some heavy topics as it related to my boys and finalizing our parenting agreement as part of the divorce. Within a two-and-a-half-hour time frame, two different dragonflies crossed my path. One literally flew into me outside my home, the other one flew inside my car and wouldn't leave. It was my personal wake-up call that this little insect was on a mission for me to change. It gave me an opportunity for deep reflection and offered time for me to pause, process, and release my struggles that were no longer serving me.

While there is no "cookie cutter" answer as to why spirit animals visit, their visits are an opportunity to more deeply understand your own personal journey of growth and healing. Everything is connected in the Universe and all coincidences serve a greater purpose that will lead you on your path for the higher good.

I chose to hang several dragonfly suncatchers in my healing center as a symbol of light for my guests. I wanted them to have constant reminders of things that we connect with on a spiritual level.

Also, my son Michael connects with dragonflies as well. As I previously shared, part of both our spiritual names include the reference to being light. Additionally, I recently learned that dragonflies are actually deaf. They have no ears or tympanum and only feel low sounds in very low frequencies. There was such deep significance found in this tiniest of creatures. When Michael was in the third grade, his teacher asked him to select an animal to do a research project on. And he chose the dragonfly! I was blown away by his selection. At his age, I didn't even know that a dragonfly existed. This was no coincidence in my book. Michael is a light beam that is being called intuitively to share his light for those to see around him.

Do you have any past awareness about a purpose for spirit animals visiting you? Are there any spirit animals you connect with and what is the symbolism you associate with them? What connection do you feel? How does it sustain or nourish you?

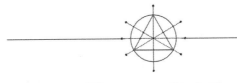

Day 145

"Don't be pushed around by the fears in your mind.
Be led by the dreams in your heart."

Unknown

Your dreams are an indicator for connecting with your Third Eye as it provides people with insight to solutions during altered states of consciousness. Dreams are such a powerful form of intuition; they bypass the ego and logical mind and can offer clear intuitive information. Despite your memory or lack of memory, everyone dreams nightly. Dreams can reveal the path that is meant for your highest good, the path you need to change or avoid, and possibly the future.

No concrete evidence exists about the consistency of dreams, but it has been accepted that dreams represent a collection of thoughts, struggles, emotions, events, people, places, and symbols that are relevant to the dreamer in some way.

Some people may also experience spirit guides who communicate to them in the form of dreams while they sleep. These guides may appear as angels or loving voices. The spirit guides often provide helpful and compassionate information which can help you live a more spiritual and peaceful life.

During the quarantine from March to May 2020, before I decided to move out of my house, I remember experiencing the most intense messages that I described as "my angels told me to do this."

I believe my spirit guides were alerting me to assemble the puzzle pieces together of my life so I could live for my highest good.

On Day 63, I described the "fire in my belly" for wanting to write my own book and the journey of self-healing that writing gave me. However, what I failed to mention was that I began to write because an angel told me to start doing it. The truth was that writing was never a fun activity of mine or something I enjoyed doing. However, I trusted my angels and quickly learned that writing became ridiculously healing and soothing for me in a way I never experienced before. I am so grateful that I trusted my spirit guides because it led me to a path that supports my purpose to help others find their own light through my journey.

Dreams are real and offer important spiritual and healing messages for those who possess the faith to believe in the power of their own intuition.

Reflect on a time when a message from a dream influenced your path or when a dream has come to life outside of your sleeping hours.

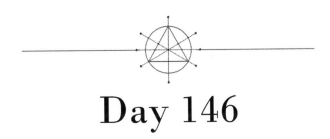

Day 146

"Imagination is everything. It is the preview of life's coming attractions."
Albert Einstein

Oxford Languages defines imagination as "the faculty or action of forming new ideas, or images or concepts of external objects not present to the senses; and the ability of the mind to be creative or resourceful."

Using your imagination to change your life may help you determine the necessary steps needed to get you where you want to go. It all starts with an idea in your mind: the ability to imagine something from your wildest dreams. The energy to imagine in your life is sourced from the sixth chakra. Where your mind goes, energy flows with it.

Giving yourself the opportunity to creatively think and imagine a world of endless opportunities also provides your mind with a break from being productive in the "real world." In fact, creating a relaxing environment for your mind can improve your concentration. Imagination is a seed that you are planting for the future for you to cultivate, grow, and develop over time.

My imagination has been on overdrive since I received the keys to my healing center. All my ideas now have a "home" to come to life; the opportunities for me to use my healing energy to put out into the Universe are now endless. To me, this warms my heart because it means I will now have the ability to help transform, shift, and heal people who live in my area. At the end of the day, that is my focus: to heal others using God's love and light.

How have you benefited from utilizing your imagination?

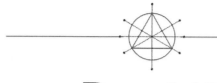

Day 147

*"You'll never be bored when you try something new.
There's really no limit to what you can do."*

Dr. Seuss

Constantly stimulating your brain to try something new is a way to expand your mind and learn, both about the new things and about yourself. This action also strengthens and connects with the sixth chakra.

There are numerous benefits to trying something new. For example, overcoming the fear of the new thing, or building the courage to become vulnerable to leave your comfort zone for the unknown.

This also sparks your creative side and builds your resumé of life experiences.

You will get to know yourself better. The more you try, the more you'll learn about your likes, dislikes, and more importantly, what sparks joy within you. Thus, what was "new" may end up remaining in your life for the long-term. It may provide great happiness and more positive experiences.

In summer 2020, my boys wanted to try stand-up paddle boards on the lake at our country club. Due to their age, they were not allowed on the boards in the middle of the lake without an adult. Despite my fears and initial doubts, my angels really wanted to try it with some friends.

They were over-the-moon excited while I was dying inside as I tried to make sure I understood all the instructions and safety measures. Also, I must note that I was not wearing a bathing suit and was wearing a white skirt. My lack of appropriate attire was a big factor for me; if I fell in, it would be a tad embarrassing to return to land drenched from the lake water.

Mind you, I put my own personal fears aside and focused on the shared experience with my boys. After we understood how to maintain balance and control of the board, we were on our way, and it was liberating! I felt strong, powerful, and full of joy. Plus, the fact that I delivered to my boys an experience that they wanted to do despite my fears was priceless.

Now we have a new summer activity to enjoy with each other and a memory that will last a lifetime. And I'll make sure to pack my bathing suit and leave the white skirt at home!

Recall a time when you tried something new that filled your life with joy.

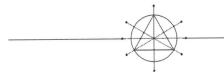

Day 148

"Silence is essential. We need silence, just as much as we need air, just as much as plants need light. If our minds are crowded with words and thoughts, there is no space for us."
Thich Nhat Hanh

Silence is peace for your soul.

I used to fear silence. It scared me—I always felt like I should be doing something. For years I believed that I thrived on productivity, accomplishing things, and following my to-do list. Silence meant I should be acting, doing something. Anything but being silent. I thought I should be productive during that time. There was an overachiever A+ grown up in me. Just existing was never something I was comfortable with.

Now, though, I crave the peace and calmness that my mind and body feel without a care, worry, or bother.

A week before Christmas 2021, I recognized while I was getting my nails done that, for the first time, my mind was not racing in my head, reciting my to-do list. I was very proud to recognize this huge moment of growth. The stillness in my mind allowed my soul to fully enjoy the pleasure of my nail salon experience. I could feel how glorious and relaxing my hands felt as the technician massaged them. I could enjoy the transformation to freshly painted nails and sit in peace without a care in the world as they dried.

I knew where I had to be and what I had to do when I left the salon. I chose for the very first time to not let my future cloud up my present experience—a time that was for my own personal self-care.

It is a simple story but the awareness is critical—giving your mind the peace it desperately deserves is a gift of love.

Do you allow your mind to sit in silence? And when you do so, what do you notice? How does your day change? Are there any benefits throughout your day?

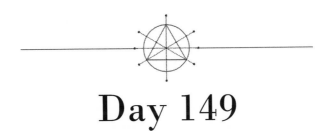

Day 149

"He who has peace of mind disturbs neither himself nor another."
Epicurus

To me, being in a state of "peace of mind" feels like I am floating through life with a mental state that is light, easy, calm, and tranquil. With this state, I have the ability to be prepared when I am faced with unexpected challenges, and I can feel free from external worries or anxieties.

Life is never meant to be free of pain, stress, or challenges. The key is to not lose yourself by going into the dark side to process and handle the external stressors that cross your path.

Having this peace takes work with regular, conscious practice; for me, that includes meditation and breathwork. I personally feel a difference in how I manage my responsibilities and response to my kids when I do not give myself the love and peace my soul and body craves from pausing in meditation.

Have you ever had something negative happen to you and, at the same time, your child or another external distraction needs your attention? And because you are frustrated with the initial issue, you proceed to respond in a harsh tone to your innocent child who just happened to need your attention at the worst time. As a result, they experienced a dark reaction that was not intended for them, but because your mind was clouded with unnecessary darkness, they also became an innocent bystander caught in the crossfire. This painfully describes how I managed difficult situations prior to my spiritual awakening, when I lacked knowledge and tools to create a peaceful state of mind.

The good thing now is that I am aware of my potential triggers which take me away from a place of light to the dark side—and these take with them my feeling of peace with myself and others. Thus, because of this awareness, I have the ability to proceed cautiously, recognize, process, and release that which caused my mind to no longer be full of light.

How do you feel when you have "peace of mind"?

Day 150

"You have the power to heal your life, and you need to know that. We think so often that we are helpless, but we're not. We always have the power of our minds . . . Claim and consciously use your power."
Louise L. Hay

I am proud of my personal growth when I recognize that I am no longer reacting, agonizing, or stressing over a situation like I would have previously done in the past. This is because I am consciously choosing to keep my body, mind, and soul in a peaceful state by living in a present frame of mind. With the awareness that healing is a continual process, I take comfort in knowing that my own efforts to heal my spirit are working.

I love this quote by Lao Tzu: "If you are depressed, you are living in the past. If you are anxious, you are living in the future. If you are at peace, you are living in the moment."

Historically, I've been governed by an anxious mind because I was constantly trying to control the outcome of my future. Thus, in a sense, I was really living in a future state of mind. But I missed so much beauty, love, and gratitude for myself and others around me because I didn't enjoy the calmness of my present. Especially since the present is the only thing that is truly existing at any particular moment.

Learning how to engage your physical senses helps to ground you in the present moment by drawing your attention away from your thoughts and into your experience. This creates a feeling of being safe and helps create a calm, peaceful internal feeling throughout your mind and body. An easy way to practice this is to acknowledge five things you can see, four things you can touch, three things you can hear, two things you can smell, and one thing you can taste. It's an anchor. Anyone can do it anywhere.

As I was completing this piece, I had my monthly alone time with my son, Michael. Michael chose to play the "Game of Life" while we watched a Christmas movie on my phone. I watched him in awe as he set-up the pieces and proceeded to get so excited about the type of house he selected, his job, and the fact that he got triplets! He even named all of them as he proudly added them to his car with his wife and dog. I was just living and enjoying all the beauty of his presence. He was full of wonder and joy—a gift he gives to himself on a regular basis. And I was filled with wonder and joy to witness and learn from him about the marvel in everyday life when you choose to consciously stay focused, in the calm of the present.

Reflect on a time in your life when you were filled with the wonder and joy of living in the present moment.

I Am

Divine

I Am Divine
DAYS 151–180

The seventh chakra, located at the top of the head at your crown, is the highest chakra and your connection with the Divine. It is the energy center of supreme consciousness, which allows you to fully experience life in an awakened state. Allow yourself to be guided by a higher power, to trust and have faith in the unknown on your path to Enlightenment.

To live life boundlessly means recognizing that spiritual elevation is our true awakening process. Feeling a sense of fulfillment is a way to add magic to your life, and eliminating what is no longer working can illuminate what will work for you. It is the purest form of light, represented by a pure white light or violet color.

As it relates to the seventh chakra, you will understand that:

- The crown chakra encompasses most of the brain, with the right and left hemispheres supporting a different role for your soul, and you can manage brain function by implementation of different breathing techniques.
- The pineal gland, which is included in the crown, has an impact on your healthy sleep habits; getting high-quality sleep keeps the body working optimally, plus it is great for your mental and emotional well-being.

- Cosmic energy is the unrestricted flow of the Universe that is representative of our consciousness through the crown chakra. Likewise, through this energy center you will learn that "OM" is the first sound of the Universe. It is a unifier that connects all living beings to nature and the Universe.

- It is often depicted as a thousand-petal lotus flower in full bloom at the crown with the ability to generate energy up through the seven chakras, but also regenerate and move the energy back down as well.

- Believing in the existence of angels strengthens this energy center, plus everyone has the ability to be a "walking angel" for others in the form of friendships. This is motivated by love to help others.

- The eagle is the spirit animal of the crown because of its strong connection to God.

- Letting go of attachments and fully surrendering is key to opening your crown chakra.

- There are no accidents in life; they are synchronistic experiences designed to guide you on your path.

- Death is a part of life and should be embraced, not feared.

- There is beauty in being vulnerable, in becoming something new, and making the world around you beautiful.

- When you emit your own positive frequency and intent into the Universe, you can live a life full of authenticity.

Tune In with the Adi Mantra
"Ong Namo Guru Dev Namo"

To center yourself in the higher self before practicing Kundalini yoga, chant the Adi Mantra three times.

"*Ong Namo Guru Dev Namo*" translates to "I bow to the Divine wisdom of all that is" and "I bow to the Divine teacher within."

HOW TO PRACTICE

- *Posture:* Sit in Easy Pose, with the spine erect.
- *Eye Position:* Eyes slightly closed, focused at the Third Eye, which is the point between the brows.
- *Mudra: Prayer Pose.* Place the palms of the hands flat together to neutralize the positive (right, or male) and negative (left, or female) sides of the body. Your thumbs should press against the sternum and your forearms will be parallel to the floor.
- Consciously begin to breathe. Gently inhale through your nose, feel the breath fill up your belly, fill up your lungs, and expand your rib cage. On the exhale from your nose, recognize the breath leaving your body. When ready to "tune in" with the Adi Mantra, inhale and exhale deeply from the nose and begin chanting the mantra three times.

Asanas

The asanas listed below focus on strengthening the energy center at the crown area. It is recommended that you hold each posture for one to two minutes with a slight rest in between. Remember to stay within while holding the postures and while resting, keep your eyes closed, focusing on the Third Eye, the point between the brows. This will allow you to focus on yourself and build your intuition, plus learn to trust your own power and ability.

- Cobra Pose
- Spinal Flex
- Bridge Pose

- Tree Pose
- Stretching Backward

Find a description of each posture in the Appendix on page 423.

Meditation

"Left and right nostril breathing + alternate nostril breathing"

In this chapter, I discuss the positive benefits of brain function through implementation of various breathing techniques. The reason this has an effect on the brain is because the quality of prana processed through the two nostrils differs corresponding with the qualities associated with the two sides of the brain. The left hemisphere of the brain is connected to the right side of the body and nostril; the right hemisphere of the brain is connected to the left side of the body and nostril.

You may use the technique of inhaling and exhaling exclusively through either the left or right nostril in order to benefit from the quality associated with that nostril.

If I need to relax and calm my body, especially before bed, I focus on left nostril breathing. Breathing through the left nostril is associated with apana (the cleansing energy), coolness, calmness, and empathy.

If I need to energize and concentrate my body, I focus on right nostril breathing. Breathing through the right nostril is associated with prana (the nurturing energy), warming, vigor, alertness, and concentration.

To balance both hemispheres of the brain, creating a deep sense of well-being and harmony, I focus on alternate nostril breathing.

Therefore, for this month's meditation, I invite you to practice any of the breathing techniques described depending on how you are currently feeling and/or the benefits that you hope to achieve.

How to practice left nostril breathing:

- Begin by sitting in a comfortable position with your eyes closed
- Close your right nostril with your right thumb
- Slowly inhale through your left nostril for a count of four seconds and exhale through your left nostril for a count of six seconds
- With practice, you can increase the counts to inhale and exhale in the following ratios: 4:8, 5:10 or 6:12
- Work up to a practice of three minutes

How to practice right nostril breathing:

- Begin by sitting in a comfortable position with your eyes closed
- Close your left nostril with your right index finger
- Slowly inhale through your right nostril for a count of four seconds and exhale through your right nostril for a count of six seconds
- With practice, you can increase the counts to inhale and exhale in the following ratios: 4:8, 5:10 or 6:12
- Work up to a practice of three minutes

How to practice one round of alternate nostril breathing:

- Begin by sitting in a comfortable position with your eyes closed
- Close the right nostril with your right thumb
- Slowly inhale through your left nostril
- Hold that for a moment
- Let go of the right nostril and close the left nostril with your right index finger
- Exhale through your right nostril

- Slowly inhale through your right nostril
- Hold that for a moment
- Close the right nostril with your right thumb
- Exhale through your left nostril
- Begin with one or two rounds, relaxing in between rounds, never forcing your breath. Work up to a practice of three minutes

Deep Relaxation

- *Posture:* Lie on your back in Corpse Pose. With your eyes closed, place your arms at your sides, with palms facing up. Allow your body to rest, process, and absorb the movement of energy.
- *Time:* One to three minutes minimum.

Ending Prayer

To close your Kundalini practice, chant three long *Sat Naams.*

Sound Healing

Enjoy this month's ten minute Sound Healing ensemble to further relax your mind and body. Consider listening during deep relaxation or at another time during your day when your body could benefit from and enjoy the beautiful healing gift of sound and vibrations.

Access this month's asana videos, meditation, sound healing audio, and more at www.LisaAnnese.com/i-am-light

Day 151

*"I looked in temples, churches and mosques
but I found the Divine within my heart."*
Rumi

Oxford Languages defines Divine as "of, from, or like God or a god; and devoted to God; sacred."

The seventh chakra at the crown, which is also referred to as the "Sahasrara", is the highest chakra and our connection with the Divine, the supreme self, and allows for spirituality to integrate into our physical lives. Thus, we all possess the ability to be Divine, as reflected in the mantra for this chapter, "I am Divine."

The word "Sahasrara" in Sanskrit means "thousand" or "infinite." Awakening of the crown means a universal flow of energy and Enlightenment represented by pure white light or violet color.

I learned about a spiritual teacher named Arkan from New Mexico who shared his definition of being spiritual as, "What spirituality is really about is one's capacity to be guided." Thus, it is allowing ourselves to be guided by a higher power, or a God— whatever you connect with is the path to the Divine.

You can deepen your connection to the Divine by letting go of expectations, releasing attachments to and expectations of how things should be, listening to the voice of your inner wisdom, and having faith in what you cannot see but can feel as the truth.

For me, releasing the power that attachments and expectations had over me was the realization I needed to understand that they were weighing me down. I tended to allow things to take over my life, and to attach to someone or to something, and I'd attach myself to that person. I'd follow their dreams instead of following my own. The attachments weighed me down because I wasn't being myself.

Once you realize you don't have to attach, you can have healthier relationships and can coexist with someone without having an unhealthy attachment. I'm still a work in progress, and nobody is ever 100 percent healed, but the key is the awareness of the effect that holding onto something has over you. Your end goal is always to be full of light and free-flowing. How I feel once I finally release something is how I want to constantly feel. It's a feeling of consistent faith that what is right in the moment will come, and that if something doesn't work out, it might not be meant for me. And letting things go allows for something else to come in. I return to this in times of struggle and when I am not living from a place of my highest good.

Also, this quote is true of my experiences with the Divine. I didn't experience true divinity from attending weekly Mass at my church. Divinity came through consistent, internal, spiritual work. While I have deep respect for my church and the services offered, for me they are separate. The church gave me a place to go when I was struggling and felt lost. It was a community of people who took me in with open arms and no judgment. There was only love. I hold both my spirituality and my connection with the Church as part of my healing, but they helped to heal me in separate ways and for that I am eternally grateful.

How do you define divinity? Is it present in your life? If not, would you like it to be? How might you begin to invite divinity into your life or start to notice the Divine?

Day 152

"Wahe guru can convert your present dreams into future reality."
Unknown

"Wahe Guru" is one of the most powerful Kundalini mantras, and translates from Sanskrit as "The Wonderful Lord." More specifically, *"Wahe"* is an exclamation of awe and ecstasy, and *"Guru"* is the one who brings us from the darkness to light. Taken together, it is an expression of ecstasy through knowledge and experience, which triggers your destiny.

In ecstasy, the self is lost. The ego is lost and you become "One" with everyone and with God. This is a process of being whole and free in the way "He" originally created "you" to be. Thus, you will see the expression of God's powers in everything. As a result, chanting *"Wahe Guru"* brings you very near to God in each moment and circumstance, in both the good and the bad.

For me, the year 2021 can be defined as *"Wahe Guru."* I'm in complete awe of the magnitude of transformation of my spirit but also grateful that I am now fully living my purpose with divine light. As the year was about to close, I was reflecting on my two biggest accomplishments: writing this book and opening my healing center. I am filled with a feeling of ecstasy that I was able to create two masterpieces out of nothing. They are two things that were not in existence at the start of the year, but they have now come to life in the Universe with the ability to further help myself and others. The magnitude of the effects of *"Wahe Guru"* is infinite; I feel my connection with God's powers and am forever grateful to be living this life.

Reflect on your own "Wahe Guru" moments. How did they make you feel?

Day 153

"The brain is like a muscle. When it is in use, we feel very good. Understanding is joyous."
Carl Sagan

The crown chakra encompasses most of the brain. The brain is a complex organ that together with the spinal cord makes up the central nervous system. In addition to regulating basic life functions, such as breathing and heart rate, the brain controls thought, behavior, emotions, and memory.

The brain itself splits into the right and left hemispheres and each has a specific role for the soul. The left is known as the logical side: it is linear, objective, responsible for language, numbers, and analytical thinking. The right is known as the creative side: it is holistic, subjective, responsible for expression, emotional intelligence, intuition, and imagination.

My Kundalini training taught me that it is important to balance the functions of both hemispheres of the brain for optimal growth and well-being. You can accomplish this through meditation, breathing techniques, and various mudras (which are a position of the hands that seals and guides the energy flow and relaxes the brain).

For me, I notice an immediate difference in my brain function when I implement several breathing techniques. If I need to relax and calm my body, especially before bed, I focus on left nostril breathing. If I need to energize and concentrate my body, I focus on right nostril breathing. To balance both hemispheres of the brain and create a deep sense of well-being and harmony, I focus on alternate nostril breathing.

The reason this has an effect on the brain is because the quality of prana processed through the two nostrils differs correspondingly to the qualities associated with the two sides of the brain. The left hemisphere of the brain is connected to the right side of the body and nostril; the right hemisphere of the brain is connected to the left side of the body and nostril.

I invite you to practice inhaling and exhaling only through the right nostril to energize your body or through the left to relax your body. Listen to whatever your body needs right now. Reflect on any difference you may experience in your mind and body.

Day 154

*"Keep the pineal gland operating and you will never
grow old, you will always be young."*
Edgar Cayce

The pineal gland is a small, pinecone-shaped endocrine gland located deep in the brain, where the right and left hemispheres join, and thus it is included in the crown chakra energy center. The pineal produces melatonin, which helps regulate sleep, wakefulness, and fully regulates reproductive hormones. All of these affect brain activity.

The pineal is commonly associated with spiritual thought and mystical experiences. Spiritually, I learned that the activation of the pineal gland in the crown will open the Third Eye, which we discussed earlier in the "I am Intuitive" chapter. Ancient philosophers have also regarded this gland as the principal seat of the soul and the place in which all our thoughts are formed.

If you experience sleep disorders, it could be a sign that your pineal gland is not producing the correct amount of melatonin. Getting high-quality sleep every night is important to keeping the body working optimally, plus it anchors your mental and emotional well-being.

This was the case for me when I first moved out of my house. The emotional stress and upheaval of my life completely changing caused a disruption to my sleep cycle and menstrual cycle. I was waking up hourly instead of experiencing a continuous block of sleep and my body was producing an excess amount of estrogen, which caused infrequent cycles, breast pain, heavy periods, cramping, and hair loss.

Dr. Chris facilitated a hormone cycle test and recommended the addition of supplements to manage and support my body. A year later, everything has settled and my hormones are operating consistently. Although the pineal gland is small, it is powerful.

> ***Reflect on your sleep patterns. Is there a correlation between when you sleep or don't and the effects on your body? Are there things that happen during your day that could be impacting the quality of your sleep?***

Day 155

"Om is the mysterious cosmic energy that is the substratum of all things and all the beings of the entire universe. It is the eternal song of the Divine."
Amit Ray

Om is the first sound of the Universe. It is a unifier that connects all living beings to nature and the Universe.

When chanted, the sound "OM" vibrates at the frequency of 432 Hz, which is the same vibrational frequency found throughout everything in nature. When pronounced correctly, it sounds more like "AUM" and consists of four syllables: A, U, M, and the silent syllable representing the deep silence of the Infinite. Symbolically, the three letters embody the divine energy of Shakti, representing the feminine energy that moves through the Universe. This energy is characterized as creation, preservation, and liberation.

Just as "OM" is representative of the Infinite, the flow of energy from the crown chakra allows you to experience endless creative infinity as well. "OM" is the Bija Mantra affiliated with this energy center.

I learned from my sound teacher that Bija Mantras are one-syllable sounds that are known as the sounds of the chakras, and each energy center has its own, unique mantra. Therefore, chanting a particular mantra can help to activate the energy related to that chakra.

When I host a sound session using my Tibetan singing bowls, I often utilize the Bija Mantras while I am helping to heal a particular chakra energy center for a client. Plus, I regularly chant, "Om Mani Padme Hum," the Buddhist mantra commonly translated as, "The jewel is in the lotus." This is a mantra for Enlightenment, designed to connect you with your innately loving and compassionate nature. I chant this beautiful mantra over the heart center as I connect my heartfelt energy with others. According to the Dalai Lama, this mantra can "Transform your impure body, speech, and mind into the pure body, speech, and mind of a Buddha."

Reflect on your personal experience with alternate nostril breathing these past few days. Were you familiar with this before? Does it appeal to you? Or has another meditation appealed more?

Day 156

"The Universe is saying: Allow me to flow through you unrestricted, and you will see the greatest magic you have ever seen."
Klaus Joehle

Cosmic energy refers to the unrestricted flow of the Universe; it is the energy of the seventh chakra and representative of our consciousness. It is the highest form of prana, the energy that animates life and maintains balance—the energy that makes everything possible. This is our life energy source.

As we discussed yesterday, "OM" is the first sound of the Universe, chanted as "AUM", and the three letters symbolically embody the divine energy of Shakti. Similarly, the cosmic energy is representative of the "Divine Mother" energy and is responsible for all creation. It represents power, strength, and capability.

For me, I feel the magic when my soul is unrestricted and free-flowing. In this state, I am "just being." I'm out of my head and in my heart. I'm trusting and believing in a power greater than me on my path. It is quite enchanting, mystical, and remarkable to release control, trust in a higher power, and allow the cosmic energy to do its thing. This is possible because that will always be what is best for me and my highest good.

I felt the cosmic flow when I decided to write this book. As I have shared before, writing became an extremely therapeutic tool that I enjoyed privately for my own healing. However, with my son's disability, I became vulnerable and expressive through my writings on social media. This awakened me to the fact that others are benefiting from my light, just as much as I am.

The cosmic flow came in the form of Divine timing, simplicity, and ease at identifying a spiritually-minded publisher, then understanding and agreeing on a book theme/idea, and then finally accepting that it was time to switch gears and officially become a writer.

I am still in awe at the transformation of events that have progressed since August 2021 as it relates to my book. It was initially written for others, as I didn't realize that I would benefit. To date, however, I'm experiencing the deepest healings as I am processing and releasing unhealed topics that have been weighing me down for years. Everything connected beautifully, like magic, and I knew I was in the right place at the right time.

If we learn to let go and trust, it can be an opportunity to remember that the Universe is constantly working in our favor.

Recall a time you felt the cosmic flow of energy from the Universe flow through you naturally. What transpired? How did you feel?

Day 157

"To be conscious of being, you need to reclaim consciousness from the mind. This is one of the most essential tasks on your spiritual journey."
Eckhart Tolle

Oxford Languages defines consciousness as "the state of being awake and aware of one's surroundings." The energy to live consciously is sourced from an open and developed crown chakra.

Being conscious is the ultimate goal. I lived the first forty years of my life unconscious and unaware of the world around me. My regular Kundalini yoga classes were my first introduction to the idea of "living consciously" versus living like a robot, mechanical and scripted. However, due to my current spiritual nature, I can look back at myself before my spiritual awakening with grace and forgiveness for not knowing any better.

Attending the Khalsa Way prenatal yoga training in Miami in January 2020 was when I first really understood that I was not living consciously during my pregnancy and the births of my two boys. Likewise, since I was not conscious during their births in 2011 and 2013, I wasn't living consciously before that time either. As a result, I was left with a feeling of disappointment and sadness for not questioning more and living in the clouds. I'd just been going through the motions.

Today, decisions related to food choices and medical care are top of mind for me and of utter importance. Although I cannot go back and change decisions from the past, I can ensure that all current and future decisions are made from a place of consciousness and awareness.

How do you live consciously? Have you noticed any difference in your life when you are approaching something from a place of consciousness versus unconsciousness?

Day 158

"Enlightenment is the 'quiet acceptance of what is.' I believe the truly enlightened beings are those who refuse to allow themselves to be distressed over things that simply are the way they are."

Wayne W. Dyer

In 2021, I became intrigued by the unalome: the Buddhist symbol that represents each individual's transcendence, path to Enlightenment, and our existence on Earth.

The base of the unalome symbolizes your birth and the starting point of life, depicted as spirals.

The zig zag lines are shown next, which signify the wandering we do in life, the twists and turns. These are the life-altering events and experiences that are derived from our path. These experiences ultimately lead us to our greatest versions of ourselves.

Then it is followed by straight lines toward the top, which signifies becoming centered and aligned with the Divine. There's a sense of being wiser, more mature, and closer to Enlightenment.

Lastly are the three dots at the top of the unalome, which symbolize reaching your goals, freedom, peace, and Enlightenment.

The symbol was a perfect depiction of my current state of awareness and understanding that I was on my very own path to Enlightenment. Obviously, it was no coincidence that I learned about its symbolism and meaning. It was a sign from my angels, alerting me to my strength and inner healing work as I transcended.

Our paths are never straightforward. They are meant to be filled with suffering and challenges. Analyze your actions and learn from them. Let them motivate you to keep seeking the ultimate goal of awareness, bliss, and harmony as your journey unfolds. According to Buddha, "Suffering is temporary, Enlightenment is forever."

Have you considered your own path to Enlightenment? Looking at the unalome symbol, what point of your journey are you experiencing now?

Day 159

"Like a lotus flower, we too have the ability to rise from the mud, bloom out of the darkness and radiate into the world."
Unknown

The seventh chakra is often depicted as a thousand-petal lotus flower in full bloom at the crown of your head. A beloved symbol in many spiritual practices, the lotus symbolizes purity, calmness, wisdom, Enlightenment, self-regeneration, new beginnings, rebirth, and being grounded. But it also speaks to always remembering your roots.

Its roots are grounded in the Earth as its petals flow out from the crown and back down through the chakras as a stream of Divine wisdom and awareness. As such, to open our crown chakra we need the ability to generate energy up through the seven chakras, but we must also be able to regenerate and move the energy back down as well.

For me, this flower is the perfect example of the path to Enlightenment and a true analogy of my life. In order for the lotus to blossom, it has to grow through slime, pond scum, and murky waters, but it always blooms. It's a perfect symbol because it demonstrates that you and I have the power to grow even in the darkest of circumstances. By staying true to our heart and soul through the dark and rough times, we will eventually rise and flourish in the light, face the sun, and radiate for all.

The lotus is a perfect visual for my journey. Most recently, I grew through the murky waters of releasing difficult areas of my past, as I wrote about them in relation to the different chakra energy centers. It is fascinating that, as I completed each chapter of this book, I have simultaneously felt lighter. And in a sense I can literally feel myself blossoming toward my own path of Enlightenment. I'm becoming perfectly radiant and full of light—a light to shine on others and heal along the way.

Reflect on a time you felt yourself bloom like a lotus flower and how it felt. If you haven't experienced this before, what steps could you implement to begin this healing journey for yourself?

Day 160

"Let the angels help you feel an aura of protection each day and each night. Let them surround you in this halo of love, and feel safe and protected always."

Unknown

Through the crown of the seventh chakra, the Divine self manifests in a physical body and is the gateway to God; likewise, when a person dies, the soul exits through the top of the head. As previously shared, this area is associated with the element of light; as a result, halos are often depicted near the top of your head.

The halo indicates an awakened and active crown chakra and is depicted in ancient artwork around heads of angels and other ascended beings. It's featured in religious icons all over the world. Often halos appear as a glowing, transparent gold energy aura around the head; the more activated the chakra, the more energy is present at the crown and the greater the illuminated brilliance. The halo or aura is shown as a sun-circle or crescent shape around the head. People have been awarded this glory as a "gift" of recognition because they understood divinity and wisdom at a higher level than most of us. Thus, the halo is a symbol of the divinity in those specific souls and should be honored as such.

When you speak as a projection from your halo, you speak from a place of higher sense of self, purpose, truth, and Enlightenment; The source of this energy is derived from the crown chakra.

When I practice Kundalini yoga, the postures and breathing

techniques generate and circulate energy up my spine. In order to prevent that energy from escaping my body and to allow it to recirculate in my body, I wear a turban over my crown and halo area. This results in a feeling of euphoria and it allows me to fully reap the benefits of my practice. As a result, I can exist with a higher vibration/energy state and project from my halo area.

Are there situations where you feel you speak from a higher motive, and thus speak from your halo? How does this impact you and the situation?

Day 161

"The more that you trust and believe in angels,
the more they will pour the blessings upon you."
Denise Linn

I have felt a deep connection with angels since I was a child. Belief in the existence of angels connects you with the Divine and strengthens the crown chakra. In fact, as part of my spiritual awakening and awareness, I have even questioned the fact that maybe I am a walking angel in disguise, clearly here to help and heal those around me. And it's something we all have the ability to do.

As a regular collector of items depicting angels, my collection continually expands with reminders about the presence of angels, from my "everyday" angel decor to my specific "Christmas" angel decor. Seeing angels regularly is a reminder of my deep faith that angels support us every day in our lives.

Angels guard, protect, and inspire us. They also communicate messages as they watch over us. They encourage us through signs and guide us on the path we need to go. Angels also influence our good thoughts and invite us to do good. They continually surround us and are here to help us become the best versions of ourselves.

During the week of Thanksgiving in 2021, Roco and I missed getting run over by a car by milliseconds. It was a surreal experience that left me scared and with chills for a couple days. I truly believe my angels blessed us on that beautiful day and saved us.

Ironically, right before the incident, as I was waiting for the light to change (giving us the right of way to walk across the street), I recall looking up at the gorgeous sky with gratitude at how perfect everything was.

An immense river of joy filled my heart and soul with warmth and love. I wasn't distracted; I was aware of my surroundings. And then a car came barreling around a corner. Luckily my senses were on alert and I had the ability to swerve out of the way. Had I been on my phone or distracted by a different type of external influence, there may have been a different outcome. However, it was a reminder that things could've changed in just a millisecond. I'm forever thankful to my angels for their protection.

Recall a past experience when your angels helped you in a difficult situation. Do you remember the lesson learned?

Day 162

"Not all angels reside in heaven. Some walk the Earth. Just like you."
Unknown

Angels do exist on Earth—in the form of friendships motivated by love to help others.

My beautiful son, Michael, was eventually diagnosed with permanent hearing loss by the audiologists at the Children's Hospital of Philadelphia on August 20, 2020. While I had known something was "off" about his hearing for a few years, I was not mentally prepared to hear the words, "Your son will require double hearing aids, for the rest of his life, in order to function."

His audiologist prepared me for his long journey, with follow-up tests, appointments for services, and navigating his future learning and understanding at school. They also shared the reality that his hearing may continue to worsen as he aged. I was beyond grateful for the tremendous support and path that his medical team provided, but I was also scared and fearful of the unknown and Michael's future.

This diagnosis was a huge mountain that was yet to be discovered by Michael and me—and we were currently still on the ground at the base. I understood that the only way out was to start climbing. Hearing loss became my mountain—something for Michael and me to tackle together.

After Michael's appointment, we went to visit my good friend Linda, who'd been watching Anthony while we were at the appointment. Linda and her husband are like angels to me. As I expressed my fear to her husband, Mike, he said, "Well, it sounds like you had a great day today!" I looked at him with a fresh perspective and said, "You are correct." It was a great day because we had an answer: we finally discovered why my son was experiencing difficulties and we had a plan to fix it!

Changing what may appear as a "negative" into a positive situation is how everything should be approached as everything is a Divine blessing. And everything doesn't always feel amazing—it's important we recognize all those feelings and emotions. Sometimes I look at the "deaf child" signs around my complex and there is sadness. But sometimes I look at them and think, "I accomplished this." In the end, we all face challenges which help us to learn, grow, and be stronger. I am grateful for those challenges as they push us to live for our highest good.

I'm also forever grateful for the friendships in our lives; they are proof that God and the Universe give you exactly who you need, when you need it. The key is to be aware and open to the abundance of gifts from the Universe in the form of those who are walking beside you.

Michael's journey began at diagnosis and is constantly unfolding, like the beautiful lotus flower. Because of hearing loss, we now have a network of "angels." They're mothers with sons who have hearing loss at different stages of life to help guide us; we share the ultimate goal and belief that, despite their disability, our boys can do anything and everything!

Reflect on friends who became "angels" in your life. What transpired? How did it make you feel?

Day 163

"May you soar on eagle wings, high above the madness of the world."
Jonathan Lockwood Huie

The spirit eagle is man's connection to the Divine because it flies higher than most other birds. It conveys the powers and messages of the spirit. To me, it is the spirit animal associated with the crown chakra as that is the chakra that connects with God.

In the fall of 2021, during a reiki session, the spirit eagle appeared on my forehead in my energy field. Intrigued by its existence, I was on a mission to understand its connection to my life. Areas of its symbolism that I connected with were: truth, the Divine, foresight and psychic awareness, freedom, and independence.

While I was already living my own path of truth, this was confirmation for me that when I am living in my truth, I have the power to soar higher than I could have imagined. Seeing an eagle is a reminder that the Divine exists in all of us—everything is sacred.

Eagles have extraordinary eyesight and can see eight times as far as humans can. Thus, despite the fact that they can soar to immense heights, they still have the ability to see the miniscule details of what is happening on the ground; they are symbols of foresight and psychic awareness, blessed with keen eyesight to see things from a viewpoint that humans cannot.

The eagle reminds us that freedom starts in the mind. But if an eagle makes itself known to you, it may be a sign to exert more freedom and independence, in the sense of trusting yourself with your dreams and inspirations.

I understand that nothing is a coincidence; the timing of this was impeccable because, at this time, I was in a groove with my purpose. I had plans laid out for me to pursue in my future. However, I was scared to take the steps to implement my dreams as I was safe on the ground. The eagle was my sign that it was time. I was ready to soar—I was ready to fly like an eagle and further pursue my dreams.

The biggest step for me was opening my own healing center, which happened about two months after this reiki session with the awareness of the eagle spirit. I want to implement my healing for others in a way that helps them see that "the sky's the limit," just like the eagle. Having my own center is an opportunity to implement programs, events, and services for people. All of these offerings can educate about the importance of living with light, connecting with your spirituality, and choosing the path of truth.

In what ways have you connected with the symbolism of the spirit eagle in your life? Is there an animal you see with frequency that has then revealed meaning or symbolism?

Day 164

"Self is a sea boundless and measureless."
Kahlil Gibran

The seventh chakra is about living as a boundless person with energy sourced from the crown area. Also referred to as the "tenth gate," it is the meeting point between the physical body, the Universe, and the soul. It is the highest level of sensing and functioning using intuition with all the open chakras.

Oxford Languages defines boundless as "unlimited or immense." In other words, living your life as limitless and without bounds. You can experience things infinitely. Life feels spontaneously free-flowing as you connect spiritually with the Universe, to the beat of your own soul.

Our soul's movement and way of being is similar to the sea. It is boundless and free. This is the feeling I experienced in the summer of 2021 when I rediscovered my passion for lap swimming after a twelve-year hiatus. I returned to this type of exercise as my forty-one-year-old body was in desperate need of low impact activities.

As I swam my laps, the major feeling rushing through me was freedom. My body and soul felt free—free from physical pain, but also from mental pain and distractions. It was a great opportunity to return my Pisces soul back home to the water and heal my inner child. I felt boundless, like the very water I was swimming in, full of joy and life. Definitely as it should be.

Do you recall a time when you felt boundless? What transpired for you?

Day 165

"Separation before elevation. You have to let some people and things go so you can go to the next level."
Tony Gaskins

Spiritual elevation means true awakening. It's connecting with our pure existence and the Divine with an open crown chakra.

Oxford Languages defines elevate as to "raise or lift something up to a higher position." From a spiritual perspective, this means to elevate your soul to a higher dimension and vibration. Understand that when you do this, your views and interests will naturally change; you begin to look at people, situations, and things differently.

It's an opportunity to let go of what is no longer serving you, in order to elevate to a higher place. It is freeing to release the energies of the past and make room for new energies to enter in the present.

Adding things to your life shifts from your needs to your wants when you understand that, from a soul's perspective, you are already complete as it is. Whatever's not meant for you goes; by allowing things to move freely, the things you want have space to enter. You experience less grasping when you're aware that making space for a new addition to your life can add deep value. This continues and feeds your higher vibrational living.

For me, there are television shows and movies that I thoroughly enjoyed before my spiritual awakening but cannot tolerate now. I am aware that my time and energy are limited and priceless. This motivates me to be selective with my attention and, consequently, my energy will be maintained at a high frequency.

I also recognized that some excursions with my boys at our local country club felt enjoyable in the past but do not energetically feel right to me now. It has been a struggle because these events felt like second nature to me, but my choices were made unconsciously. Now I choose to make conscious decisions where my energy goes and who has access to it.

In addition, the popular kriya for elevation was the very first kriya that I taught to my yoga teacher training group in December 2019. It's a very special kriya that holds a place in my heart; it exercises the spine and aids in circulation of prana to balance the chakras. The kriya energizes the body and refreshes the breath, leaving you feeling calm, clear, and elevated. In preparation for this kriya, I practiced the postures and prompts until I had them memorized. It was an opportunity to fully benefit and elevate my energy, as intended.

> *Reflect on your own path of elevation. Is there anything you had to release in order to elevate your energy? How was that process for you? If you are interested in elevating your soul, what steps can you start to take to get there?*

Day 166

"The art of fulfillment is the ability to experience not only the thrill of the chase, but also the magic of the moment, the unbridled joy of feeling truly alive."

Tony Robbins

Oxford Languages defines fulfillment as "the achievement of something desired, promised, or predicted; satisfaction or happiness as a result of fully developing one's abilities or character." Possessing a strong and open crown chakra will bring you an unconditional state of total fulfillment, magic, and joy. This satisfaction and happiness will engulf you in a true feeling of being alive.

Feeling a sense of fulfillment also allows you to feel illuminated by the magic that exists when you make the impossible possible and when everything feels like it fits together perfectly, like a puzzle. This sense of alignment can only happen when you are awakened, conscious, and believe in the power of magic. As Roald Dahl says, "Those who don't believe in magic will never find it."

As a parent, I always feel the magic from my boys on Christmas morning. They go to bed with no presents under the tree and awaken to the "magic" of gifts for all to share and exchange. The day is full of wonder, light, and mystery behind the delivery and execution of beautifully wrapped packages. Our Christmas in 2021 was full of surprises as my youngest son, Michael, tested positive for COVID on Christmas Eve. A surge of cases hit our area and the inevitable happened. Luckily, I was able to care for him with my mother's instinct and love to ensure he felt safe and healed quickly considering the circumstances. That Christmas morning, he was feeling better as his eyes were illuminated and sparkling as he observed the packages around our tree. It was a beautiful sight that can only be described as magical. He jumped on my lap, held me tight, and just wanted to exist in the moment of the beauty of Christmas. A magnificent sense of fulfillment flowed through me as I know I delivered a memory that will last a lifetime, as there is magic in the memories.

Recall the last time you felt fulfilled. What feelings were associated with it? Did it feel like magic to you?

Day 167

"If you eliminate what no longer works, you illuminate what does."
Cheryl Richardson

Albert Einstein is quoted as saying, "Everybody is a genius. But if you judge a fish by its ability to climb a tree, it will live its whole life believing that it is stupid." This is a perfect analogy to understand that everyone has their own gifts and skills that they can excel and be successful at. The key is to stop doing what you cannot do well, so you can illuminate, shine, and excel at what you are meant to be doing.

Oxford Languages defines illuminate as "to make something visible or bright by shining light on it; light up." I am constantly sharing with my boys that they each have their own unique gifts. It's important to increase their time with the things they excel at. When that happens, they are illuminating their energy for the world to see, as when they are illuminating, their crown chakra is open.

Making my boys aware of their unique gifts, especially as young souls, is a great blessing for them as it supports them in living their lives from a place of spirit. They are learning to trust their intuition and, in doing so, will shine brightly for themselves. In the future, they can illuminate what works for them.

As previously shared, my awareness of my purpose became clear as I approached my fortieth year. While I have zero regrets for my life's progression, as it was all divinely orchestrated to teach my soul a lesson, I have the opportunity to shape my boys' future based on my journey from dark to light.

In my life path, I eliminated the need of, "I should work in public accounting to support myself financially because I earned my CPA." By letting this go, I am able to illuminate my spiritual healing gifts to help myself, my boys, and those in my community who cross my path for help. It's a beautiful gift for others, but also for myself as I am following the truth in my heart and soul.

By following your purpose, life flows with ease. Things are simpler and illuminated when you trust your own spirit as your guide.

What have you found that you can eliminate from your life in order to allow you to illuminate elsewhere? What has become illuminated?

Day 168

*"According to Buddhist psychology, most of our troubles stem
from attachment to things that we mistakenly see as permanent."*
Dalai Lama XIV

One of the shadows of the crown chakra is attachment. Having an attachment to something or someone will keep you in the dark. It prevents you from seeing the light; as your shadow, it impedes your ability to live consciously.

The key to life is to learn to let go of any and all attachments that you may have. Attachments often lead to expectations which can cause pain and suffering. Allowing yourself to cut ties and let go of attachments will open your crown chakra; this connects you with the cosmic energy and your higher self.

To be clear, when you let go of an attachment, you don't forget about it. What I mean is that you remove the feelings associated with it so that they no longer consume you. We become consumed and enter the dark side when we agonize or make up scenarios in our minds based on false expectations. This was my motto before my spiritual awakening. I always agonized over past discussions and potential future outcomes. It was painful and added no positive value to my life. I was only harming myself with this negative pattern of abuse. It led to very dark moments.

Now when I feel I am starting to "enter the dark side" regarding a situation or connection with a person, my goal is to talk it through with a trusted friend, spend time resting my mind in meditation, or listen to soothing mantra music.

Choosing to focus on my present and what is currently affecting me at that moment helps tremendously. Also, I visualize myself as a light beam; this attracts light to my crown through my chakras and helps ground me.

To open your crown, focus your energy at the top of your head and fully surrender; release the power an external influence may have over your focus and ability to stay calm, present, and full of peace. This will open you to new opportunities and possibilities, as well as awaken the crown and remove you from any past attachments.

What is your experience with attachments? Is it a struggle to let go? How do you feel when you do disconnect from the attachments?

Day 169

"Paradise is not a place. It is a state of consciousness."
Unknown

"Paradise Found." This statement was printed on a light blue wood hanger that I purchased at a small shop I visited while traveling to Rhode Island. It was the fall of 2008 and I had just begun to date my husband. The sign was perfect because I believed that I had found paradise. Plus, the color matched my newly painted bathroom in the condo I had recently closed on, and I had just started a new job at my company. My life was a living paradise because everything was perfect: new home, new boyfriend, and new job.

Reflecting back on this time, I am proud of myself for recognizing that paradise was not a place, but a state of mind, a state of consciousness. In religious terms, paradise is a place of happiness and delight. It's a place where existence is positive, eternal, and harmonious. When you understand this, you can turn any existence into a paradise based on your own personal awareness and perception of your physical surroundings and mental state.

Reflect on your state of consciousness. Can you define it as paradise? How could you make it a paradise?

Day 170

*"There are no accidents or coincidences in life. Everything is synchronicity—
because everything has a frequency. It's simply the physics of life and the
Universe in action."*
Rhonda Byrne

Oxford Languages defines synchronicity as "the simultaneous
occurrence of events which appear significantly related but have no
discernible causal connection."

This term was originally coined by Carl Jung regarding mysterious occurrences; when you experience synchronicity, you'll
have experiences that seem far too significant to be mere day-to-
day encounters. They are serendipitous in nature or discovered by
chance in a happy and beneficial way.

To me, synchronicities are a sign from the Divine that can only
happen once your soul has elevated, and thus you are fully aware and
can observe with your eyes. Plus, you can feel significant energy shifts.
These become "little clues" alerting your consciousness to signs that
all add up to you being on the right path for your soul. Thus, when
you follow the right path for you, it will feel that everything has just
miraculously fallen into place with ease. Your spirit will remain at a
higher vibration. You'll feel joy, fulfillment, and peace.

I shared on Day 111 about our dog, Roco, and how he was the
missing piece for our family. He is exquisitely perfect and the companion I did not know that I needed in my life.

Choosing Roco was a synchronistic occurrence as we originally went to the pet store to purchase a different breed of puppy. However, upon meeting that puppy, I didn't feel that he was a good fit for us. Still, I was determined to find the perfect addition to our family; I noticed this adorable, two-pound, apricot toy poodle with deep eyes who was in a container with a different breed of puppies.

Aware that toy poodles remain small and are very smart, I was intrigued. To me, the synchronistic occurrence that made me know that he would be "our dog" was his given name: Frankie. This was my sign. At that time, my good friend, Frank, had been providing emotional support and assistance through the divorce process. The name sealed the deal in a sense and so I am very grateful for all that's transpired after bringing our new addition home.

Trusting the power of synchronistic events and occurrences from the Universe is a leap of faith. It can be hard to follow the feeling and believe in a power greater than you to guide you on your way. But it's worth it to breathe deeply, release control, and to "just let things happen" naturally as they should.

Reflect on occurrences in your life. Do you recognize any of them as synchronistic encounters?

Day 171

*"We do not fear the unknown. We fear what
we think we know about the unknown."*

Teal Swan

One of the qualities of the crown chakra is the relationship to the unknown, as the chakra offers an opportunity to lean in and trust the power and love of God. It's about learning to rely on, believe in, and have hope that you will be guided to exactly where you need to be. It's getting you out of the thoughts in your head and into your heart.

The truth is that we don't actually need to know about the unknown, as nobody has any certainty to predict the outcome of the future. All any of us can do is have faith and to practice a new habit of saying, "I trust in you, God." It is easy to praise and thank Him when things go right or as expected, so why don't we rely on Him when the opposite is presented to us?

When we understand that God has a hand in everything, it removes the fear and pressure out of our hands and places it into the hands of God. I've previously shared how my connection with the Church helped me have a place to go and feel safe during my darkest moments. And at the end of 2021, I was experiencing a downward spiral with a triad of heavy issues. Meditation and journaling helped me tremendously that next morning and I gained some clarity in an answer from God to begin Bible journaling.

While I have never really studied the Bible in detail, I trust that I was led to learn more about the teachings through journaling as it combines my passion for creativity and my connection to God. It's a new adventure for me to embark on in 2022 and at the top of my list of New Year's Resolutions. I have an opportunity to be still and trust the power of God and the unknown.

Reflect on and describe your understanding of the unknown.

Day 172

"Death is but a transition from this life to another existence where there is no more pain and anguish. All the bitterness and disagreements will vanish, and the only thing that lives forever is love."

Elisabeth Kübler-Ross

Having a fear of dying is a shadow side of the crown chakra. Fear of pain and suffering, how death will happen, and what happens next make death anxiety a very real phenomenon.

From a spiritual perspective, we are spirits having a human experience, in a physical body. As a result, what dies is the physical body, but your spiritual energy lives forever. Our human experience is full of lessons and learning experiences and we are here at this moment to clear karmic lessons from our past lives. This is how we grow and ensure that we accomplish our purpose on Earth in a physical body.

These are my understandings as learned from my Kundalini training, which originates from an Eastern philosophy. Those who believe in this philosophy view death as a transition and understand that accepting the harsh reality is the most effective way to manage it.

This contrasts with modern Western society where the reality of death is not openly discussed and is feared by many. As such, it is often one of those taboo topics that people make assumptions about.

For me, I've embraced the Eastern philosophy and believe that I am fulfilling karmic lessons from my past. At the age of forty-one, I learned that in one of my past lives I died in a war, standing up for something I believed in and, as a result, I carried a lot of fear with me into my current life. Learning this truth illuminated for me why I carried an extreme amount of fear even as a child.

Thus, my karmic lesson was to live from a spiritual perspective, learning to focus on love, which is the opposite of fear, as I fulfill my purpose as a human in this lifetime.

Reflect on your own understanding and relationship with death. Is it from a place of acceptance or fear?

Day 173

*"A man may be born, but in order to be born, he must first die,
and in order to die he must first awake."*
George Gurdjieff

Are you fully awake to the happenings of your world around you, or are you coasting through life with your eyes open but not truly awake to your surroundings?

I am only truly living now because I allowed the "Old Lisa" to die with my separation from my husband. It was a result of me finally waking up to recognize that I wasn't living as God intended for me. I had so much more potential, opportunities, and growth awaiting me once I was ready to wake up for the first time.

I have shared before how my path of truth was symbolic of a rising phoenix. A phoenix is a symbol of rebirth, renewal, and hope; the bird rises from the ashes of its dead, old self and predecessor. That was me. In order to live, to be awake and experience life for the first time, I had to die.

While my family was in quarantine in spring 2020, music became my lifeline. I started to really listen to, connect with, and understand the deep meaning behind song lyrics in a way I'd never experienced before. Maybe it was because at this time my interest in writing was piqued as it was the beginning of my internal healing process.

During this time, I came across a Swedish singer named Fia. It was no accident I encountered this artist whose songs were about light and spirituality—the Universe always presents you with what you need on your path.

Fia's songs introduced me to the concept of a rising phoenix and I made the connection that I was indeed on my own unique journey of death and rebirth. Her music gave me strength and wind beneath my wings. They helped me accomplish the unthinkable on the start of my journey to a new life.

Are you walking around awake in your life? How was the process to get you there?

Day 174

"What makes you vulnerable makes you beautiful."
Brené Brown

On Day 20, I shared that Brené Brown taught me what it means to be vulnerable and how to live authentically while expressing my own vulnerability. According to Brown, "The definition of vulnerability is uncertainty, risk, and emotional exposure. But vulnerability is not weakness, it's our most accurate measure of courage."

The crown chakra is associated with a person's inner and outer beauty. Therefore, when you share something that makes you vulnerable with another, it shows your deep feelings, truths, emotions, and imperfections—the essence of your true beauty.

Emotional vulnerability is the ability to express your emotions and allow yourself to truly connect, to be seen, and be intimate with another. When you don't follow this, you don't allow yourself to be known by others or even really know yourself. Until recently, this was my relationship with my father.

Growing up, I never had a comfortable or close relationship with my father as I wasn't comfortable communicating my true feelings. I'd put an emotional barrier between the two of us for my own protection and survival when I was younger.

However, my perspective and connection with my father changed in February 2022 when, at eighty years old, he broke his ankle and required surgery, leading to a massive infection and dependency on his family in a new way. Roles changed and I began to take the lead with his medical team on decision-making, asking insightful and challenging questions; I was fully aware that we had to advocate on his behalf.

During his darkest time, his light began to shine, allowing me to truly see him for who he is. For the first time, I felt compassionate toward him and understood him better.

I practiced my Tibetan bowls near his broken ankle and asked Nicole to do intuitive reiki to encourage the movement of energy and further heal his injury. We often practice together to heal clients; however, this was a first for my family.

Previously, I'd hidden this part of myself from my family because I feared their disapproval. My vulnerability allowed me to be truly seen for who I am. The real me. And because I allowed myself to be vulnerable, the wall between us came down, allowing my truth and light to flow freely.

I am blessed to have this interaction with my father as an opportunity to help and serve, just like I would try to heal another. It is also a new beginning for our relationship, and I recognize that we have never spent this deep quality time together before. Reflecting back on this moment, it saddens me that forty-two years have passed before our "new beginning," but I have faith that, as it says in Ecclesiastes 3:1, "God is always on time."

Reflect on a time you felt beautiful as a result of being vulnerable? If you haven't experienced this yet, how would you like this encounter to take place?

Day 175

"Luxury is not a necessity to me, but beautiful and good things are."
Anaïs Nin

After my spiritual awakening, I chose to live with a simpler and less complicated spin on my life. While I was rarely attracted to brand names or fashionable trends, I did have a thing in the past for high-end handbags and jewelry.

Since my style was clean lines, solids, and often monochromatic outfits, I enjoyed accessorizing with key pieces. These key pieces were often luxury items. Not essential, but highly desired and associated with wealthy people.

As I prepared to pack my belongings to move out of my home and into my new apartment, alone with my boys, I recognized the magnitude of luxury goods that I had rarely used in my closet and in my drawers.

As a busy mom who is active physically, I rarely wore jewelry or spent the time changing what I was already wearing. As far as bags go, I would often just bring my keys and phone as my pants have side pockets or I utilize casual, less expensive side satchels that allow me ease of movement, convenience, and simplicity.

As I started to become more aware of the power of sound and my interest in becoming a sound healing practitioner, I decided to use my already existing "jewels" of handbags and jewelry and exchange them for my new "jewels" of ancient Tibetan sound bowls. I sold the majority of my pieces and used the money to purchase my new sound healing tools.

It was a true energy transfer from the "Old Lisa" to the "New Lisa" and unlike anything I could have predicted. A beautiful path was in front of me the whole time, waiting to be discovered. My old luxury items no longer brought me joy or added any value to my life.

However, I was wonderfully intrigued and swept away to a peaceful place through my sound tools. The vibrations transformed me from strained and stressed to still and serene. I found a beautiful sanctuary for my soul to inhabit that was calm, relaxed, and lifted my spirits.

What beautiful things in your life are your necessities? How has your definition of what is beautiful in your life changed?

Day 176

"If you ever fall apart, find the beauty in becoming something new."
Caelus

There is something quite beautiful and extraordinary about trusting the path of your life to allow everything to completely fall apart and experience it becoming something new again.

My spiritual awakening became an opportunity for me to let go of the person I've always been. I could trust and lean into God and allow my highest self to emerge.

I started a new tradition with my boys for Christmas 2021: a very special Christmas dinner with just the three of us. It was a memorable time for my boys and me to be together and celebrate the beauty and love of life at Christmastime. We ate a special dinner at a restaurant that we wouldn't normally dine at and had a memorable meal filled with games. The boys had my undivided attention.

As I was preparing for our dinner, I shared with my dear friend, Ali, how completely happy and in love I was with the strong, single mother I have become. Out of all the different versions of Lisa— child, adolescent, young adult, married, married with kids, and now a single mother with kids—I am completely in love with the version of myself that I've become. I'm proud of what I've accomplished throughout this change, rather than being complacent, sad, or upset. I'm proud of the fact that I'm doing it alone and trusting my own intuition. I trust that this Lisa knows the way to go and how to guide her kids along the way.

This version of me is only possible because I chose to live the path of truth—alone. I allowed it all to fall apart in order to allow what is best for me to remain.

I understand now that in the fall, "The trees are about to show us how lovely it is to let dead things go." We also must be like trees at times and allow what is no longer living to die within us. Only then can we embrace the new blooms of life that emerge with time.

Remember a time you let go, trusting the beauty of something new to happen in your life. How did you feel?

Day 177

"I'm going to make everything around me beautiful. That will be my life."
Elsie de Wolfe

In the fall of 2020, this beautiful quote captured my eye as I was shopping in Kings, a local supermarket near my home. It was printed on a neutral background, in a typewriter style font, in a simple frame. I was perusing their floral department, which always has great gift items, and it made me stop in my tracks. Yes! My goal and purpose is to make everything around me beautiful: that has always been my life. Despite the challenges and struggles that I was dealing with on the inside, I always ensured that everything was still beautiful on the outside.

Well, around the same time that I became aware of this quote, I was asked to be the featured family on the cover of our town's magazine for the March 2021 edition, something that I have previously shared. My story was about challenges being our greatest blessings and how my strength, positivity, and light had carried my boys and me to success. In my day-to-day life, I fully accept that challenges are no easy task and so I don't promote my business or share my struggles with many people, as I believe that there are things that should remain private. Despite this, I always maintained the same exterior and continued to share my light and make everything beautiful.

As shared on Day 95, I always feel fulfilled when I share my love and light with everyone. It is an infinite energy exchange of love as I simultaneously feel the same love that I extend to another. Also on this day, I discussed how I share my light regularly with others and, in particular, I mentioned my regular interactions with my friends at the UPS store in town. It feels good to have camaraderie with others and to feel a connection while pursuing day-to-day activities. As I mentioned, when this magazine was distributed, my friends at the store were thrilled, shocked, and in denial that I had experienced all that was shared in the article as, whenever they saw me in person, I was bubbly, happy, and care-free. It felt like a true testament to the desire of, "I'm going to make everything around me beautiful. That will be my life."

How do you make things around you beautiful? How would you like to make things beautiful in the future?

Day 178

"Everything changes when you start to emit your own frequency rather than absorbing the frequencies around you. When you start imprinting your intent on the Universe rather than receiving an imprint from existence."

Barbara Marciniak

When you start to emit your own frequency, you are living a life full of authenticity and at your own vibration. You begin to trust your spirit as a guide with your own set of rules instead of following the path of others, understanding that we were meant to expand ourselves. Living this way, you are in full alignment with yourself and the world around you. As a result, the Universe takes your lead, and as Ralph Waldo Emerson said, "Once you make a decision, the Universe conspires to make it happen."

Frequency is the rate of vibration measured over a specific period of time; it is basically a repeating sequence. When your energy vibrates at a high frequency you attract more positive emotions and are more spiritually inclined. This could be emotions like love, happiness, joy, peace, and acceptance. Alternatively, when your energy vibrates at a low frequency you attract negative emotions stemming from an ego-based mindset, such as anger, sadness, fear, stress, and anxiety.

Another interesting fact is that when a frequency rate increases, matter becomes lighter. Therefore, when you vibrate at a high frequency, your body can become lighter as a result.

At the end of 2021, I struggled with a "Bermuda Triangle" of issues: intense topics that all would be difficult on their own, but I was blessed to handle three at one time—all culminating on the same evening.

The evening that this transpired, I had just completed a four-and-a-half-hour mediation session, leaving me completely exhausted and distraught. I recall going to sleep in my clothes fairly early because that was what my soul needed. When I woke the next day, I felt like my body was entering a downward spiral and was extremely heavy. I was vibrating at a lower frequency. In addition, I had gained about three pounds from the day before, with no diet change to explain it.

Subsequently, a lot of soul searching transpired, followed by some decisions and internal healing. I was finally ready to comprehend (and act on) these decisions that were healthy for my soul. These intense recognitions resulted in an emotional purge of decades of negative energies that I had been holding onto, mainly as it related to my relationship with men and my co-dependency with them.

During the emotional purge, my weight began to steadily increase, again without a diet change. However, after thirty-six hours, I began to feel like myself again. My head was clear, I felt strong, and I lost four pounds overnight. Since I was now vibrating higher, my weight naturally reduced as I was no longer holding onto energies that were no longer serving me. This speaks to the idea that the wrong emotions can wreak havoc on your body, weighing you down in more ways than one.

What is your own experience with emitting a positive versus negative frequency? How does your body feel?

Day 179

"Everything that is happening to you is being drawn into your life as a means to help you evolve into who you were really meant to be here on Earth. It's not the thing that matters, it's what that thing opens within you."

Oprah

Are you ready to allow the Universe to move through you? To fully open you and evolve your spirit beyond your wildest dreams?

When your crown chakra is open and strong, you allow your connection with the Universe to move through you on your journey to your highest and greatest good.

When you understand that you can't control what happens to us, it just makes sense to relax and allow whatever is supposed to move through you to take the lead and be in control of the "story of your life." Remember, it is all being exquisitely planned within the powers of Divine timing for your life, because only then will you be ready to fully accept the gifts that are meant to fully blossom in you.

For me, the thing that I allowed to move through me was the healing power of sound vibrations. I trusted and followed the signs that were presented to me because they filled me with an immense joy and uplifted my spirits in a way I'd never experienced before. I was ready to allow the beautiful energies to flow through me. The positive effects could direct, change, and heal all who came within my path. It was then that I felt and experienced my healing gifts and became forever changed, trusting that the Universe truly has my back.

What are your experiences trusting the Universe? What have the effects been for you?

Day 180

"And the people stayed home. And read books, and listened, and rested, and exercised, and made art, and played games, and learned new ways of being, and were still. And listened more deeply. Some meditated, some prayed, some danced. Some met their shadows.

"And the people began to think differently. And the people healed. And, in the absence of people living in ignorant, dangerous, mindless, and heartless ways, the earth began to heal.

"And when the danger passed, and the people joined together again, they grieved their losses, and made new choices, and dreamed new images, and created new ways to live and heal the earth fully, as they had been healed."

Kitty O'Meara

This quote kept my head above water and my soul centered during the unknown times of March 2020, when the world was in quarantine from COVID-19. It was a time of great fear, anxiety, and uncertainty as everything went dark and our way of life changed. However, this quote represented the light of unprecedented times.

It helped me view life from a different place because the world had indeed changed—but all for the better. It reminded me to become more aware of the big picture and to see the blessings and love that exist in the present moments of life.

This was a life that was in desperate need of being viewed from a changed perspective because that was the only solution to move from the dark to the light for our world. It was an opportunity to experience life using the right side of the brain, full of creativity, emotions, and to "feel" the way through the confusing experiences.

It was also important for me during this time to manage my own personal anxieties and remain grounded for my young boys who were watching my every move. They were also navigating immense changes to their day-to-day experiences. I often would remind myself that they were picked up from school one day in March and not allowed to return again for six months. Their school was on a computer screen, there were no organized sports or activities, and they were forbidden from seeing extended family or close friends for fear of getting too close and spreading germs. Life as we knew it was unlike anything ever experienced before, for both the little and big people of the world.

For me, my yoga was my saving grace, and when I felt overwhelmed, I would find beauty in the moving clouds of the sky. These activities were very calming for my mind; they kept me focused on the present and away from the fear of the unforeseen future.

How did you choose to heal from experiences during quarantine from COVID-19?

Afterword

Dear readers,

Thank you for your dedication, energy, time, and love to complete this 180-day journey of light for . . . YOURSELF! Having kindness for yourself is the light you give to others. That's what goes out into the world.

Remembering that our lives are in a constant state of motion, it is important to go with the flow, understanding that the source of your truth and healing will always begin from within you. This will be the secret on your journey and beyond toward your path to Enlightenment.

You are light.
You are divine.
You are intuitive.
You are love.
You are power.
You are joy.
You are truth.

My hope is that you have ingrained these key life mantras into your consciousness, taking them with you wherever you go, as they are now part of your soul and existence.

I encourage you to continue to utilize the teachings in this book as your personal guide to healing. Reread quotes and reflections as appropriate based on the ever-changing and unique flow of your life. Continue to generate and move the energy in your body with yoga postures, still your mind with meditation, and relax your body with the power of sound vibrations.

Life is a continuous gift. Always remember that you deserve all the beautiful benefits that life has to offer you. Be present and awake to what is around you in the moment. For example, the sun's beauty is a gift. You can carry that beauty with you and allow the beauty to uplift you. Everything in life is a gift if you're open to receiving it.

You deserve to stop and see those things, to let them change you. They can change how you view your day—from awful to good. Through this work, you can become aware that something is making you feel bad in the moment, and you can consciously turn it around. The only way to change your circumstances is to change your perspective.

Every day I'm learning and healing something. It's a continuous cycle that's not ever gonna stop. I try to stay open to the understanding and awareness that we can always be helping ourselves, loving ourselves, and healing what's happening in our lives.

You know what to do! You are the leader of your life.

Love to all. Light to all. Peace to all. Sat Naam.

Appendix

POSTURE DESCRIPTIONS

I AM TRUTH

Neck Rolls

Sit in a comfortable, easy position with a straight spine and your neck lengthened. Inhale as you begin to rotate your neck and right ear toward your shoulder in a clockwise fashion; exhale as your head hangs forward; inhale as head comes back to the top. Repeat the movement, gently switching directions halfway through.

Cat-Cow

Begin on your hands and knees with your hands under your shoulders and knees under your hips. Inhale in Cow with a flat back and head up. Exhale in Cat with an arched spine, head down, pressing your chin into your chest. Repeat the movement.

Crow

Begin in a standing position. Squat down with wide knees and feet. Heels flat on the floor or on a cushion for comfort. Lengthen your spine. Extend your arms in front of you, perpendicular to the floor. Hold the position.

Cobra

Begin by lying on your stomach, hands under your shoulders, palms flat on the ground. Gently lift your chest, heart, and last your head as you extend your arms and lean back. As an alternative, you can leave your forearms on the floor instead of holding a full arm extension. Hold the position.

Pelvic Lifts

Lie on your back with your knees bent and feet flat on the ground. Hold your ankles or as close as you can reach toward them. As you inhale, lift the hips up from the navel as you exhale, lower your hips using the thighs and buttocks. Repeat the movement.

I Am Joy

Butterfly

Begin in Easy Pose with the soles of your feet together. Gently grab underneath your feet as you lengthen and pull the spine up. Continue to bounce your knees with your breath.

Cobra

Begin by lying on your stomach, hands under your shoulders, palms flat on the ground. Gently lift your chest, heart, and last your head as you extend your arms and lean back. As an alternative, you can leave your forearms on the floor instead of holding a full arm extension. Hold the position.

Nose to Knee

Lie on your back, bend your knees and hug them to your chest. Raise your head, bringing your nose toward your knees or between your knees, if possible. Hold the position.

Back Rolls

Begin by lying on your back and bending your knees up into your chest, pressing them with your arms. Gently begin to roll on your spine, inhaling as you roll forward and exhale as you roll back. Continue with this movement.

Baby Pose

Begin by sitting on your heels. Bend forward, placing your forehead on the ground, arms at your sides, with palms facing up. Hold the position.

I Am Power

Sufi Grind

Sit in Easy Pose. Grab hold of your knees and begin to rotate your hips and spine in a big circle. Inhale as your body rotates toward the front and exhale as you rotate backward. Gently switch directions halfway through.

Spinal Twist

Sit in Easy Pose or on your heels. Gently grab your shoulders, with thumbs in the back and other fingers in front. As you inhale, rotate your torso to the left, and as you exhale twist to the right. Repeat this movement.

Bow Pose

Begin by lying on your stomach. Gently grab your ankles using your thigh muscles to pull your upper body off the ground. Then lift your legs off the ground, followed by the chest and head. Hold the position.

Triangle Pose

Come down to your knees and lean forward, placing the palms of the hands with the fingers spread wide and the soles of the feet on the ground approximately hip width apart, creating a triangle with your body. Pull your chin in, elongating your neck, and roll your armpits toward each other. Hold the position.

Leg Lifts

Begin by lying on your back, hands either under your buttocks to support your back or at your sides. As you inhale, press your lower back into the floor using a pelvic tilt and lift your legs up to a desired angle of 30, 60 or 90 degrees. As you exhale, gently lower your legs down. Repeat this movement.

I Am Love

Bear Grip

Sit in Easy Pose. Place your left palm facing out from your chest with the thumb down, place the palm of your right hand facing the chest and bring your fingers together. Curl the fingers of both hands so the hands form a fist. Apply tension, trying to pull your hands apart, and hold the position.

Yoga Mudra

Sit on your heels coming into Baby Pose, bringing your forehead to the ground. Interlace your fingers, with the palms facing down toward the head, and extend your arms overhead, making them perpendicular to the ground. Hold the position.

Baby Pose

Begin by sitting on your heels. Bend forward, placing your forehead on the ground, arms at your sides, with palms facing up. Hold the position.

Yoga March

Begin in a standing position with your feet under your hips. Place your hands in Gyan Mudra by connecting the tip of your thumb with the tip of your index finger. As you inhale, raise your right knee and both arms overhead; as you exhale, drop your arms and drop your leg. Repeat exercise on your left side. As you inhale, raise your left knee and both arms overhead; as you exhale, drop your arms and drop your leg. Feel free to leave your eyes open for balance. Continue with this movement.

Windmill

Begin in a standing position with your feet 2–3 feet apart. Extend your arms parallel to the ground, palms facing the floor. Inhale, turn to your right, then exhale, bow down, and touch the ground at your right with your left hand. Inhale up, turn to your left, then exhale, bow down, and touch the ground at your left with your right hand. Continue with this movement.

I Am Intuitive

Shoulder Shrugs

Begin by sitting in Easy Pose or on your heels. Place your hands on your knees. As you inhale, bring your shoulders up to your ears; as you exhale, release them down. Continue this movement.

Yoga Mudra

Sit on your heels coming into Baby Pose, bringing your forehead to the ground. Interlace your fingers, with the palms facing down toward the head, and extend your arms overhead, making them perpendicular to the ground. Hold the position.

Sitting Bend

Begin by sitting on your heels. Interlace your fingers behind your neck, pulling your elbows back. As you inhale, elongate and stretch your spine up. As you exhale, fold your body forward, continuing to lengthen your spine, bringing your forehead to the ground. Use your legs for assistance to push you up as you inhale, bringing your body back to the original position. Continue with this movement.

Front Bend

Begin in a standing position, with your feet hip width apart. As you inhale, lift your spine up, raising your arms overhead, and as you exhale, bend forward from your navel, continuing to lengthen your spine, bringing your head in toward your legs. Reverse the position as you inhale to come up by pushing your feet into the ground slowly, pulling yourself up, with your head coming up last. Continue with this movement.

Rock Pose

Sit on your heels with a lengthened and straight spine. Eyes focused on your Third Eye point, sit and meditate. Remain in this position.

I Am Divine

Cobra

Begin by lying on your stomach, hands under your shoulders, palms flat on the ground. Gently lift your chest, heart, and last your head as you extend your arms and lean back. As an alternative, you can leave your forearms on the floor instead of holding a full arm extension. Hold the position.

Spinal Flex

Sit in Easy Pose and grab your ankles. As you inhale, rock your pelvis forward, pushing your chest forward and up. As you exhale, round your lower back, rocking your pelvis back. Continue with this movement.

Bridge Pose

Begin in a sitting position, with your knees bent and feet flat on the ground. Your arms will be behind your body, palms flat on the ground, with your fingertips facing your feet. Gently lift your hips up and keep your head up, parallel to the floor with an elongated spine. Hold this position.

Tree Pose

Begin in a standing position. Starting with the right side, place the right heel either on the inside of your left calf or above your knee on your thigh, close to the groin. Stretch your arms up with the palms together in Prayer Pose, hugging your ears. Focus on a point in the distance to maintain your balance. Hold this position before switching halfway to perform the posture on your left side.

Stretch Backwards

Begin in a standing position, with your feet parallel to each other and a few inches apart. As you inhale, engage your navel, stretching your arms above your head, and gently lean backward as you lengthen your spine. Hold this position.

Resources

Reference for all asanas and mantras:
The Aquarian Teacher KRI Instructor Yoga Manual & Textbook

Access and supplement the activities referenced in the book

- *Monthly Yoga Postures, Meditations and Sound Healing Videos:* www.LisaAnnese.com/i-am-light
- *My Spotify Playlist* with "I AM Light" Book References for soundtracks to the mantra meditations: Search for "Lisa Annese" on www.spotify.com

Suggestions for further exploration which are mentioned in the book

- The Kundalini Research Institute (KRI) kundaliniresearchinstitute.org
- Khalsa Way Prenatal Yoga Teacher Training khalsaway.com
- Singing Bowl and Sound Institute of New York katherinehamer.com

- *The 5 Love Languages* by Gary Chapman
  5lovelanguages.com
- *Broken Open* by Elizabeth Lesser
  elizabethlesser.org/broken-open
- *The Healing Power of Sound* by Dr. Mitchell Gaynor
- Brené Brown
  brenebrown.com
- Layne Redmond
  layneredmond.com
- Fia
  fiasmusicofficial.com
- Myers-Briggs: My MBTI Personality Type
  myersbriggs.org
- Balance Wheel Activity: you can find numerous examples online, but here's one example.
  wheeloflife.noomii.com

Further topics you might want to explore

- Number sequences
- Spirit animals
- Mandala
- Unalome
- Pisces and other astrological signs
- Spiritual intimacy
- Yin/yang energy

Acknowledgments

Thank you for reading about my journey. This book is the result of my deep internal healing process. It's my unique story and a missing piece I needed to turn the dark situations and experiences in my life into a form of light for myself and my boys.

I am blessed to have not walked this healing path alone, and grateful to the Universe for always giving me those I needed to support me in my travels to recovery.

Thank you to my therapist, Pam, for putting me back together in a discovery of myself with love and patience. I'm grateful to Dr. Chris, one of my spiritual guides who educated me about the power of faith and the utmost trust in God's light above all things. I'm indebted to Frank, my honorary brother and divorce coach, for the magnitude of support needed to navigate and rebuild my life during my darkest moments. Love to Nicole, my soul sister and closest confidante; our paths are parallel and intertwined for our highest good in support of each other and the wide range of those whom we will heal. I'm honored by the teachings of Kathy, my sound teacher and my biggest supporter, who held the keys to the door of my purpose; plus, my other spiritual teachers who have helped me along the way.

I'm appreciative to the Church of the Most Blessed Sacrament for giving me a safe home and place of community during a time of great difficulty and beyond. Thank you to Monica, my editor, and Bryna, my publisher, for your magic and believing in me and the fire inside of me.

To my son's medical team at the Children's Hospital of Philadelphia (CHOP), there are no words to express my deep and sincere gratitude for your care and support in navigating Michael's hearing loss diagnosis. My son is thriving in leaps and bounds because I have the confidence and feel secure with a plan for his future.

To those who have supported me on my journey and believed in me when I didn't always believe in myself, thank you. To my parents, for the foundation and gift of life, I am forever grateful for you. Blessings to my boys for their love, patience, and trust as I create a new life for us, and to my first husband for the karmic lessons. Finally, I thank you, my reader; I am proud of you for your interest in enhancing and creating light in your own life.

About the Author

Lisa Annese is a dedicated practitioner and teacher of Kundalini yoga and meditation, sound healer, spiritual guide, and owner of The Divine Sound, a yoga and sound healing studio. As a divorced woman, single mother, and hearing loss advocate (supporting the needs of her son who has permanent hearing loss), she chose to walk the path of truth, trusting her own spirit with strength, grace, love, and light as the answer to her darkness. A testament to the truth that challenges are your greatest blessings, Lisa became a true "guru" at heart in her ability to turn the dark into light in her own life for her and her two boys. This act of bravery, courage, and her ability to be vulnerable changed the narrative and future for her family.

Lisa openly shares her path to finding her own light; she is currently living her second life as a "Rising Phoenix." She shares stories from her past as an opportunity to educate and help others to do the same for themselves.

She understands that life is full of learning experiences for your soul and that the light in your life can only exist because of the darkness that you had to endure. The main takeaways from her teachings are: to express your own personal gratitude for all the blessings that come your way, remain present, live simply, and go with the flow. Truly embrace the gifts that are waiting for you.

Prior to this, in her first life, Lisa worked in public accounting as a CPA and human resources professional for approximately ten years at Ernst & Young, before she chose to stay home and raise her boys.

Lisa currently lives with her two sons, Anthony and Michael, and their toy poodle, Roco, in Franklin Lakes, New Jersey.

Learn more about Lisa's virtual and in person book club offerings, workshops, events, and more at lisaannese.com or on Instagram @ lisaannese.

About the Publisher

Founded in 2021 by Bryna Haynes, WorldChangers Media is a boutique publishing company focused on "Ideas for Impact." We know that great books change lives, topple outdated paradigms, and build movements. Our commitment is to deliver superior-quality transformational nonfiction by, and for, the next generation of thought leaders.

Ready to write and publish your thought leadership book with us? Learn more at www.WorldChangers.Media.

Made in the USA
Middletown, DE
13 September 2022

72851120R00267